CW00926580

THE
LUXURY
STRATEGY

THE
LUXURY
STRATEGY

BREAK THE RULES OF MARKETING
TO BUILD LUXURY BRANDS

J.N. KAPFERER AND V. BASTIEN

KoganPage

LONDON PHILADELPHIA NEW DELHI

Publisher's note

Every possible effort has been made to ensure that the information contained in this book is accurate at the time of going to press, and the publishers and authors cannot accept responsibility for any errors or omissions, however caused. No responsibility for loss or damage occasioned to any person acting, or refraining from action, as a result of the material in this publication can be accepted by the editor, the publisher or any of the authors.

First published in Great Britain and the United States in 2009 by Kogan Page Limited
Reprinted 2009 (twice), 2010 (twice), 2011

120 Pentonville Road	1518 Walnut Street, Suite 1100	4737/23 Ansari Road
London N1 9JN	Philadelphia PA 19102	Daryaganj
United Kingdom	USA	New Delhi 110002
www.koganpage.com		India

ISBN 978 0 7494 5477 7

British Library Cataloguing-in-Publication Data

A CIP record for this book is available from the British Library.

Library of Congress Cataloging-in-Publication Data

Kapferer, Jean-Noël.
    The luxury strategy : break the rules of marketing to build luxury brands / Jean-Noël Kapferer and Vincent Bastien.
        p. cm
    ISBN 978-0-7494-5477-7
    1. Luxuries--Marketing. 2. Luxury goods industry. 3. Product management.
I. Bastien, Vincent. II. Title.
    HD9999.L852K37 2009
    658.8--dc22

                        2008034402

Typeset by Saxon Graphics Ltd, Derby
Printed and bound in India by Replika Press Pvt Ltd

Contents

About the authors

This unique book on luxury strategy could only be written by two complementary authors, both experts in the field at the highest level, each with a very specific angle.

Jean-Noël Kapferer is one of the very few worldwide experts on brand management. His book *Strategic Brand Management* is the key reference of top-level international MBAs. Professor at HEC Paris, the luxury research centre in Europe, he holds the Pernod-Ricard Chair on Prestige and Luxury Management. He consults extensively and is a member of the board of a major luxury brand. Jean-Noël Kapferer holds an MBA from HEC Paris and a PhD from Northwestern University USA. He directs executive seminars on luxury all around the world.

Vincent Bastien is one of the most experienced senior managers in luxury business. He has directed some of the most prestigious luxury brands, mainly as Managing Director for six years of Louis Vuitton Malletier, or as CEO of Yves Saint Laurent Parfums and Sanofi Beauté. He is now Affiliate Professor at HEC Paris, where he teaches Strategy in Luxury. He holds a MS from the Polytechnique School of Paris, an MBA from HEC and is an alumnus (SEP) of the Stanford Business School.

Introduction: To be or not to be luxury

Luxury is in fashion, and the fashion is for luxury. To be 'in', just as you must be young, you must be 'luxury'. Moreover, eternal youth is the luxury of those who are able to frequent the most sublime spas, the famous cosmetic surgeons, and purchase the fruit of the latest scientific research from prestige cosmetics brands, with the rarest ingredients.

Today, luxury is everywhere. Managers and marketing people regularly invent new terms to qualify luxury: true luxury, masstige, premium, ultra-premium, opuluxe, hyperluxe. Instead of clarifying the concept of luxury, this semantic creativity only adds to the confusion: if everything is luxury, then the term 'luxury' no longer has any meaning. What, therefore, constitutes a luxury product, a luxury brand or a luxury company?

The current confusion masks a profound reality: luxury does exist, it is not just a trade, restricted to some cars or fashion accessories, but a different and global way of understanding a customer and of managing a business. The concept of luxury is as old as humanity; a discriminating understanding of it makes it possible to define the rigorous rules for its effective management. Such is the goal of this book.

Just as the marketing of mass consumption goods was invented in the United States, and developed by large American groups such as Procter & Gamble, and then conquered the planet, so luxury strategies were invented in Europe, and developed worldwide mainly by French and Italian companies.

The highly original methods that were devised in order to transform, in less than half a century, small family businesses such as Ferrari, Louis Vuitton, Cartier or Chanel, but also Bulgari, Gucci, Prada and Ferragamo, into great global brands are in fact applicable to many trades in almost all cultures.

Written by two specialists of complementing professions, each with a long experience of luxury, this work encapsulates and rationalizes the management of this new business concept, based on the successful experiments, and the failures encountered, by these European pioneers. From these, the authors draw practical conclusions, both on the rules to be applied to the luxury marketing mix, often diametrically opposed to those of classic marketing, and on the specificities of implementing a luxury strategy within a company, both at the financial and the human level.

Far from being simply a descriptive work, it delivers clear principles for becoming and remaining luxury, as well as when and how to depart from luxury, if such is the strategy. It also builds a theoretical framework taking into account the dynamic of luxury through time and history, making it possible to understand the *raison d'être* of these principles in the highly internationalized markets of today.

One of the advantages of this work is that the management principles described are applicable well beyond the restricted circle of luxury trades such as we know them today.

PART 1

Back to luxury fundamentals

1 In the beginning there was luxury

It would surely be unthinkable for a book on the management of luxury brands to be nothing more than a set of rules and an assortment of formulas. Luxury is a culture, which means you have to understand it to be able to practice it with flair and spontaneity. The reason why marketing – the child of the industrial society and the father of consumer power – doesn't seem to work with luxury goods the same way it does with everyday consumer goods, even top-of-the-range consumer goods, is because the two are fundamentally quite different.

If we want to be able to market luxury, we need first to understand what luxury is all about. Before continuing, therefore, we need to make a brief historical detour. There is no denying that these days luxury has its own special peculiarities and its new business models, but for all that it still lays claim to be called 'luxury'. In order to be able to deduce from them the paradigm of luxury with all its coherent internal rules, you first have to understand its inner dynamics.

A brief history of luxury

The fact is that the history of luxury goes back to the dawn of humanity. To the time when our species parted company with its ape ancestors? Perhaps... who knows? But it is not our intention to get into that old debate – still less to discuss the legitimacy of Darwin's theory of evolution! Having said that, this question is paradoxically the reason behind this book: wanting to manage a firm specializing in a luxury line efficiently, and finding that tried and tested conventional marketing methods that worked well with standard consumer goods were somehow ineffective – positively harmful even – when applied to luxury products, we needed to find the underlying principle or principles of the mechanics of luxury. Now, as you delve deeper into the subject it soon becomes apparent that the appeal of luxury is so deeply rooted in human nature that you have to look for its origins a long way back in our history – indulge in a little bit of anthropology, in fact.

The origins of luxury

It seems legitimate to start from the fact that we bury our dead – proof that we are aware of our own mortality – is what truly sets us apart from animals. In other words, humanity is as old as the period since we started to bury our dead. And what, apart from skeletons, do we find in these graves? We find objects that with the passage of time are more and more refined, until eventually we start coming across long-lost tombs whose occupants had been buried together with their most precious jewellery and symbols of their power – such as weapons, horses and even ships.

Very soon (on a prehistoric timescale) it appeared that everyone was desperate not just to bury their loved ones but also to bury along with them the food they would need to survive in the other world, as well as objects that were so much a part of them that they had to accompany them after death.

Since the dawn of humanity, then, there have been organized societies, leading groups and, of course, objects, symbols and lifestyles specific to these leading groups. It is in the appearance of these leading groups and of the symbols and objects specific to them that we need to look for the origins of luxury. If we accept this analysis, luxury is part and parcel of humanity and of life in society.

Closer to home, as regards the ancient civilizations about which we know quite a lot thanks to the invention of writing, whether we're talking about the Egyptians, Mesopotamians, Chinese or Amerindians, the situation is very clear and we are well beyond the theorizing stage: we know their social dynamics and their beliefs, which confirm this close link between socialization and luxury.

Let us come back to this vital aspect to human beings, that is, the certainty that sooner or later they will die, and the question of life after death, because it tells us a great deal about the fundamental (and eternal) mechanisms at work behind the whole concept of luxury in humankind, both ancient and modern. The moment we become aware of our own mortality, the ultimate in luxury, well beyond any notion of possessions or status, is to be able to live on – and live on comfortably at that – after death. Every great civilization has come up with its own and often remarkable way of answering this craving for immortality – metempsychosis (a transmigration of the soul to some other human or animal body), the idea of Nirvana, and suchlike – but it is the Egyptian 'way of death' that interests us most in the context of this book.

The case of Ancient Egypt is in fact the most spectacular, for the desert climate of the Nile Valley has miraculously preserved everything for the benefit of future generations. And what do we find? We find the remains of a highly hierarchical and stable society, with its own very precise and extremely sophisticated codes and rules for living; Egypt clearly practised all the codes of luxury, and apparently invented many new techniques for doing this, the best-known being the discovery of glass to protect perfumes.

Two aspects of this luxury are ever-present: great pomp and splendour during life and a highly ritualistic approach to the afterlife. During life, as in all human society, this splendour was expressed by every available means and spurred the invention of exclusive products such as perfumes, which were reserved for the gods, the Pharaoh, the High Priest and those around them. After death everything became even more spectacular: the pyramids, the tombs in the Valley of the Kings and the Valley of the Queens… the most sophisticated means, both artistically and technically (the building of the pyramids) were invented and then applied to ensure that this pomp and splendour lived on in the afterlife.

According to Egyptian beliefs, it was the survival of the body that guaranteed the survival of the soul, and this survival called for some amazing expertise: highly sophisticated techniques had to be developed (embalming of mummies, erection of the pyramids or excavation of tombs), which were very costly. For obvious economic reasons this great luxury was reserved for a very small elite: the Pharaoh, his wife or wives, the High Priest and a select few important dignitaries.

Based on archaeological discoveries in the Nile Valley and on deciphered hieroglyphics, it seems fairly certain that the evolution of this 'luxury industry' followed much the same path as that which we have today: democratization. What the unearthed mummies and tombs tell us is that this luxury gradually spread downward to other more ordinary mortals and a few 'sacred' animals, and later, during the Low Period, to all Egyptians and even to domestic animals. This 'dispersion of luxury' would be a feature of all societies that had the time and resources for it.

By the same token, it might be supposed that the debate about the usefulness of luxury was already raging in those far-off days: while some looked upon such things as a pointless extravagance (the lives of peasants were undoubtedly extremely hard), others saw in it a powerful driver of artistic and technical discoveries that gradually spread throughout society and eventually benefited everyone. Besides, the recent discoveries around the Giza plateau have forced us to exchange the conventional image of the pyramids built by slaves subjected to ceaseless lashing for one in which they were in fact raised by resourceful engineers and a skilful workforce: the luxury of the Pharaohs was not built on slavery but on the expertise of those who were not only capable but also free.

From Greek antiquity to the 19th century

Throughout the period that stretches from Ancient Greece to the present day the concept of luxury has been the subject of constant hot dispute between the proponents of luxury as an aspirational and improving force in society and those that see luxury as an enemy of Virtus (one of the elements of virtue as understood by the Romans):

- In Ancient Greece it was the secular conflict between Athens and Sparta that perhaps best illustrated this contrast between social concepts. The rivalry between these two city states went on for centuries and has been thoroughly explored by numerous historians.
- In classical Italy, when the military might of Rome was able to shield the city from its external enemies, it was the conflict between the supporters of the Republic, its austerity and its belief in Virtus (Cato the Elder being the principal evangelist of this position, with the famous sumptuary law, the Lex Oppia, passed in 215 BC and repealed in 195 BC), on one side, and on the other those advocating a more elegant and sophisticated Republic. It was the latter group that eventually emerged victorious, and Imperial Rome will forever be remembered for its refinement and luxury. The bitterness and the recurrence of this conflict between two fundamentally different kinds of society (one warlike, masculine and austere, the other pacifist, feminine and sophisticated), with a definite taking of sides for or against luxury even culminating in civil war, shows just how important is the idea of luxury.

And these conflicts were not confined just to classical antiquity – not even to the Western world: sumptuary laws have been around for thousands of years, both in periods of (relative) social stability (the Tokugawa shogunate in Japan, 1603–1868, or the reign of Elizabeth I of England) and in periods of serious social unrest (for example, the French Wars of Religion in the latter half of the 16th century). However, we shall not be elaborating any further on this period of history (those interested are referred to the outstanding book by Christopher J Berry entitled *The Idea of Luxury* (1994)).

Without ever reaching quite the same degree of violence, whether actual or legal, this conflict has been going on for all time in human society everywhere (see also p. 77 on court etiquette), and continues to this day in our Western societies, and especially in France: the debate between luxury as an insult to the poor and luxury as a source of skilled and steady jobs; somehow it is all right to produce luxury goods, but certainly not all right to buy them.

The thing to remember is that luxury is – and always has been – a major sociological issue in any society, because it has to do, at one and the same time, with:

- social stratification;
- the notion of practical utility and waste;
- decisions relating to the distribution of wealth.

In other words, the concept of luxury is not a socially neutral one; quite the contrary as, in a manner of speaking, it is society that defines what luxury is. This is true of all societies, even contemporary ones: in addition to the time-honoured methods of deterrence, we have a veritable arsenal of taxes to determine whether a product is a luxury item or not… in fact, this is often the best way of arriving at such a definition!

It is hardly surprising therefore that the fundamental shake-up of Western society in the 18th century, the 'Age of Enlightenment', which contributed to both the French and American revolutions, should have had such a profound impact on luxury, on both a philosophical and an economic level.

Turn of the 19th century

The consequences for luxury of the philosophical and social upheavals of the 18th century started becoming apparent in the 19th century:

- Liberalism (Adam Smith) was very favourable to trade and to luxury as the driver of economic growth, provided the first true economic rationale for luxury as the means to creating wealth for all.
- In parallel with this growing liberalism, English philosophers of the 18th century, and especially David Hume (his essay titled *Of Luxury* was published in 1752) were to separate 'luxury' and 'morality', until then considered mutually irreconcilable in Christian Europe, and would provide a philosophical justification for luxury.

- The general democratization towards the end of the 18th century gradually made luxury accessible to all.
- Following the Industrial Revolution, which brought about a considerable rise in living standards, more and more individuals found themselves with the financial means to afford luxuries.
- The beginnings of female emancipation, which would not percolate all strata of society until the middle of the 20th century, could already be seen at work in the 19th.

We have already seen that it was the pacifist, feminine societies that most readily and completely accepted luxury. As the 20th century progressed, the situation gradually turned in favour of the social legitimization of luxury. Today, this process of legitimization is not yet complete, even in developed societies, but it is irreversible.

We are now going to look more closely at this sociological evolution and its consequences, and in particular at what we shall call the driving forces behind luxury.

The 20th century and the democratization of luxury

Let us go back to Darwin: one could compare the world of luxury until the turn of the 20th century to the animal population of a large island, long isolated from the rest of the world (as South America once was, or as Madagascar and Tasmania are today), and on which a varied and totally original fauna has developed in a specific ecosystem.

One fine day, due to continental drift or falling sea levels, a spit of land joins this island to the continent; suddenly, the fauna on this island find that they have all this vast space into which to expand, but at the same time have to compete with much larger fauna that have adapted to their own ecosystem. In what way do the new fauna need to evolve in order to conquer new territory? Which species are going to disappear, and why? Is hybridization going to lead to the appearance of successful new species?

Let us pursue the analogy: since the dawn of humanity right up to the turn of the 19th century, the world of luxury has been virtually totally isolated from the rest of the economy, its pleasures and delights reserved for a very small elite; practically the entire population were living in a subsistence economy, firmly rooted in their rural environment or living a life of misery in towns and cities, without any access to culture. So this world of luxury, with its own economic rules, has gradually developed and, over the centuries, acquired a truly idiosyncratic character.

From the 20th century onward, this world of luxury gradually ceases to be a world apart. An ever-growing slice of the population is beginning to have access to it, partially at least: an ever-widening spit of land now connects Luxury Island to the continent of the industrial and consumer society. Luxury can now set out to conquer the world, but at the same time it must overcome fierce competition from industrial products and their sophisticated marketing. It is equally true to say that luxury has to set out to conquer the world as it cannot remain holed up on its small island, otherwise it would disappear, as almost all the endemic South American species have disappeared, failing to adapt to the new situation that resulted from the joining of North America with South America, or as the Australian marsupial fauna are in the process of disappearing following the arrival of the Europeans accompanied by placental mammals.

As it sets out to conquer the world, even though its idiosyncratic nature does not at first really prepare it for such a venture, and even though it has to overcome some powerful adversaries along the way, luxury does hold some major trump cards, with many drivers of social and economic change taking place in the second half of the 20th century working in its favor.

The drivers of change

The two fundamental sociological trump cards that luxury have today are, of course, female emancipation (though there has always been a market for luxuries among the rich societies, even in those as unfeminist as the Ottoman Empire) and world peace (however theoretical, but nevertheless publicly proclaimed). These two aces in the hole were boosted in the 20th century by four new and powerful drivers, and in order to understand what is happening today and be able to come up with practical strategies for luxury it is vital to have a detailed understanding of how they work.

Democratization

This is the most important driver of luxury and the one that explains its current success, for democratization implies two things:

- First, that everyone has access to the world of luxury, which is why the client base has grown exponentially. Having said that, clearly this fabulous opportunity for luxury carries with it a major risk: that of vulgarization, which is a major trap to be avoided in the process of democratizing luxury (we will have occasion to come back to this point quite frequently, especially in the chapters on setting up a luxury strategy) Staying in the realms of the metaphysical, here is an example of complete democratization without any vulgarization whatsoever: while democratizing the idea of 'eternal life' for everybody, Christianity has nevertheless avoided vulgarizing the concept of 'the individual soul'; it is not because everyone has a soul that mine or yours is no longer worth anything... The aim of this deliberately slightly provocative example is to show that democratizing something, that is to say making it accessible to all, does not necessarily entail its vulgarization, that is to say a total loss of value.

- Second, that historical social stratification is gradually disappearing. We shall be returning at length to this point in due course when discussing the cardinal role that luxury plays in this context of a democratic and open society, a central theme of this book that we will call the 'paradigm of luxury'.

The offspring of social stratification in inegalitarian societies, luxury has become its father in democratic societies.

Logically, the democratic process, which favours transparency and levelling out (not so much economic as cultural), should have signalled the demise of luxury by bringing about the disappearance of 'transcendent' leading classes. However, paradoxically, the very opposite has happened: luxury, the offspring of the 'transcendent' stratification of society, does not die just because this stratification has disappeared; instead, it has become its creator and driver.

There is something very important that needs to be said at this stage: in a democratic society, luxury may lead to social stratification, but it also encourages humanity, something that is often lacking in our modern cities. We shall be reverting frequently to the systematic and very important affective relationship that tends to form between a luxury brand, a luxury product and a client; if no such affective relationship exists, that is because in the client's eyes the product is not a luxury product. It's an absolute given.

There is one final important point to make in this context: architecture, a particularly social and ostentatious form of art, quite clearly has very much to do with luxury – you need only think of the pyramids of long ago, the French palaces of the more recent past, and today's flagship stores! The more or less free access to luxury, which we can readily see from architecture, is a measure of democracy: the extravagant splendour of Ceaucescu's palace in Bucharest, standing right in the centre of a wretchedly poor city, was a far more eloquent testimonial to the true state of democracy in Eastern Europe's 'people's democracies' than any political treatise ever could be. And it was no less true of medieval villages in Europe, which existed in the shadows of the all-powerful church (or cathedral) on one side, and of the mansion (or palace) of the local ruling classes on the other: both symbolic of the total absence of democracy.

Increase in spending power

This is the most obvious driver of the growth in luxury goods: increased spending power means increased availability of money and time (both indispensible to luxury, as we will see later). Having said that, closer analysis shows a possible alternative in how this increased spending power can be applied:

- A qualitative and quantitative linear growth in the consumption of most products (people eat, clothe themselves and live 'a little better'). It is this linear growth that will underpin the development of the consumer society and current marketing strategies, culminating in 'top-of- the-range' or 'premium' products.
- For some products, and for some users, a sharp and non-linear increase in expenditure of money and time: a very large proportion, or even the entirety – or more – of the surplus is spent on a specific activity, occasionally to the detriment of all other activities; this is the notion of bingeing, of extravagant consumption, that we find at the basis of luxury.

This choice (between spreading 'discretionary spending power' among many products and concentrating it on just a few products) will play a very important part in our subsequent analysis designed to distinguish between 'premium' strategies and 'luxury' strategies. Let us assume for the moment that the increase in spending power benefits both luxury products and premium products equally: this particular driver is not luxury-specific.

Globalization

In addition to its role in accelerating the rise in spending power, through wage increases and falling prices of most manufactured products, globalization plays a dual role as a driver of luxury:

- It offers accessibility to completely new products that can be sources of luxury (silk, spices, sugar in the 16th century for the West, French wines for the whole world in the 20th century), to new cultures, a source of new emotions and new desires ('Japonisme' – or obsession with all things Japanese – in France in the 19th century) and, looking at it from the opposite perspective, opens up new markets: for the French fine leather craft trade in the 1970s, Japan was the key to development on a considerable scale.
- At least to the same extent as democratization, it is a factor in doing away with social stratification. Globalization leads to a levelling out of all cultures and a relativism in all religions: a perfectly globalized society would have just one language and one religion.

Here we come across the same problem as the one discussed in the context of democratization – and therefore the same social utility of luxury – but this time at the level of an entire culture, rather than of a single individual; in this context, it will no longer be just social stratification but also the roots, a cultural and precise geographic localization in an undifferentiated world, that people are going to look for in a luxury product – it would have to show evidence not only of social stratification, but also of being rooted in a particular culture.

A luxury product is rooted in a culture. In buying a Chinese luxury product (silk, let us say), you are buying not just a piece of material but a little bit of China as well – a luxury product comes along with a small fragment of its native soil.

This does of course mean that a luxury brand has to stay absolutely true to its roots and be produced in a place that holds some legitimacy for it: by remaining faithful to its origins, the luxury product offers an anchor point in a world of cultural drift, trivialization and deracination. A luxury brand should not yield to the temptation of relocation, which effectively means dislocation: a relocated product is a soulless product (it has lost its identity), even if it is not actually anonymous (it still bears a brand name); it no longer has any business in the world of luxury. We shall be returning to this later and in greater detail, but we need to understand one thing right away: a product whose production centre has been relocated loses its right to be called a luxury product.

And there we have another major difference between a luxury product and a premium product: it is perfectly legitimate for a 'premium' product to seek out the most suitable and most economical manufacturing location possible, so long as quality and service levels can be maintained.

A luxury product, which carries a whole world with it, has to be produced in a place that is consistent with its world. Products by Chanel or Hermès, being manufactured in France, truly are luxury products; products bearing a Dior or Burberry label, on the other hand, being manufactured in countries where labour costs are low and not in France (Dior's place of origin) or in the UK (Burberry's place of origin), are no longer entitled to be called luxury products: this kind of relocation for cost-cutting reasons is proof that these brands do not have (or no longer have) a sufficiently high level of quality or creativity – as regards the products concerned, at any rate – to justify a price level that would allow them to continue to be produced in their country of origin. The public outcry that arose when Burberry announced that it was closing down one of its production facilities in the UK and moving it to an area with low labour costs in China certainly left its mark!

Interestingly, this relationship between luxury and local production does not only apply to 'fashion accessories' but to all products: one of the reasons behind BMW's success with the Mini is that it managed to continue building it in the UK. And that is also true of Rolls-Royce, of course.

All of that holds especially true when the luxury brand sets out to conquer the world. Now, as we have seen previously this is something it has to do: a luxury brand that cannot go global finishes up disappearing; it is better to have a small nucleus of clients in every country – because there is every chance that it will grow – than a large nucleus in just one country, which could disappear overnight. That's the law of globalization.

If this globalization does bring a luxury brand financial success and durability, the major risk then is that it forgets its roots – like some people who, their own success having gone to their heads, forget or even reject their parents; once separated from its roots, the brand ceases to be a luxury brand and is immediately relegated to the category of just another competitor in consumer goods brands – a battleground for which it is particularly unsuited.

Communications

This is the last of the great present-day drivers of change that has an impact on luxury. The development of global mass media – television in particular – and the growth in international travel have made everyone aware of the cultural richness and diversity of our planet and of the many other possible ways of living, even in our own society; everyone can vicariously live the high life along with the great and the good whom they have 'met' through television or read about in celebrity magazines.

What this means is that, before each and every one of us, there opens up a vast so-called 'field of possibilities', where we can pick and choose what best suits us personally to come up with our very own social stratification. Looking at the flip side of the coin, the wealth of possibilities available to us is now so great that anxiety of choice, a favourite theme of Jean-Paul Sartre's, weighs so heavily on some individuals that it ends up alienating their freedom, very often to the point where they prefer the power of decision to be taken from them, thereby abdicating their free will.

We shall be coming back later to discuss one of the key consequences of this situation: where the luxury brand becomes the be-all-and-end-all for some individuals, guiding them in their social choices, so much so that sometimes they behave as if they belonged to a sect. The annual Steve Jobs show at Apple is just like some ancient religious ceremony conducted by a High Priest – just as the purpose behind the sacrificial ceremonies of the Aztecs was to keep the sun in orbit for another cycle, so the Apple Show is designed to reassure its worshippers that revolutionary new products are going to be able to sustain them for one more year.

The non-return effect

So, we have identified four powerful drivers at work here: democratization, increase in spending power, globalization and communications – when they are all working at full throttle they help propel luxury to previously unknown levels.

Before moving on to other things, we need to add a word about a well-known effect of luxury, namely the 'non-return effect', or 'ratchet effect', the counterpart of the 'non-linear increase' that we talked about earlier: once people have tasted luxury in whatever area, it is very difficult for them to turn away from it – to come back to earth. When there is a fall in spending power, we witness a symmetrical phenomenon to the one that we identified when spending power was increased: people start cutting their expenditure on every kind of conventional product (for example, they will trade their Chevrolet for a smaller and more economic Ford), but it's a different matter when it comes to luxury products (they will keep their Ferrari, even if it means leaving it in the garage and going by bicycle, on the pretext that it's more ecological). They will do without almost anything, so long as they can afford the upkeep on their mansion. And there is a point that is worth noting here, one that we shall be returning to time and again: this 'ratchet effect' of luxury affects both the personal aspect of luxury ('I really can't do without the comfort of my cashmere sweater') and its public one ('I drive a Ferrari').

On this point, one of the authors is reminded of an anecdote: back in the 1980s, the People's Republic of China was a major customer of Saint-Gobain Desjonquères, buying from them mainly small glass bottles, some for packaging antibiotics and others destined to be used for nail varnish. It was October and the time had come to draw up the budget for the following year – an annual chore for the boss of any large group. The economic situation in China at that time was rapidly going from bad to worse, and a severe cutback in orders for the year to come was predicted; it seemed obvious to him that, in critical times, the health of the Chinese population was going to take precedence over the beauty of its womenfolk, especially in a Communist state. He therefore decided to leave the sales forecast for the bottles for antibiotics at the current year's level, while at the same time drastically reducing the sales forecast for the nail varnish bottles. This proved to be a major error of judgement, because the very opposite occurred! The Communist leaders had understood perfectly that if they kept up supplies of nail varnish in their state-run stores they would be passing along the message that everything was fine… and they could even add that they were reducing their orders for antibiotics because the health of the population had greatly improved! Besides, people would never know how much antibiotics were used in hospitals anyway.

After decades of monochrome existence, Chinese women at last had the chance to wear bright colours (on their nails at least!) without being immediately rebuked and condemned; to deprive them of nail varnish would be to deprive them of a symbol (at that time a luxury in China) of what was for them a quite new and very important freedom, and that would have been far more dangerous for the powers of the day than abandoning a number of sick people to their fate.

Fortunately for the company's budget, both products were manufactured on the same machines, and the total production volume was as forecast.

The stages of change

Without dwelling too long on the historical aspect, it is interesting to see how luxury has gradually invaded the modern economy, both in terms of products and activities and on a geographic level.

If the late 19th century and early 20th century saw the first mass emergence of contemporary French luxury houses (Louis Vuitton, Cartier, Hermès), and if the inter-war period saw the second, with the development of perfumery (Chanel No 5), it was not until after the Second World War that the luxury business really took off and became an industry in its own right, and at the same time a luxury niche gradually began appearing in all the specialist trades.

Indeed, luxury is after all very much a peacetime industry, as we saw previously with the feminine societies, and the post-war period saw its moment of triumph – or rather its triumphal progress – as the process continued from 1945 up to the present day:

- the 1950s: the pioneers (perfume, alcohols, champagne);
- the 1970s: the decade of Japan and the oil-producing countries;
- the 1980s: USA and the Reagan years;
- the 1990s: globalization.

Now, at the start of the 21st century, luxury has become so popular that everyone (or almost everyone) wants to be in on it. Luxury is very much in fashion, and almost every economic player is claiming to offer it.

If we want a sound basis from which to start defining effective operating strategies, we need to go back to the origins of the concept to find, behind all the claptrap spouted about it, the true signifiers of luxury and what it is all about. At the most profound level, this 'invasion' is the consequence of what earlier we referred to as the paradigm of luxury, or the luxury paradox: the offspring of social stratification, in our present-day societies luxury has become its father.

Luxury, the individual and society

Now that it has become common to hear people talking about the end of social stratification, of open societies and of luxury goods accessible to all, we really must return to this central theme of the connection between luxury, the individual and society.

Luxury and social stratification

Let us start with what is in our eyes the most fundamental point, one that we have christened 'the paradigm of luxury':

- Originally, luxury was the visible result – deliberately conspicuous and ostentatious – of hereditary social stratification (kings, priests and the nobility, versus the gentry and commoners), a social stratification with which absolutely everyone had to fall in as it was itself based on certain metaphysical principles (the social order as ordained by the Creator, the Church, the Tao, the caste system, the Law of Karma, etc).

- Eighteenth-century rational thought and Enlightenment philosophy resulted in the gradual disappearance of the founding myths of European society that gave legitimacy to the social structure, whether in the Middle Ages or under the *Ancien Régime* in France, and, along with these myths, away went all supernatural explanations for natural events: lightning is no longer thought of as Zeus voicing his anger, but simply a phenomenon produced by electrostatic discharge; objects are no longer attributed with a soul. This is the phenomenon of 'disenchantment', or 'Entzauberung' (literally, demystification or rationalization), that the German political economist and sociologist Max Weber analysed so well, which characterizes present-day Western society and which, thanks to globalization, is inexorably conquering the world – a materialistic and fluid society in which any kind of transcendent social stratification has disappeared.

- What has not disappeared, on the other hand, is humankind's need for some form of social stratification, which is vital; without it, a person, a social being by nature, is unable to escape social chaos and imitative disorder born of undifferentiation (as French philosopher René Girard showed most ably). We need to know our place in society.

- Luxury, then, has a fundamental function of recreating this social stratification. What is more, it does it in a democratic manner, meaning that everyone can recreate (up to a certain point) their strata according to their dreams – whence a new kind of anxiety, that of freedom: before, the strata were known and respected; democracy, sexual equality and globalization have led society to lose its points of reference and opened the sluice gates to consumption, but now it lacks any hierarchical codes. These need to be recreated, and 'the anxiety of freedom' creates a demand for advice on how to recreate these codes, placing the 'luxury brand' in a position of superiority with respect to its client, a notion that we shall come across repeatedly, as its consequences when it comes to the strategy are very considerable: in addition to quality, which you have a right to expect from a top-of-the-range brand, you would want something extra from a luxury brand – some sociological advice, an instruction even: 'This is exactly the product you need to buy for yourself or somebody else', with the client's full acquiescence, if not their express demand (What should I give this person for this occasion?'). It is the brand that is laying down its law to the consumer – all quite democratically of course!

Luxury as a social marker: luxury for others

Clearly luxury is a marker, which is why there is such a need for brands.

With luxury recreating some degree of social stratification, people in a democracy are therefore free – within the limit of their financial means – to use any of its components to define themselves socially as they wish. What we have here is 'democratic luxury' – a luxury item that extraordinary people would consider ordinary, is at the same time an extraordinary item to ordinary people. The DNA of luxury, therefore, is the symbolic desire to belong to a superior class, which everyone will have chosen according to their dreams, because anything that can be a social signifier can become a luxury. By the same token, anything that ceases to be a social signifier loses its luxury status. Once, a swimming-pool was a luxury, but it is no longer so. A private elevator still is one, for it harks back to the multistorey private hotel.

The codes of luxury are cultural, inasmuch as the luxury brand lies at the confluence between culture and social success. The elite classes should (or are supposed to) appreciate luxury for themselves, even if snobs consume in imitation without actually enjoying, or understanding for that matter.

These markers of luxury are to be found all around us:

- Objects, of course: 'family jewels' to be preserved at all costs and exhibited on every important occasion. The luxury object can even become a 'social necessity' (the 'ratchet effect' referred to earlier), with the need to own the object leading, in some extreme cases, to aberrant behaviours, like those of young Japanese women using prostitution as a means to afford a particular brand of bag (the 'sugar daddy' phenomenon).

- Houses, obviously: think of those penniless old nobles, refusing to work on principle and living in abject misery – in their mansions – and from time to time (as rarely as possible) giving a great ball just to reaffirm their rank in society, and then ending up eating sardines out of the can for six months.
- Beauty, needless to say: historically the skin colour of 'chic' European women has always been an ostentatious sign associated with the luxury of free time – for centuries it was white, to show that one didn't need to work out in the fields; then for a few decades it was bronzed, to show that one did take a vacation; and now it is a deep suntan.

What we might call 'luxury among friends', which falls somewhere between 'luxury for oneself', which we shall be looking at next, and 'public luxury', which we were talking about just now, also comes under this heading of affirmative logic:

- the bottle of champagne that you take along to a party, even though you don't particularly like drinking champagne, and which was selected in accordance with very specific codes that depend on the social status of both sets of individuals;
- the art collections that are shown to the fortunate few, and in particular 'difficult' arts, reserved for the initiated (very modern or very primitive art).

Luxury for oneself

In addition to this key social function, luxury is an access to pleasure: it should have a very strong personal and hedonistic component, otherwise it is no longer a luxury but simple snobbery, and we would quickly fall into the trap of provocation ('I have the biggest automobile in the whole neighbourhood') or the potlatch – a highly complex ritual ceremony practised in Melanesia and among certain indigenous peoples on the Pacific north-west coast of the United States and Canada, especially the Kwakiutl tribe, in which the object of the exercise is to overawe the other person and outdo them by offering them the most luxurious gifts possible, which cannot be reciprocated, placing the person in a position of weakness in a society in which every gift must be followed by a return gift of equal or greater munificence.

Undoubtedly there does exist a consumer market for symbols (in answer to the question What makes people rich these days?'). But no luxury brand can hope to survive if it relies purely on clients who are only interested in the symbol rather than the substance; these people – the ones who are only interested in symbols – will drift from one symbol to another, from one logo to another: tycoons will today be drinking Dom Pérignon by the case and tomorrow something else. The luxury brand is a cultural thing and as such it has to proclaim its profound truth, the truth that brings us into resonance with it.

Put another way, although snobs do constitute a not inconsiderable proportion of a luxury brand's clientele, they could never be its bedrock; a luxury brand relies on as large as possible a core of faithful clients thoroughly imbued with the brand's culture and appreciating its world, its identity, and its philosophy.

There are several key points to emerge from this and we shall be returning to them in due course:

- Luxury is qualitative and not quantitative: the number of diamonds in a necklace is an indication of its opulence but says nothing about the taste of the wearer.
- When it comes to luxury, hedonism takes precedence over functionality. The materials used in haute couture that may be very elegant but not always pleasant to wear ('You have to suffer in the name of beauty'), designer furniture that is highly uncomfortable, the discomfort and noise of a Ferrari; these are all part and parcel of a luxury product. Products without any defects and without a soul are for 'those who don't know any better'.
- Luxury has to be multisensory: it is not only the appearance of a Porsche that matters but also the sound of it, not only the scent of a perfume but also the beauty of the bottle it comes in. It is multisensory compression.
- Luxury for oneself does of course include a strong aesthetic aspect, distinct from its hedonistic component (what we find beautiful does not necessarily have to be pleasant). We shall be coming back to this later (see 'Luxury and art'), but it is worth observing here that aesthetic pleasure is certainly influenced by the social and cultural environment but nevertheless remains highly personal; it contributes significantly to the individual component of the concept of luxury.
- Last but not least – luxury being a social phenomenon, and society being composed of human beings, luxury, whether object or service, must have a strong human content, be of human origin (as Karl Marx said about value and labour: gold and diamonds are luxuries and have a high value because it takes a great deal of labour to find and extract them): the object must be hand-made, the service rendered by a human; we shall be dealing with this specific aspect at greater length later.

Duality of luxury: luxury for oneself and luxury for others

It immediately follows from this analysis that if one wants a luxury product or service to be a lasting financial success (which is the point of this book) it absolutely must possess the following two aspects:

- a social aspect (luxury as a social statement in relation to other products or services – connecting luxury, brand status);
- a personal aspect (luxury as an individual pleasure – cocooning luxury, customer experience).

It is revealing in this respect that the Luxury Institute in the USA produces two barometers of luxury in every sector:

- The first is called the Luxury Customer Experience Index (LCEI), which is a measure of the satisfaction felt with a service. It is an expression of the perceived quality in all its facets, including reliability, fragility or flimsiness, ease of access, etc, but also the human aspect, the service.
- The second, called the Luxury Brand Status Index (LBSI), is more concerned with the intangible, the prestige associated with the given brand, its dream potential and therefore the distinction conferred on the possessor. The items in the index have to do with a feeling of exclusivity and uniqueness, the feeling of having one's social standing reinforced through the brand, the feeling of being a special person.

This duality and this ambivalence makes the concept of luxury extremely subjective and variable, both between individuals and between societies; this is the more glaring the better-known the brand and the more visible the product. Let us take the case of Louis Vuitton, for example. It is far and away the world's most valued luxury brand, which does not stop thousands of people – some of them from genuine feeling, but most of them from pure snobbery – considering it to be a vulgar brand that can no longer be counted a luxury brand at all, declaring that they wouldn't dream of buying anything of theirs, let alone be seen with it; yet this doesn't stop the very same people gladly accepting the gift of a product bearing the LV monogram and of using it ostentatiously.

One should therefore never say 'This is luxury and that isn't' without prefacing the remark with 'For me', 'To my way of thinking', or 'In my opinion', just as one should never say 'This is beautiful' or 'This is ugly' without prefacing it with 'I find that' – there again, luxury and art are closely related, and success in both can never be absolute.

Luxury and ethics

We shall now briefly consider the boundaries of luxury as a social game and also positive and negative luxury.

A luxury that is not ethical ceases to be a luxury

In this social game of luxury, it is absolutely vital to remain ethical, both with respect to others by avoiding provocation, and with respect to oneself by avoiding addiction; the purpose of luxury as we see it and advocate it is to contribute to social peace and universal happiness, rather than the opposite. This is why the future of luxury will need to incorporate sustainable concerns too, all along the production process (see also page 297).

With respect to others

The aim of 'positive' luxury – the only kind that interests us here – is to elevate somebody socially by raising one's own esteem in the eyes of others and not by crushing them (see the potlatch example above). 'Luxury by crushing' is nothing but showing off and doesn't make a great deal of sense; it only leads to a totally frustrating constant headlong flight ('We're going to really impress them, just to sicken them') – we shall be returning to this later (in Chapter 9 on price).

Likewise, the aim of this 'positive' luxury is to prevent imitative conflict – everyone at war with everyone else (see the works of Thomas Hobbes and René Girard) – an inevitable consequence of unstructured societies.

With respect to oneself

'Positive' luxury is there to make one happier; it should not become something that one cannot literally live without or, not going quite so far, it should not lead one to sacrificing one's true self to appearances. Luxury should be there to boost one's true self, not stifle it.

It must of course remain within decent limits, otherwise it's no longer a question of luxury but of addiction (the Japanese 'sugar daddy' phenomenon mentioned earlier).

Luxury is to such excessive behaviors what eroticism is to pornography: positive luxury is refinement, nuances, culture, flirtation, pleasure, and not brutality; luxury does of course often manifest itself in abundance, but not overabundance, which leads to saturation and revulsion.

Luxury is not excess and excess is not luxury

Which, in conclusion, is why one should not confuse 'having a taste for luxury' with 'having luxurious tastes'. The first suggests someone cultivated and discerning, the second acquisitiveness and excess.

Positioning of luxury in our present-day society

We shall be discussing what in our present-day society characterizes our attitudes to time, to money and to the individual, where luxury fits into this context, and what unique points of view it has to offer that make it a priceless quest.

Luxury and time

Our modern society's relationship with time is very specific: the key phrase that sums up this relationship is 'time is money', meaning that lost time is lost money and time gained is money gained. At a time when thanks to improved nutrition and advances in medicine we are all living much longer, we have this paradoxical dread of wasting this additional time; we seem obsessed with finding ways of using it instead of enjoying it.

Our society lives under this tyranny of time, having become the society of instant gratification, of the ephemeral, accelerated still further by the modern sources of entertainment, like the movies and TV, imposing their own tempo on the passive viewer, displacing books, which gave us the freedom to make time for reading; expendable starlets and public entertainers have replaced philosophers. To enjoy luxury you have to devote time to it, and conversely, luxury is an opportunity to enjoy some free time.

Let us take that a little further: one of the most significant aspects of our society is that not only have we monetized the relationship to time (interest rates), but also created from it a basis for managing it (forecast return on an investment, discount rates); time, like money, being a one-dimensional variable, this invasion of measured, quantified, time makes for a one-dimensional society – time is no longer 'the form of inner sense' in human experience, as Kant put it, but becomes an objective external variable, eventually being integrated as a single dimension of the four-dimensional universe of General Relativity, where Man no longer has any place. We shall be dealing in greater detail with this one-dimensionality, this representation of the universe, in the section on luxury and money below.

Finally, as we saw earlier, the role of luxury is to recreate social stratification; however, social stratification has a time dimension; consequently luxury, in contrast to fashion, should not be the slave of time but stand aloof from time, or at the very least it should not be dominated by it, and hence the second contradiction of luxury: a luxury item is both timeless and of the here and now. Put another way, a luxury item has to appear both perfectly modern to the society of the day and at the same time laden with history; one of the conventional ways of dealing with this contradiction is for the brand to have the stamp of timelessness while the product has every appearance of being modern or vice versa.

Luxury and the consumer society

Luxury is of course part and parcel of our present-day consumer society, in which it has found a highly fertile breeding ground. We have seen the extent to which the relationship between luxury and time has differed from the relationship between modern society and time. It is in fact totally opposed to the consumer society on three other major points, as detailed below.

Relationship to the item

The luxury item is an object loaded with meaning, to which one becomes attached (to quote the 19th-century French dramatist, poet, and novelist Alphonse de Lamartine: 'O inanimate objects, have you then a soul that attaches itself to our soul and forces it to love?'), a 'lived-in' product rather than an undistinguished, utilitarian product that we would immediately replace, or rather get rid of, as soon as it starts to fail or is technically superseded.

The luxury object is durable and even increases in value with time vintage, like a wine or a piece of Louis Vuitton luggage. It is technically designed to resist wear, uses choice starting materials that time only serves to enhance (the patina of old furniture, Vuitton natural cowhide, vintage-wine grape varieties, etc), and is of a design that also will stand the test of time (like Ferrari); thus, the very opposite of an industrially manufactured object, which is expected to wear out and go out of fashion in order to be replaced and keep the production machinery busy – as soon as a new automobile leaves the showroom it loses 30 per cent of its value.

Relationship to people

The consumer society is a child of the Industrial Revolution, whose success is essentially due to mechanization, that is to say the replacement of people by machine; its ideal, however noble, is a society of robots to relieve people completely from the tasks of production.

Conversely, luxury being primarily social in nature, and society being made up of human beings, every luxury product should bear a person's imprint. We shall be reverting to this point at greater length in Chapter 8 on the luxury product, but we can cite here the German sociologist Georg Simmel: 'A product has the less soul, the more people participate in its manufacture.'

If the standard consumer product is a product mass-manufactured by machine and sold in self-convenience stores and department stores, through catalogues or on the internet, a luxury product on the other hand is hand-made and sold by one individual to another individual. You could scarcely find a greater contrast!

Relationship to desire

This is the most subtle point and the most difficult to handle on account of the total subjectivity and the lack of lucidity when faced with this subject:

- The luxury product corresponds to a deep and (relatively) personal and spontaneous desire, whereas the consumer product is the object of a desire created from start to finish, or at least manipulated, by advertising.
- The choice of a luxury product is the result of a personal decision and not of a 'mimesis', in René Girard's sense of the word.

  (Here is a good example of this difference: when you gaze from the terrace of a villa overlooking the Gulf of St Tropez at the sumptuous yachts lying lazily swinging at anchor in view of all around, and whose only daily nautical outing is to go from the port to one of the nearby beaches or perhaps a local seafront restaurant before returning to port – there you have a caricatured demonstration of the power of this mimetic phenomenon, which has nothing to do with luxury: the yachts are quite obviously luxury products, and a cruise on one of these yachts in some out-of-the-way archipelago, either alone or in the company of close friends, for many of us would be the height of luxury!)

- The desire for luxury is based on hedonism and the aesthetic, not on overindulgence leading to saturation and revulsion.
- The key word when it comes to luxury is dream, not envy.
- Luxury is about being, for oneself and for others, not about having.
- The right time for luxury is the time of celebration, the giving of gifts.

Money, fashion, art and luxury: boundaries and ambiguities

To wind up these remarks about the basics of luxury and be able to go about the practical business of putting in place a system for managing luxury effectively, we need to consider in depth the analysis of the relationship between three sociocultural concepts closely associated with it, namely money, fashion and art.

Luxury and money

The first of the three is the one that requires us to take the analysis the furthest. 'Luxury' is so often taken as a synonym for 'money' that to confuse the two ends up seeming natural, and to call into question the idea that luxury and money are just two sides of the same coin may shock some people (see our earlier example of the yachts in St Tropez). And yet, an insufficient understanding of the relationship between luxury and money, without of course comparing the two, is one of the main causes of failure in the management of luxury.

At first sight the relationship between luxury and money may seem so obvious that one might begin to wonder whether the word 'luxury' should not disappear altogether from everyday language and be replaced by the word 'money'.

In fact, money is generally the 'brute force' of luxury in its 'public' or 'for others' manifestation, sometimes the only form of luxury in unstructured (the 'Far West') societies, or societies that have broken down. In China today, for example, people still leave the price label showing on 'luxury' clothes. Even in wealthy and socially structured countries, claiming to be 'the most expensive in the world' can be part of a marketing strategy for products that are unmistakably luxury products, whether it is Jean Patou's Joy perfume or the Bugatti Veyron. Having said that, regardless of the fact that this is a particularly ephemeral claim – for anyone can always, and perfectly easily, make things 'more expensive' – these products have never been a financial success; now, the point of this book is precisely to explain how to succeed financially and commercially, and especially when it comes to products or services whose price is not particularly high.

Let us take that a little further: there is little similarity between 'luxury for oneself' and money; the roots, the basic elements of luxury, are extremely abstract concepts ('beauty', 'pleasure'), or not very concrete in themselves, even though their consequences are very concrete ('youth', 'health', 'happiness'); they are difficult – impossible even – to quantify and therefore to connect with the notion of money. To find the connection between these two concepts of luxury and money we have to resort to myths, like the one about Faust – it is the pact with the devil, not money, that brings wealth and eternal youth. Sometimes, as in the myth of the Golden Age, it is lack of money that makes it possible to achieve this happiness.

It is therefore manifestly clear that luxury is not only money, and money by itself is not luxury.

Let us look a little deeper, from the theoretical point of view, at the complex relationship between 'luxury' and 'money', the practical point of view of which we shall be discussing later in Chapter 9 on price. In this analysis we shall be basing ourselves on the concepts developed by Georg Simmel in his celebrated book *Philosophie des Geldes* (Philosophy of Money), published in 1900, the most profound and complete treatise ever written on the subject of money as seen from the conceptual point of view.

Luxury and money as purely sociocultural phenomena

Ever since people emerged from the subsistence society, we have had to trade in order to obtain the means of survival, and at that point money became indispensable. To quote Simmel (page 193): 'Money is the hypostasis of trade between human beings... if the economic value of objects lies in the exchange relationship that they form, money is the expression of this relationship that has achieved autonomy.'

Sooner or later, money always becomes an instrument for measuring and grading the social scale; it even has a strong natural tendency to want to be the only one, especially in our globalized and multicultural society, where it is the only universally recognized power, for it alone can provide society with the means to economic fluidity, indispensable to globalization – as soon as you have a universal currency, all products of all human societies then become comparable.

Money, like the 'public' face of luxury, is purely a social convention: as soon as this social convention ceases to be shared, money loses all value. In those places where shells (cowries, for example) served as currency, a banknote was worthless, and vice versa, just as when a local currency becomes worthless abroad if no one can be found who is prepared to change it.

So, just like luxury, money is generated by life in society, but it plays a contrasting role in creating a social stratification; in fact, money has the power to break down social castes, as indeed other cultures. Here is another quotation from Simmel (page 518): 'Monetary affairs have a democratic levelling effect.'

There is of course a strong connection between the two concepts: right from the beginning, those who had the right to luxury – the powerful – were also those who had money, but there was never any confusion of roles; the socially dominant (the nobility, warriors and religious bodies) accepted with difficulty, or not at all, anyone else who had money (merchants and financiers), and who often had to stay out of sight.

This contrasting role in the stratification process is the point of departure for understanding the fundamental difference between luxury and money in the 'social comedy'.

The unidimensionality of money and the multidimensionality of luxury

Money is a unique and universal measure because it is the collective and unidimensional abstraction of value; it is not the product of social stratification, for it is a continuum: you are a member of the aristocracy or you are not, but when it comes to money you can have more or less of it.

The unidimensionality of money is boundless alongside the complex and ever-changing multiplicity of human beings and their social life; money, if it is the sole criterion, creates an 'anomic' society, as French sociologist Émile Durkheim (1930) defined it, therefore unlivable for people – a person's place in society cannot be reduced to the money they possesses.

To quote again from Simmel's *Philosophy of Money* (page 260): 'The man of money pure and simple is quickly threatened with a loss of social status... money all too readily becomes an aim in itself, in all too many people it concludes the teleological series once and for all.'

Let us go further down this road: the abstract, semantic void of money is opposed to the concrete, the semantic richness of luxury.

Money as such does not bring on longing; what brings on longing is not money itself, but what you can get with it. There is nothing luxurious about a banknote; it is only in our dreams that each one of us converts it into a luxury and in this way gives it a concrete meaning. For a concert pianist the money received for playing is not enough: what they also want (and even want above all if they are a true artist) is the public's applause. If you give a child money or a cheque as a birthday gift, basically it means that you don't know the child, or that you cannot be bothered to get to know them – this gesture distorts the nature of the gift by reducing human relationship to nothing more than a sum of money, to a mere material act.

The objectivity of money and the subjectivity, both personal and social, of luxury

Let us come back to what we said at the outset: price, and therefore money, is not a determinant of luxury.

It is quite obvious that price on its own does not make something a luxury; an ordinary automobile will cost more than a luxury purse, and it is a common error to believe that to turn any product into a luxury product all it takes is to raise its price, which will soon bring about financial failure – a product that is more expensive can often turn into a product that is too expensive, one that nobody wants, rather than a luxury product that people long for.

For anyone looking for financial success (which is the point of this book), things are even more clear-cut: within a given range, the most expensive products are never the most profitable, and a company that makes only very expensive products does not generally have any financial success (as in the case of Rolls-Royce, for example), or is likely to find it outside of its core production (designer jewellery and haute couture, for example). Too narrow a client base would entail crippling costs; Volkswagen has publicly admitted that each Bugatti Veyron costs the company over €4 million to produce, whereas it is sold for (only!) €1 million.

Money is society's language, luxury is its grammar

In the early 20th century, in his Course in General Linguistics, Swiss linguist Ferdinand de Saussure (1972) likened the exchange of terms in language with that of currency, the structural dimension of language corresponding to the exchange value and its functional dimension to the usage value. If we take up this analogy and take our current analysis to its logical end, we come to the conclusion that money inexorably becomes the language of any constituted society, or rather it becomes the vocabulary, for it designates everything in an explicit and unique manner – if the economy is fluid, a product or service has at any given moment a fixed price, just as it has a name (or a barcode!).

Seen from this angle, luxury plays the role of the grammar for the language of this society: just as the grammar does for vocabulary, it is luxury that brings monetary signs together to create a language. And the more elaborate and structured this grammar is, the more elaborate the social structure.

We can compare money taken in isolation to the language we speak in a foreign country after reading one of those slim volumes aimed at tourists in a hurry (*Armenian in Ten Easy Lessons* or *Finnish in Ten Days*, etc): we can manage to ask where to eat, where to sleep, how much this or that costs (indeed, that's all these slim volumes ever talk about – the price, more about the price, and nothing but the price...), but it is completely impossible to use just this language, with no grammatical structure, to communicate meaningfully with another person, who remains a foreigner.

Just as pidgin, a language that uses a basic English vocabulary without any grammatical structure and devoid of any trace of British culture is the common language of mass globalization, so money is the lingua franca (the pidgin of the Roman Empire) of societies:

- that have shorter histories – in such a case, some form of social stratification has to be invented. In the USA, it was in the beginning that the Founding Fathers, having a core of shared values centered on the Bible, were able to structure North American society on clear foundations; but this society has not had the time to establish firm roots or create a powerful history. The mass immigration of the 19th century has buried this too recent and too feeble a structure, and money, with its 'dream machine' that is Hollywood, has gradually (and hopefully only temporarily) taken control of the society.
- that have been completely torn apart by one political or economic upheaval after another (Communist countries like the former USSR or, right now, China), for that is the only common reference point in this case;
- that have not yet succeeded in uniting around common cultural and political concepts (the global and multipolar society of today).

But this stage does not last for ever: gradually society becomes civilized and 'luxury' becomes its grammar (cf *The Idea of Luxury*, by C Berry).

Let us sum up this relationship between money and luxury in a couple of sentences:

- Money fuels the luxury engine but is not the engine; the engine is the recreation of vertical hierarchy / social stratification.
- Luxury converts the raw material that is money into a culturally sophisticated product that is social stratification.

In placing ourselves in the territory of Value, so dear to economists, we could say that luxury introduces a new notion of value that goes beyond the classic dialectic of use-value and exchange-value: symbolic value. The use-value of a product being a non-monetary value, and the exchange-value representing its price, the luxury-value of a product is its symbolic value, also non-monetary, emanating not from work or exchange but from social stratification. It will be greater or lesser, depending on everyone and on the social context, but it will have to be higher than the exchange-value (the price of the product) for a large enough number of individuals for there to be a market for the product.

'Luxury and money' summarized

Having concluded this analysis it is now clear to us that luxury plays a key role within any organized society, and that this role has nothing to do with money.

This is very much in line with the aim of this book, which is to define the conditions that would allow a luxury brand to conduct a luxury strategy, and to explain in concrete terms how to go about it: if the word 'luxury' were no more than a synonym for the word 'price', there would have been no reason to look any further, and it would have been sufficient simply to raise the price of one's product – always provided more clients could be found – to do a bit of 'trading-up', in order to succeed. However, luxury is something radically different from trading-up, which does not have the sociological and historical impact of luxury.

On the other hand, if price doesn't mean luxury, then the possibility opens up for many brands to successfully conduct a 'luxury' marketing strategy – and it can be called that because it takes its inspiration from strategies developed with success by great luxury houses like Cartier or Louis Vuitton – in trades not traditionally regarded as 'luxury' trades, as for example Apple has done in consumer electronics or Nespresso in the coffee market (see also page 284).

Luxury and fashion

Let us now address ourselves to another ambiguous and confusing relationship, namely that of luxury and fashion.

Right up to the turn of the 19th century, fashion belonged to the luxury world; only the favoured social stratum could afford the luxury of not having to keep their clothes until they had worn out, and of buying others without being driven by necessity to do so.

In the 20th century the fashion world started finding a degree of freedom, then to diverge from that of luxury, and today the overlap between luxury and fashion is in practice extremely slight – although this fact is not generally publicized.

Luxury is now 'fashionable'. Fashion claims to be a luxury (an affordable one, if possible)

Many luxury brands adopt the behaviour of fashion brands. Sharing certain aspects of luxury, including the quality of not really being essential and a certain element of showing-off, fashion would like to think of itself as belonging to the world of luxury in order to improve its status.

One consequence of this 'two-way traffic' is that the semantic confusion between luxury and fashion is greater than ever these days, and some clarification is definitely called for.

We have considered the social function in the present day of luxury, but what is it in the case of fashion? It is in fact a dual function, responding to two recent social 'novelties': massification and urbanization.

In fact, if the importance of luxury in our modern democratic societies comes from its role of social stratification, the equally great importance of fashion derives from the negative consequences for human beings of urbanization – anonymity and an unnatural life; one of the most common collective responses as a way of regaining lost time, or even of creating an illusion of time, is through the frenzied use of fashion.

It is worth mentioning here that though living in a large conurbation is gradually becoming the norm for many of us, 99 per cent of humanity's life was spent in small family units closely bound with nature; it is this way of living, as opposed to living in vast anonymous housing developments, that represents the ecosystem to which our psyche is best suited. Being unable to adapt quickly enough to this new universe, people have had to find ways of adjusting, as once they had to adjusting to living in caves.

It is the sociological role of fashion these days:

- In our 'unnatural' societies, fashion has artificially given back a rhythm to time by marking the seasons and the years by something other than figures (we talk about 'summer fashions', not 'third-quarter fashions'), thereby giving the vital reference points back to the city-dweller. As French philosopher Jean Baudrillard put it in his *Symbolic Exchange and Death* (1976), 'Modernity simultaneously sets in motion a linear time, which is that of technical progress and history, and a cyclical time, which is that of fashion.'
- In our anonymous and undifferentiated societies, where there is a major risk of 'mimetic crisis' (as René Girard meant it), fashion creates an artificial differentiation, but this time it is 'horizontal' instead of 'vertical', as it is with luxury, because it allows us, even in the middle of all the crowd, to make ourselves recognizable to everyone and at first glance, as a member of this or that tribe. Going back to Georg Simmel: 'There are fashions each time social differences seek visibly to express themselves... mobile classes and individuals find in fashion the rhythm of their own physical movements.'
- For some people, finally, fashion is their way of rejecting social stratification, of escaping the vertical organization of social positioning: to everyone his or her fashion, his or her style, his or her way of mixing everything with everything. Social differentiation is not stratification.

As we saw earlier, our Western societies had need of luxury to make them suitable to be lived in by us primates; as they are also urban societies, they also need fashion to be livable. In fact, they need both luxury and fashion:

- luxury, by recreating a social stratification that was done away with by democracy; and
- fashion, by recreating the rhythm of the seasons that was done away with by urbanization, and a social differentiation while avoiding being engulfed by the anonymous crowd.

On the other hand, if luxury and fashion both play a key role in our social life – and therefore in the economy – for all that, there should not be any confusion between them. Fashion is no more a luxury than is money, and vice versa. It is interesting to note on this point that civilizations that are still living in an isolated natural environment and in small communities (on Pacific islands, like present-day Vanuatu for example) have a social stratification (chiefs), luxury objects (jewels), but no fashion.

Looking at the evidence before us – that they have in common the need to appear different and be differentiated socially – it would be easy to rush to wrong conclusions, not realizing the extent to which luxury and fashion differ from each other in two fundamental respects:

- relationship to time (durability versus ephemerality);
- relationship to self (luxury is for oneself, fashion is not).

The best example of this is in haute couture, which we shall be looking at later in some detail, and whose *raison d'être* is precisely to be both the height of luxury and the height of fashion. With the notable exception of Chanel, the financial collapse of haute couture is today virtually complete, for the good reason that it is no longer relevant to present-day sociological issues, as we have just seen. It is so-called 'streetwear', as epitomized by the likes of H&M and Zara, that is very much alive and well financially, while haute couture is for the most part forced to convert its financial deficit into an investment in the brand in order to obtain a return on investment through other derivative products – which in fact become the real stars of fashion shows, the dresses shown there being not so much to be worn as to show off the accessories.

Luxury and fashion, then, represent two worlds – both economically important, but still very different (the 'luxury streets' are not to be found in the 'fashion quarters') and they overlap only marginally (limited to haute couture); in these cases, success relies on a tandem arrangement, where you have a brand (which covers the luxury side) and a creator (who covers the fashion side), and the best example of this is Chanel and Karl Lagerfeld.

A final point – a major source of confusion between luxury and fashion can be put down to the current economic climate: short-term stock exchange pressure is forcing luxury to take a leaf out of fashion's book:

- constantly launch new products (perfumery) without worrying too much about their relevance, except financially;
- cannibalize existing products;
- join the ephemerals and so lose any pretence of luxury.

Hence the temptation of those large houses that are on the stock exchange to get out (successful leveraged buy-outs) or to hide themselves within a large group (like Louis Vuitton Malletier in LVMH).

To be more explicit on the differences between luxury and fashion today, and introduce the world 'premium' whose relation with luxury will be discussed in depth in the next chapter, we can place luxury, fashion and premium on the three points of a triangle in which any brand with a minimal status has to be positioned (see Figure 1.1).

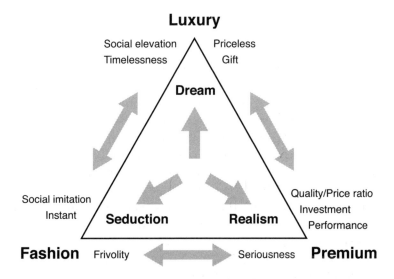

Figure 1.1   Luxury, fashion and premium positioning triangle

Luxury and art

The two concepts are very closely interlinked – so closely, in fact, that it seems impossible to separate them completely; indeed, they are two related concepts.

In the first place, both go back to the dawn of humanity – many of the objects found in early tombs are both *objets d'art* and luxury items; it is very likely that luxury and art came into being at the same time, or were perhaps for a long time indistinguishable. Even today many traces can be found of this long common infancy, and there is clearly a considerable overlap between the two concepts.

First of all, they have in common the importance of aesthetics – the *raison d'être* of art, but also an indispensable condition for luxury – and increasing value with time. Next, for both, practical utility is of secondary importance; in the case of an *objet d'art*, the use-value is often zero, whereas the symbolic value is very high. Luxury and art are powerful and very closely interlinked socio-logical markers: designer jewellery is a luxury and an art, as is the architecture of a mansion or a museum. Another point they have in common is sociological and psychophysiological relativity. In art as in luxury, it is virtually impossible to get a consensus among all individuals and among all peoples, for one is dealing with the subjective ('tastes and colours are things you can't talk about'), and, what is more, you should never seek this consensus, except at the risk of losing your magic and therefore your worth in the eyes of those who love you; the aim is to seduce enough 'clients' to exist.

But there are differences between them of which one could scarcely be unaware. Even if the use-value of a luxury product is small, especially when compared to its symbolic value, it is never zero, in contrast to that of a 'pure' *objet d'art* – the luxury object has nevertheless to have some usefulness. This usefulness of the luxury article is expressed as a use-value, but also as a real exchange-value. Luxury is rooted in the real economy – it must quickly find a solid market, otherwise it will disappear. On the other hand, the myth of the artist as an accursed genius, who only lives after death, is a perennial one in the art world... even if, these days, to be unknown and poor is no longer any guarantee of talent! Picasso showed the way, and many have rushed to follow. The fact nevertheless remains that there is still a very wide gulf between luxury and art in this domain: the creator of luxury lives off their trade throughout their lifetime, while the artist seeks eternal survival through their work.

When it comes to certain aspects, it is no longer a question of differences, but of a conflict between luxury and art:

- Art seeks to be universal – despite the sociological and psychophysiological relativity, art can eventually reach everyone; luxury has to be selective and cannot be within reach of everyone, unless it is to lose its soul.
- The work of art is a unique object in both time and space – it's what makes all the difference between the painting and its reproduction, or what distinguishes the live spectacle (theatre, dance, opera) from the film or record industry (see Walter Benjamin's *The Work of Art in the Age of Mechanical Reproduction* (2006)). The luxury object is designed to be distributed: a luxury object can of course also be a unique object, but this aspect of luxury is not the purpose of this book.

From this duality spring several conjunctions and complementarities:

- Luxury is the driving force behind art in the economic world.
- Luxury is a great patron of the arts. In the United States, as in Classical Antiquity (with the famous example of Maecenas, advisor to the Roman Emperor Augustus), it is well-off individuals who fund (are the patrons of) art. However, this is not the case in Europe – without today's big luxury groups, like LVMH in France, it would not be possible to hold any major exhibition of paintings.
- Luxury is the artist's means of financial subsistence. Working for the luxury industry allows an artist to live decently while pursuing his artistic work – a talented sculptor like Serge Mansau is also the designer of bottles for fine perfumes.
- Art is the aesthetic and social guarantor of luxury.

- Contemporary art helps to ensure that luxury brands with timeless products remain topical and relevant. Luxury brands are a major player in contemporary art; Cartier's Alain-Dominique Perrin has shown the way with the setting up of the Foundation for Contemporary Art in 1984, at Jouy-en-Josas on the outskirts of Paris; he was quickly followed by many others, and today any house that likes to think of itself as 'luxury' has its own Modern Art foundation (the latest being the Louis Vuitton Foundation, expected to open in 2010 at the zoological gardens in Neuilly also on the outskirts of Paris).
- Contemporary art is a source of inspiration for designers of luxury goods. As we saw earlier, luxury was the means of subsistence for many an artist; by the same token, immersing its designers and product managers in the world of contemporary art helps a luxury brand ensure that its products stay topical and relevant. Otherwise, the quest for timelessness leads to creations so irrelevant to the present day as to be considered old-fashioned (this is the sad lot of a few prestigious houses in the Place Vendôme in Paris), and therefore unsellable.

One open question: today, contemporary art is no longer using high-quality materials; on the contrary, it is more and more using 'rubbish' as raw material. This strategy is totally opposed to the strategy of luxury. Are they now departing from each other?

2 The end of a confusion: premium is not luxury

Luxury is everywhere, or at least the word 'luxury' appears everywhere: luxury is in fashion, and the fashion is for luxury. Every product declares itself to be a luxury product, aspires to be a 'true luxury' for everyone... or for the chosen few. The word 'luxury' has become commonplace, and a commonplace word becomes progressively emptied of meaning. We no longer speak of 'luxury', but of 'accessible luxury', of 'true luxury', 'new-luxury', etc. The systematic adjunction of the adjective is there to remind us that the word 'luxury' has become an imprecise one. How can a subject be correctly dealt with when such haziness hangs over the name?

As it is with many concepts, so it is with luxury: everyone understands it, but nobody can agree on exactly what it means, on its contours, its frontiers or its members. It is true that the concept of luxury is not an absolute category, but a relative group, and one that cannot be dissociated from the social and political structure of the century in question. Moreover, as our societies fragment, what is luxury for some is not luxury for others: to each their own luxury. Finally, what luxury is today is not what it will be tomorrow, bearing in mind the industrial capability for making what was once the preserve of the few accessible to everyone.

Another source of ambiguity is linked to the multiplication of concepts such as new luxury, mass luxury, opuluxe, masstige, and so on. This blossoming reveals the desire for trading up among the traditional brands, and at the same time the drift of luxury brands seeking among the public at large the profits that they can no longer create in their original business, luxury. All together they create a multiplication of names that could suggest the existence of a staircase between mass brands and luxury brands, one that may be descended or ascended. However, this is not the case. Luxury requires another way of doing things, almost opposite to that which flourishes in mass-consumption and upper range goods.

These confusions may be damaging, both from a conceptual and a manage-rial point of view. The previous chapter presented the too-often forgotten essence of luxury: the conclusion of this clarification was that luxury is not managed in the same way as non-luxury, even upper range. Traditional marketing stops at luxury.

The multiple approaches to the concept of luxury

Various avenues have already been used to pin down the concept of luxury and define its territory of meaning. Of these, six principal avenues can be identified:

- The first way to define luxury is democratic. Since there is no agreement on one meaning of the word 'luxury', it is possible to refer to the percep-tion of the market, by asking potential clients what luxury means to them. The problem is that different groups of the population have very different, even opposing, understandings of the concept of luxury: a large gold watch studded with diamonds would be the epitome of luxury to some, and of bad taste for others.
- The second is the elitist route. This consists of turning one's back on democracy and choosing what only a few call luxury, the leisured classes, for example. The difficulty becomes manifest when this logic is followed at an international level. Luxury as viewed by a rich Japanese person does not map the same criteria as luxury as viewed by a rich American or French person, still less a rich German, for whom the concept of luxury is suspect: for a German, poor quality is always too expensive. This route hardly assists the luxury company to define a global range.
- The third route consists of trusting the experts. How could the average person possibly understand all these concepts? In this case, however, it is necessary to know who the right experts are, of which nationality, and which culture. This brings us back to the previous problem.

- The fourth route is empirical. This means using the word 'luxury' to refer only to the circumscribed group of so-called luxury brands. Is not the brand the basic unit of all analysis of the luxury industry? The question then arises as to whether certain brands should or should not be included within this perimeter. For example, is Lacoste a luxury brand? Yes, for the Chinese, according to *Time* magazine (October 2007), it currently is: they rate it among the three best-known luxury brands, having discovered it through the new Shanghai Tennis Masters, in department stores and its few exclusive boutiques. But this is not the case for the Spanish or the Italians, since distribution of the brand is very extensive in their countries.
- The fifth route is corporatist. It consists of calling luxury those things that are luxuries, or 'the' luxury, seen by a country that produces luxury. In France, this is what the Colbert Committee does; but this route has little value on a global scale.
- A sixth route is to ask the creators of luxury themselves what they do, according to which criteria, concepts, and values. Here, again, who should be interviewed?

Since none of these different routes offers a problem-free answer, there is another, more radical option: to deny the specificity of luxury.

Denying the specificity of luxury?

In this case, luxury is considered not as a category, but simply as the extreme limit on a certain number of attributes, none of which (for example high price) would be sufficient by itself to define luxury. It would therefore be the extremism of all limits, elevated to a doctrine of design, manufacture, distribution and communication to describe luxury (Sicard, 2006). The classical marketing books (Doyle and Stern, 2006) also follow this line of thought: for many of them, 'luxury' is only the trading up from 'premium' products to 'super premium'. Thus luxury is the ultimate version of a range, marked by all the well-known criteria of rarity, high price, sensuality, creativity, attention to detail, age, quality, imagination.

The advantage of this approach is that it makes it possible to integrate the diversity of luxuries, rather like positioning the cursor differently over this or that dimension.

The problem with this approach is that it does not correspond to the reality perceived on the ground. If this position of negating the specificity of luxury were true, L'Oréal or Procter & Gamble would be the 'emperors of luxury', and Silverstein and Fiske's *Trading Up* (2005) would be the bedtime reading of every luxury manager; and conversely, Louis Vuitton, Chanel, Cartier and others would be no more than small, admittedly prestigious, but local and family companies.

This is simply not the case: neither L'Oréal, despite its acquisition of Lanvin in the 1990s, nor P&G or Unilever have succeeded in the luxury field, and, as its name implies, the book *Trading Up* (Silverstein and Fiske, 2005) is a (moreover excellent) summary of the methods to use in order to successfully move a brand upwards, not a guide to a successful luxury strategy.

The financial markets, furthermore, make no mistake: in 2008 Millward Brown valued the Louis Vuitton brand at US$26 billion, whereas the L'Oréal brand was valued at $16.5 billion, almost two times less for a turnover that is around five times higher. The same study valued the Toyota brand at $35 billion and BMW at $28 billion, although the number of vehicles sold was eight times smaller for BMW than for Toyota.

The financial markets, therefore, recognize the specificity of luxury. We can therefore legitimately go further, and examine the fundamental differences between 'luxury' and 'premium' in the everyday management of a brand, and the reasons why it is impossible to simply 'trade up' from 'premium' to 'luxury'; and that in particular, raising the prices of a 'premium' brand is not sufficient to turn it into a luxury brand.

There is no continuous movement from premium to luxury

There are plentiful examples of attempts to achieve luxury status through continuity with the premium, by increasing the prices without changing the strategy... and the failures are equally plentiful. Another strategy for entry into luxury entails the acquisition of a luxury company that you believe you can manage better than the current owners. These two types of strategy, while they generally work well in the world of industry and mass consumption goods, generally lead to painful defeats when applied to the field of luxury. We will take a recent and clear example, since all the figures are public, and the sector and actors are known to all: the case of Ford.

In the late 1980s and early 1990s (the purchase of Jaguar took place in November 1989 for €2.2 billion), the Ford motor group decided to develop into luxury, creating a 'pole' known as Premier Automotive Group (PAG), through the acquisition of prestigious (Jaguar, Aston Martin) or premium (Volvo, Land Rover) brands, and applying 'Ford methods' to make it a profitable group.

In spite of several years of massive investment, PAG remained immovably 'in the red'; Ford decided to throw in the towel and divest itself of its 'luxury subsidiary' in 2007. While Aston Martin was sold at a good price (around $1 billion) to a fan of the brand, Jaguar – losing money heavily – had to seek out the Indian Tata group as a purchaser.

In contrast, the Volvo and Land Rover brands (LR was bought for €2.4 billion in 2000) suffered less: pompously renamed 'luxury brands' upon their acquisition by Ford, they are in fact 'premium' brands; a 'Ford' management strategy was therefore able to improve their results, whereas Jaguar and Aston Martin, being genuine luxury brands, could only be seriously damaged by this kind of strategy. Luxury is not 'premium at its best'.

At the beginning of 2008, Ford sold Jaguar and Land Rover to Tata for €1.4 billion; those two brands had been bought for €4.6 billion.

As the systematic failure of this type of strategy is that of large, well-managed groups, it cannot be attributed to simple management errors, but to a failure to comprehend what luxury is. We can, however, deduce from it that to succeed in luxury it is necessary to add other things, and in particular prestige, which Ford lacked, and all would have been well. If this analysis is correct, the inverse strategy, moving downwards away from luxury, should work very well, since luxury would mean a little 'more' everywhere; it would be enough to put in less, to reduce prices, and the job would be done.

It is not easy to exit luxury through a 'downwards' strategy

Is the strategy of lowering prices on a 'luxury' brand in order to make it 'premium' and develop it (or turn it around), or of launching (or purchasing) a 'premium' brand by a luxury brand to extend its market, an effective one?

One famous example is Mercedes: this luxury brand decided some 15 years ago to opt for a volume strategy, offering models in all market segments. Its 'downward' diversifications via other brands were not successful: Smart has been a financial failure to this day (2008); and the purchase of Chrysler was disastrous. Worse even than the financial disappointment was the damage done to the brand: Mercedes was forced to launch its luxury model under another name than its own: that of Maybach... unthinkable only 10 years ago.

Ford had failed in its climb towards luxury, because it was a classic company; Mercedes failed in its exit from luxury, because the methods that had made it successful in luxury were impossible to transpose into the world of classic or even premium consumption. To attribute the failure of the Mercedes purchase of Chrysler to differences between American and German cultures is to underestimate another, sizeable cultural difference: that which exists between luxury management and premium management.

As in the previous case of 'trading up', the companies that tried this downwards extension strategy were generally good, well-managed brands; their failure was therefore not one of incompetence, but of an incorrect understanding of what luxury is. There is only one conclusion, therefore: if 'premium' is the 'upwards' extension of classical marketing strategies, luxury obeys other laws.

From where has the current confusion arisen?

From where, then, has the current, widespread confusion between upper-range branded products ('premium' products) and luxury products arisen, with its costly consequences, even to the point of creating the neologism 'masstige'? From two essential mistakes: one stemming from confusing luxury with high price, and the other from the accumulation and convergence of genres.

Confusing luxury with high price

Products other than luxury have high prices; if there was once a clear difference in price between luxury products and other products, there is no longer an absolute separation between premium and luxury, with certain premium products being now more expensive than the equivalent luxury products (see Figure 2.1).

What does Figure 2.1 show? Household purchasing power has grown over the years. Mass consumption products have seen their prices fall over the years, as a result of economies of scale: the fall in prices for electronic goods (TVs, PCs, telephones, etc) is indicative of this. Certain mass consumption

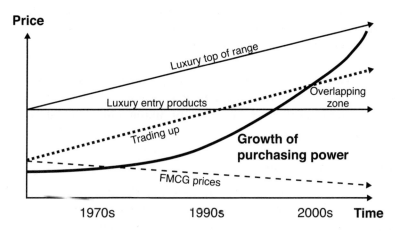

Figure 2.1   Why the confusion between premium and luxury?

goods have followed the 'trading up', premiumization approach, which has raised their prices to the point that they have caught up with entry level luxury products (see page169).

Therefore nowadays there is a zone of price overlap between premium and luxury, which may be found in many sectors (Lancome vs Guerlain in perfumes, Lexus vs BMW in cars, etc) confirming that price, by itself, is no longer today a characteristic of luxury. It is clear that, in settling for analysing things from the one-dimensional aspect of price, total confusion has been created.

The accumulation and convergence of genres

This is the second essential source of the confusion, and it relates to a behaviour typical of many brands today, although its origins are ancient.

The accumulation of genres

There is accumulation of genres in the sense that one house may sell both luxury products and upper range, or even mass, products. Thus 'Yves Saint Laurent' was:

special edition

- a luxury *griffe* when Mr Yves Saint-Laurent was creating his haute couture gowns, unique models manufactured by seamstresses in the workshop on Avenue Marceau in Paris;
- a luxury brand, Yves Saint-Laurent Rive Gauche, a variation on haute couture, created by Yves Saint-Laurent himself, and sold only in Yves Saint-Laurent shops;
- an upper-range brand, Yves Saint-Laurent Variations, manufactured in France by the Mendès company under the remote supervision of the creator;
- an upper-range brand once again for perfumes and make-up;
- a mid-range brand for fashion accessories.

Likewise, Chanel is a *griffe* under the hand of Karl Lagerfeld, and a luxury brand for its watches or handbags. Its glasses sold at Optic 2000, however, hark back to a brand that is barely even premium, either in price or in style and distribution.

The convergence of genres

There is convergence of genres inasmuch as the non-luxury brands are strongly inspired by luxury behaviours. American Express practises systematic 'trading up' by inventing ever more selective cards, such as the Platinum card; with the Black Centurion, Amex is following a luxury product strategy, while

annual fee @
top $450

made of titanium
annual fee @ $2500
plus set up @ $5000

Gold card annual fee $125
Green card annual fee $95

retaining the American Express name, the same as that of the basic card, sold with the classic promotional tools. H&M called on Karl Lagerfeld to create limited editions. Lacoste organizes fashion shows in New York and Shanghai.

The upshot of all this is a blending of frontiers, of genres, and a multiplication of concepts, all incorporating the term 'luxury' to a greater or lesser extent, to attempt to classify this profusion.

Exiting the confusion: the case of the car

Even if the current confusion does not worry customers unduly, since each can in fact say what they consider and do not consider to be luxury, in contrast every manager must have a clear view of the situation, in order to profit best from the potential of the luxury market and in order to know exactly what to do to remain there. Luxury must be continually redifferentiated, unceasingly recreating the distance between itself and its avatars. This is what its customers expect.

In order to answer all these questions: 'What is luxury? What is it not, or no longer? What is upper range? Premium? Shouldn't we recognize an intermediate category between these two concepts – the ultra-premium?' the automobile sector provides an ideal terrain for making these concepts explicit.

All carmaking groups have sought, with varying degrees of success, to add a few more labels to their portfolio of brands. Volkswagen bought Bentley, Lamborghini and Bugatti; BMW seized Rolls-Royce; Fiat runs Ferrari, and has added Maserati. As for the world's foremost carmaker, Toyota, it decided to create its own very-upper-range brand, calling it... Lexus!

The automobile sector is an industrial one and subject to rare technological and economic stresses. The rise in investment and the risks attached to new models is considerable. It is necessary to play on the synergies in research and development (R&D), at the industrial and the human resources level. This seems a particularly delicate exercise when a large group within the sector tries an assault on luxury: as discussed above, Ford threw in the towel in 2007. Can a luxury car brand be developed in isolation, or only with global technical partnerships, to remain at the cutting edge?

The car raises questions among luxury analysts in many respects. Noble descendant of horse-drawn carriages or coaches, it is considered the very symbol of luxury among men. The car signifies for all to see the progression and status of the driver. It provides an ideal space in which to examine the differences and links between the usual categories and concepts such as luxury and upper range, even with intermediate categories such as top-of-the-range or ultra premium. The car gave birth to brands that by themselves define luxury. It brings together both old brands, with prestigious histories, created by mechanical geniuses (such as Enzo Ferrari) and newly minted ones, such as the Swedish Koenigsegg, or the Japanese Lexus, created from scratch and launched in the USA in 1989 by Toyota.

Finally, in addition to the link with history, the car makes it possible to deepen the relationship between luxury and high-tech: we are too prone to link luxury with artisanship, tradition. How is this relevant in the highly mechanized and now electronic world of cars? Would they resist the examination of a modern Aston Martin or Bentley?

Relativity of luxury in cars

We know that luxury is relative. What may be luxury for one may be premium for another. Mercedes enjoys luxury status in China, India and Russia, where its black limousines, well beyond any affordable price, are the most visible local attribute of political power. This is not the case in the USA: the brand has lost the power of dreams. This is why Toyota was not mistaken in aiming at Mercedes owners to ensure the sales success of its first Lexus cars.

Lexus was a great commercial success in the USA: the brand imposed itself there in the space of 10 years. JD Powers, which establishes the reliability ranking of cars in the US, placed Lexus at the head of the class for the seventh consecutive year; it also measures the customer satisfaction index, and says that Lexus is now, by volume, the 'premier imported luxury car brand in the USA'.

The Luxury Institute, a specialized company, produces an index each year known as the Luxury Customer Experience Index based on the responses of a sample of 2,100 wealthy Americans (recruited based on their declared income and capital: annual earnings of more than $313,000 and $3 million on the stock market). The questions relate to their experience of the brand in all its aspects:

- It completely meets my needs, and even exceeds them.
- The brand's staff are polite, attentive, enthusiastic, very trustworthy.
- These cars are well maintained, beautiful, aesthetically pleasing.
- Number of mechanical or other problems encountered (reliability).
- Quality and rapidity of problem resolution.

Lexus quickly moved to the fore on all these criteria. Buoyed by these successes relayed by the media, the brand is building a reputation little by little, carried by the word of mouth of enthusiastic new adherents. It did not win its spurs through F1 Grand Prix or mythical Indianapolis speedways, but through the prizes of institutions dedicated to surveying satisfaction and market perception. Its reputation-creating approach is summed up in its slogan: 'The relentless pursuit of perfection'. There is no brand heritage here, but what Americans refer to as meritage: Lexus is the car without flaw.

For the Japanese, however, Lexus is perceived as an extension of Toyota, and therefore as a super-Toyota, but without the essential attributes of luxury: the prestige, the intangible, the dream, the imagination: outclassing a model is one thing, but possessing an identity is another.

Is automobile luxury the pursuit of perfection?

Is a Ferrari a perfect car? Anyone who has driven it knows that it is not. A Ferrari has fragilities that are part of its charm, its weaknesses as a mechanical beast that, like its rearing horse emblem, is not easily mastered. You have to know how to drive it, accept its vagaries, its unique character. A BMW is not perfect and aroused the anger of many reviewers who regretted, when scoring the brand new 5 Series, that so little legroom had been provided for passengers in the back seat, as if the comfort of their legs was of little importance to the Bavarian brand. At Porsche they explain that it is better not to have electrically opening windows or air-conditioning in a 911, since it weighs 60 kg and would reduce the lap time by a second.

Seen in these terms, luxury is therefore not the category above the top-of-the-range: luxury and upper range are not on the same trajectory. Their criteria are not the same: upper range will be judged on its polyvalence, its comfort, its boot space, its manoeuvrability, its comfort, all criteria defined by clients... upper-range clients. In luxury, it is the creator who defines the criteria; there is a reversal of the relationship to the client. The objective of luxury, automobile or otherwise, is thought of and created not according to an order (as was the case with the artisans of old: the silk weavers, the lacemakers, etc) or a request (as is the case in marketing), but according to an inspiration, a challenge to which the media, those modern trumpets of fame, are summoned.

Top-of-the-range, upper-premium and luxury cars

Armed with these examples, we can sketch the core identities of these categories called 'luxury', 'upper-range' and 'top-of-the-range'. These categories are porous: their frontiers are permeable, but their core identity is clear. If they are forgotten, the yardsticks can merge, or even become mixed up, leading to internal management errors, a phenomenon accentuated by the use of managers from traditional marketing backgrounds. Ford's handling of Jaguar after acquiring it in 1989 illustrates the mix-up of genres between luxury and traditional marketing. Having bought Jaguar for more than its objective price, Ford worked ceaselessly to increase penetration to make its acquisition profitable. In fact, Ford paid for Jaguar twice: the purchase price of $2.5 billion in 1989 and the price of bringing the Coventry staff up to the level of upper-range automobile technology and know-how. The models had certainly increased in quality in reliability, thanks to the platform policy, but the dream had gone. It had been exploited to sell small Jaguars, without immediately recreating it. The feeling of exclusivity, of being apart, without which there is no luxury, was eroded. What became of the real and symbolic separation, including social separation, between a Jaguar and a generalist upper-range car when:

- the smaller Jaguars had a Ford Mondeo engine;
- their diffusion led to a multiplication of Jaguars on the roads (the CEO of Porsche is generally credited with the statement: 'When I see two Porsches in the same street, I begin to worry');
- there were no more upward innovations: the brand only knew how to launch cheaper products, given its inability to make more expensive ones; luxury is a permanent elevation of both customers and creators;
- executives read the economic press, which revealed the Fordian industrial antecedents of all Jaguars;
- Jaguar no longer excelled at the races, where prestige and the emotional attachment of the public can be won.

The extra price of a Jaguar thus paid for an intangible that was itself in decline, accession to an ever less selective club and a non-revitalized brand myth (typically British luxury), signified only by its appearances (the elm burr dashboard and Connolly leather).

What top-of-the-range means

As the name suggests, this is the upper end of a brand's range, the shop window for the brand's know-how. Thus the Toyota Prius is the top of Toyota's range, as Passat is the top of Volkswagen's. The generalist (multi-target, multi-segment) brand makes use of a large range to accompany and instil loyalty in its clients over their lifetime: from the small car to the family saloon, to the estate, to the minivan for the larger family or the family with teenagers, then finally the upper-range saloon, with its optional extras that give a touch of personal, intimate, hedonistic pleasure to the standard car.

The upper range is thus doubly relative:

- it is the upper range, and therefore offers more technological innovations than any other level of this range;

- it carries the brand's name, and therefore its image. From this point of view, not all upper ranges are created equal.

The upper range is judged by the famous price–quality ratio: do you get enough for your money? It signals a progression of the purchaser through the range, to its extremity, and therefore their personal progression in terms of income, standing and status. To this end the upper range should receive more than its fair share of advertising investment, since it must be socially recognized as the upper range by all (the eyes of others must be able to perceive this social progression), and at the same time lend its aura to the rest of the range of stock cars under the brand's aegis.

The upper range is measured and compared, both with the lower level of the range, and with the tops of other ranges, but also with downward extensions of so-called 'luxury' brands, which are weakening themselves through this extension. Luxury is superlative, not comparative. Comparisons must be avoided at all costs. Measured against the entry levels of prestige brands, the upper range is now brandished with pride, since it proclaims a rational legitimacy, an implicit criticism of luxury. What is the point of paying a higher price, when the upper-range car gives you a high performance for a lower price, and with a greater distribution?

Upper-premium

In order to signal a more clear-cut change in one's life, it is therefore necessary to change brands. Car brands, through their known average price and their recognized prestige, are the social milestones of their owner's income progression. Two modalities now enter into the equation, two car categories: luxury, and what we must call 'upper-premium': Aston Martin or Lexus. We must learn to distinguish between them even if the latter do everything in their power to dissipate the distinction and borrow the codes of the former. Luxury and upper-premium are not differences in level of the same quest. In reality the quest is different.

In a super-premium car (Audi, Lexus, etc) the first question remains that of the usage value, even if it is crossbred with intangibles: you buy an Audi A6 for everyday use, in all weathers, on all roads, for all kinds of travel. This is not the first expectation of someone buying an Aston Martin, still less a Lamborghini. The upper-premium is recompense for hard work and remains ontologically on the side of work: hence it is counted among the bourgeois, in its structural and symbolic opposition to the aristocracy, which was prohibited from working and could only enjoy its wealth and show off its rank, be entertained, hunt and fight. This doesn't prevent the City golden boy from buying a Ferrari: we are talking about the semiotic power of luxury brands.

The upper-premium brands desire to be chosen rationally for their excellence. The price of a Audi A8 is that of its excellence. *Automobile Magazine*, the best-read car magazine, will ask if it is 'The best car in the world?'. Everything in this type of car, A8 or Lexus SR, is designed to eliminate pressure, stress, discomfort, risks, insecurity, both for the driver and the passengers. It also aims to be polyvalent in order that it can be used in the essential function of all cars: for moving people.

Upper-premium brands remain comparative, whereas luxury is superlative. The price of any upper-premium car must be justifiable by its utility curve. The high price admittedly signals the owner's social standing, but also the fact that they are buying more of what today is considered quality (more passive security, better handling, more electronics, more connectivity, more energy-saving, more space for passengers, more interior comfort, more recyclability, less pollution, less vibration and noise). Lexus used comparative advertising claims to promote its first car.

The luxury car: creation, mythical models and social prestige

Let us now turn to luxury cars. These can be recognized by the price of the products, their rarity derived from their quality, and the prestige of the name. These are sacred products or models, offspring of a sacred brand. What is the origin of this sacredness? We must return to the foundations of modern luxury to understand it.

The society of Louis XIV's court had to justify their rank, and thus their social pre-eminence, by the purity of their blood lineage (an essential temporal dimension) but also in the present by their expenditure, their glory and their heroic exploits... everything but work. The bourgeoisie, made rich by work, continually measured themselves against this class that made disdain for money their mark of distinction. The modern car is the technological, but also the symbolic, descendant of equestrian rites and objects. The luxury car can therefore be divided into two types of object: gilded coaches and thoroughbreds. Each carries a patent of nobility: a renowned brand, a myth incarnated in a brand. This myth is constructed by the heroic acts of war or by the Sun King himself, that is, the incarnation of supreme power.

Among luxury cars, Rolls-Royce is the reincarnation of the gilded coach: nothing is too comfortable, sumptuous or beautiful for the king, for Queen Elizabeth II. The excess is in proportion to their symbolic rank, beyond the norm. In the United States, Cadillac was the brand of the oil, steel or movie magnate.

For their part, Ferrari, like Porsche, embody the line of thoroughbreds. It has built its prestige in deadly mechanical jousts, where these elegant hyper-technological chargers clash, ridden by heroes in the service of their country: Ferrari is the standard-bearer for Italy, Porsche for Germany, Aston Martin for Great Britain.

These two sources for the sacralization of the brand also explain why the upper-premium brand divides its range into two groups, in order to mimic the codes of luxury and yet offer a rational progression to the potential client, compared to the upper range:

- Some cars offer the apogee of functional pleasure: they are therefore a reasonable Rolls-Royce.
- The upper-premium brand also offers coupés, tamed versions of the luxury-brand coupés.

The upper-premium is therefore a reproduction of luxury, in both senses of the word: it reproduces through imitation, through picking up the manners and codes of luxury. It is also a reproduction because of the far higher volume of production.

Whereas the upper range takes on the codes of luxury, but remains essentially earthly and tangible in its arguments, luxury – here the luxury car – draws its additional value from a sacred dimension, linked essentially to its relationship with time, history, death and life (Lipovetsky and Roux, 2003). Each model embodies, reproduces, modernizes or revives a myth, the myth of its brand. This myth is built over time: history makes brand myths.

Luxury cars incorporate time. Luxury loves time and takes its time: whether through constant reference to the brand's origins, or through the rejection of the typical productivity of series cars, subjected to the diktat of 'best price–quality ratio'.

Each Rolls-Royce Phantom requires 2,600 hours to be completed, that is, 10 times as much as a Ford. Unlike fashion, a system of obsolescence planned to recreate desire in its audience and to keep the factories moving, luxury aims at timelessness, even if in the car it incorporates advanced technology and its progress. This is why the great models of luxury cars are regularly reinvented, such as the Ferrari Testarossa. Hence also the love that industrial groups hold for brands with a mythic potential, born and nurtured by their history, in order to relaunch them (Maserati, Aston Martin, Bugatti, etc).

Two observations need to be made at this point:

- The history need not necessarily be a long one: new genuine luxury brands will be born tomorrow.

- History alone is not enough: it is necessary to create a myth, a legendary discourse that gives birth to the dream. This is what distinguishes luxury from the brand, even from the upper-premium brand. Lexus is a case in point. Being called Lexus is not enough to become Luxus.

Lexus has a history, admittedly a recent one, but a true history created of technological flawlessness. Little by little, over time, year after year, it is building a reputation, benefiting from what Reicheld (2006) calls 'the ultimate question: its clients would strongly recommend it to others around them. This is moving beyond loyalty, and into engagement with the brand (Kapferer, 2008). Lexus clients are highly satisfied with the provisions of their Lexus: it delights them in all aspects of quality and service. However, Lexus suffers from two handicaps:

- It was designed by strategists and engineers, and not by creative geniuses. The ultimate example of the Japanese approach, Lexus was guided by a benchmark, the Mercedes E-Class, and the copy has exceeded the master. The consequence, however, is that Lexus lacks identity. It is one thing to refine what already exists, it is quite another to define the future. Where is the creative dimension of the luxury brand? In fact, on the outside Lexuses lack personality: there is a sense of déjà vu about their appearance: here a grille, there a wing, there the line of a boot is strongly reminiscent of the Mercedes. Thousands of engineers are visible in the work (they used as many as for the creation of the Boeing Jumbo Jet), but Lexus has not shown its capacity for reinventing the category, for becoming its true leader, as Apple has done with its technological brio and distinctive design, or the Jumbo Jet itself.
- Lexus does not carry any brand myth within itself, nor does it create any: it is a brand invented by Toyota's management to take part of Mercedes' market share, and not a creative act. There are no races, no myth-building glorious acts, no courts, no kings, no queens: instead there are market-share points and JD Powers titles measuring customer satisfaction.

The problem is that this history of Lexus says nothing else. It does not build an idealization of the brand beyond the functional; the models are not myths, but very good cars. The upper-premium, like the top-of-range, aims at the market share and must round off its edges to do so. Luxury goes beyond functionality. Being creative, it takes the risk of not being liked.

These facts show the true nature of Lexus, and indirectly the true nature of luxury itself. In the USA, the Luxury Institute produces two hierarchies of luxury in all sectors, particularly the automobile sector:

- The first index, known as LCEI or Luxury Customer Experience Index, already discussed, measures the perceived excellence of services. Lexus excels here, as does BMW.
- The second index, known as LBSI, Luxury Brand Status Index, defines the intangible, the prestige associated with the brand, its potential for dreams and therefore for distinguishing the owner. Its questions measure the feeling of superior quality lasting over time, the feeling of exclusivity and uniqueness, the feeling that the brand provides a strengthened social status, the feeling of being a special person. Lexus excels less here: it is Porsche that dominates. The dream, in fact, is built from ingredients other than the reputation for quality alone. What do American owners of Porsches say of this brand apart, which also sets them apart?
  - It is exciting because of its style, its power; it stimulates the imagination.
  - It is remarkably built, has superb styling and exceptional performance.
  - It keeps its value over time, and maintains a symbolic youth.
  - It has always been at the pinnacle of its category, throughout its history.
  - It incorporates mystique, a heritage, the racing spirit.
  - It has been remarkably faithful to its values: it has remained highly coherent over time.

Porsche maximizes the three levers that make for a strong brand:

- It has the power conferred by its worldwide recognition: driving a Porsche therefore sends a clear message to all non-owners, which adds value for the owners. Value is in the eye of the beholder.
- It inspires the respect of all through its coherence over time, its integrity, its ability to always push its achievements further, an expression of the virtues of Germany and its unique style. The singular price is the consequence of this.
- It resonates emotionally through its glorious deeds, both present and past: mythical races and drivers, but also glamour and celebrities.

What link does luxury have with technology?

There is no prestige without respect: modern luxury therefore does not turn its back on technology. Each new model must reinforce this credibility: due to technological obsolescence and lack of reliability, and despite its patents of nobility, Jaguar went bankrupt. The beautiful and soul-stirring Ferraris are not only the pure lines of very beautiful bodywork. The emotion evoked by each new Ferrari model is also linked to the fact that it is also an advanced technological compression.

There are niche car brands, which maintain tradition and artisanship to the letter: Morgan continues to build its 4×4s with wooden chassis. But it is not a luxury brand. The link with tradition, or at least with traditional values, is a necessary but not a sufficient condition of luxury. Modern luxury is not like antiques or collectable cars alone. It is also creative and technological, but it sublimates the technology through an excess and a finality that are not ostensibly in the order of strict functionality: we are serving pleasure, a life aesthetic, 'art for art's sake'. To appreciate it fully, it is also necessary to be a true lover of the product, that is, capable of appreciating the tangible or intangible facets. Luxury presupposes a product culture in its admirers. Otherwise, the purchaser is merely in search of emotions linked with seeming, not with feeling. This audience is volatile.

How does luxury use technology? In luxury, technology contributes to creating a separate world, beyond all constraints. It creates both objective rarity through the high price that it legitimates, and also a qualitative rarity through the extremization of technology's consequences:

- A Lamborghini Diablo is a 'monster' of technology: the word 'monster' itself implies excess, in terms of demiurge, of 'monsterization' (obviously): the superlative is the norm here. This is the realm of pure emotion.
- In a Rolls-Royce, so says the legend, a coin balanced on its side would not fall over: this is the hyperbolization of comfort. This is constructed admittedly through rare leathers, interiors made of precious woods that create a passenger cell worthy of a living-room; here we find the scent of artisanship, the aesthetic of the tradition that each model must manifest: in a Phantom Drophead coupé, as in a Riva, a bridge of oiled teak encloses the entire passenger cell of the cabriolet. However, only technology beneath this passenger cell could take this 2.6-tonne vehicle to 240 kph without any vibration.
- In any Ferrari the technology is in the service of competition, a peaceful form of war, of exceeding others, and thus exceeding the self, the only race that is never over.

As we see it, in luxury the technology serves only to maintain the objective distance, but on condition that it keeps the dream: there is a potential of imaginary and sublimation of the world running through the technology. Enlightened fanatics will discourse all night on the excess of the latest 6.75 litre, V12 engine of the Rolls Phantom, unique in the world (see also page 263).

The constituents of the myth of the luxury car

Apart from technological imagination, therefore, what are the other constituents of the progressive creation of the myth necessary for the luxury brand?

- The creator, who is more of an enthusiast and a creative genius than a pure engineer. Dr Porsche and Enzo Ferrari are the equivalents of the great names of former haute couture, or the great starred chefs of haute cuisine.
- The creations themselves, which demand respect and admiration: hi-tech and high touch. Luxury builds its myth through models that are themselves mythical. Remember the Ferrari Daytona, Testarossa, Dino... Each model has made a name for itself at the same time as being a hymn to the brand myth. These models have first names, because they must be identifiable one by one in this saga. They are almost works of art, since they must be beautiful and rare: a Lamborghini Countach parked in the street causes passers-by to stop. This beauty is not purely aesthetic, but incorporates humility before the beauty of the technological gesture beyond pure rationality – that which governs our daily life, made up of decisions made under money and time pressures, etc. It is revealing that this type of car is less graffitied and scratched than a BMW. Something sacred seems to emanate from it.
- The myth is nurtured by inaccessibility. This is linked to the above-normal price of the models, which deepens the distance from ordinary standards, even those of the top-of-the-range. From this point of view, the price of luxury is not on a continuum with that of the upper premium: it is elsewhere, it measures a dimension beyond quality and reveals the exceedance of money in the service of passion.
- The brand myth is thus built by the yardstick of the wealth of its owners, but beyond this wealth, their glory, their symbolic power, their passion, and their ability to discount everything in service of that passion. Let us remember that Rolls-Royce is aiming at only 85,400 people in the world: the UHNWI or ultra-high net worth individuals, each possessing capital of $30 million. This market segment represented in 2007 more than 30,000 cars sold at over €100,000. Rolls-Royce sells one in two cars at over €300,000, worldwide.
- Rolls-Royce and Bentley drew their prestige from being the official cars of the crowned heads of the planet. This was also the cause of their decline: there were fewer and fewer kings and queens, or they were very elderly, almost from another age, or they were a simulacra of royalty (for example Idi Amin Dada). Rolls-Royce fell from its status as the best car in the world (do we not still say 'The Rolls-Royce of...'?) to a shadow of itself, devoid of

technology, fixed in common models with Bentley, extravagant and obsolete. The additional value of Rolls-Royce and Bentley now rested only on the lustre attaching to their name through their royal lineage: this was the basis of their attraction for a new clientele of sports stars, Russian oligarchs, wishing to enjoy immediately the ennobling attributes of glory and money. This clientele modified the reflection of these brands (that is, the collective representation of their owners) and contributed to their decline both in sales and in mythical power. It took BMW and Volkswagen, two German groups known for their upper-range technology, to acquire these declining myths and cause them to be reborn from their ashes, each in its own way, by boosting them with the very latest technology, with a reinvented design, while maintaining the zest of precious artisanship, in the service of their respective identities and their British workshops.

- The myth feeds on history and authenticity: 80 per cent of Rolls-Royce buyers go to the Goodham workshop to customize their Rolls, to drive it before it is shipped. This allows immersion in the authenticity, the mystery and the history of the brand.
- The myth is built on the fields of glory that are car jousts: the Le Mans 24-hour race established the endurance of the Porsche, Formula One glorified Ferrari.
- The myth feeds on heroes: James Dean died aged 24 at the wheel of his Porsche, on a Californian highway. On every lap of Formula One, the feted heroes risk everything. Where would Aston Martin be without James Bond, 007?
- The myth needs stories, true or false, rumours or confirmed, but in any case of a type to build the legend: some say it is forbidden to open the Rolls engine; others say that even if the car was travelling with four flat tyres, the RR symbol would remain upright.
- The myth supposes mystery: what are the names of the mythical Rolls-Royces? The Phantom, the Silver Shadow. This mystery is often also that of their owners.

Luxury and expressions of national identity

Life seems to be made up of binary choices: we are commanded to opt for one option or another from a series of alternatives. Do we prefer tradition or modernity? Are we governed by functional preoccupations, or do we accept art for art's sake, design, sensuality, and aesthetics as decision criteria? The essence of luxury is to refuse such choices by exceeding them, by offering a rare synthesis. Of course, this is expensive. Very expensive.

In fact the previous developments on luxury cars show that luxury loves time: it sees itself as timeless. Whereas the upper premium or the top-of-the-range models are regularly outdone by new technology and their value as second-hand cars decreases over time, second-hand luxury cars scale the heights at auction sales. In these models of the past, there is admittedly outdated technology, but their potential for dreaming is increased: a 1971 Ferrari Daytona Spider is worth $1,395,000. Rarity and mythology make it necessary: luxury likes short series, traditional values, while remaking them to the tastes and the newest technology of the day, and the renewed inspiration of the creator of the moment.

We can therefore organize the car world along two axes (see Figure 2.2): the vertical runs from the purely functional at the bottom to the highly aesthetic at the top. The horizontal runs from the highly traditional on the left to the thoroughly innovative and modern on the right.

These axes recall the tangible/intangible dimension of the added value of brands (vertical axis) and the classic Western representation of time, which places the past to the left and progress rightwards along a horizontal axis. In the centre we find point zero, the car with no irregularities, average in every way, a simple mobility object and therefore sold at the cheapest possible price, like the Renault Logan, designed to cost €5,000, while awaiting the $2,500 Nano manufactured by Tata for emerging markets.

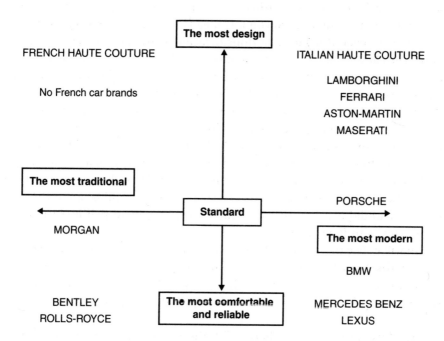

Figure 2.2   National identities and luxury cars

In this era of globalization, one of the strong sources of the sacralization of luxury brands stems from their ability to be ambassadors of national virtues, pushed to the extreme. Even if, following the demands of technology and bankruptcy, Bentley and Rolls are managed by German groups (as is Mini), the identities of these brands still sink their roots into the British national identity, its history, its glorious deeds, its distinctive values. Even technologized, a Rolls built by BMW will have to respect these: a Rolls is a land yacht. It must hark back to tradition through all those details that turn it into a true salon, where everything is a rare object, exclusive types of wood, preserved scents, while also offering the modern owner, who is no longer chauffeured everywhere, but likes to drive themself, a driving experience that is nothing but pleasure.

The Italian luxury brands, whether jewellery or cars, take the national virtues to the extreme: the art of the beautiful, the Latin sensibility and the ever-renewed, ever-surprising creative talent. Lamborghinis are technological *objets d'art*, and their beauty is made to take your breath away, just as their sleek design is made to cut through the air. Therefore they are not simply mechanical products, but also objects. Each new model maintains the mythical representation of the 'Italy' brand: where emotion, sensibility and pure sensation reign on one hand (powerful sensations at the wheel), and inventiveness, constant creativity on the other (... and breakdowns).

The lower right-hand corner of Figure 2.2 is that of constant renewal in the service of driving comfort pushed to the limit, but in a version that itself embodies the renewal of what comfort means (thus differentiating itself from Rolls-Royce): everything must be done to facilitate driving, mobility and transport. The car and the technology mounted on board are the mechanical and electronic extensions of desires and reflexes. They provide total reliability, endurance, active and passive safety, reactivity and speed where necessary, thanks to the engine's considerable power reserves. The electronics warn of danger, assist, facilitate, etc, without noise. Silence is the music of this type of car, whereas in a Ferrari you can hardly hear yourself speak. All the German virtues are found here: everything is ultra-controlled, function, nothing is useless. Others will say that the pure emotion is lacking, the emotion without which there is no true luxury. Then German luxury would be an oxymoron: Germany would excel in the top-of-the-range, a segment that it created and dominates, with Japan as a challenger.

You will notice that the upper left-hand quadrant is empty of cars: this is the site for the French conception of luxury, expressed by the brands of the Colbert Committee. Here the product is revered, a conception of manufacturing issuing from tradition, artisanship, proud of its past, but cut off from the modern audience.

There are no French cars here. With the French Revolution, the avowed egalitarianism of their national culture, the nationalization of Renault, the 'automobile made in France' brand rings hollow, and the French luxury car brands (Delage, Bugatti) have disappeared... a development that runs counter to that of French luxury in fashion, in accessories, at the table, which have conquered the world, and that of French aeronautical technology, which is universally recognized. The alchemy of luxury is a complex subject!

Beyond the product: services and privileges

The night of 4 August 1789 marked the abolition of privileges through the revolution in France: those privileges attached to the nobility, privileges by birth. Our democratic societies were born of this. On the other hand, the desire for privilege did not disappear. Luxury cars were late in recognizing this, and this time it was Lexus, the ultra-premium, that changed the rules of the market. A pure expression of Japanese courtesy, sense of detail, and attention to the guest, Lexus innovated in the USA by turning its dealerships into true salons, places that looked nothing like a standard dealership, but more like a country club. The Lexus dealership in Newport, Rhode Island has more in common with a Ritz/Carlton than a garage: it cost $70 million. Word of mouth spread quickly in Beverly Hills, Santa Barbara or Los Angeles on the thousand and one attentions that a Lexus customer could expect:

- car picked up from home by appointment, as a preventive measure, for routine check-ups;
- replacement car in case of breakdown;
- personalization of the relationship with the mechanic who works on your car (via their mobile telephone number).

These were all actions, details, concerns and attentions that were unknown in a BMW or Mercedes dealership.

The sense of privilege, however, goes beyond the dealership. In the great sporting demonstrations of which the Americans are so fond, and to which they travel by car (Flushing Meadow for the tennis, the baseball World Series, etc), there was a car park reserved for Lexus drivers. Likewise, during the two years of prior observation of luxury mores in California, Toyota's analysts had noticed the parking order of cars outside hotel exits: in general, the first are the jewels, the vehicles outside the norm, those that define luxury: Lamborghini, Ferrari, Rolls and Bentley. It would not be insignificant to ensure that all new Lexuses also enjoyed a high position. Not only would this offer the owner an honorific privilege, but in addition it would confirm the symbolic superiority of their choice, since it was recognized by the valets who only park luxury cars.

Finally, let us talk about the CRM, which in traditional marketing means *customer relationship management*. In that context, it is typically associated with client databases, with fine behavioural segmentation, targeted offers, personalized relational activities, and customer magazines.

In terms of luxury, we should instead be talking about *community recognition management*: recognizing and honouring the community of believers, the followers. Thus at Ferrari the community of 38,000 owners of old Ferraris are honoured and cajoled. They are encouraged to send their jewel for an in-depth maintenance check, at the holy of holies, at Maranello. This is the opportunity to possibly come to the very heart of the religion and collect it. At Rolls-Royce, 200,000 enthusiasts visit the site, where there is also a museum, in July and August, on the occasion of two special events.

At Lexus, exclusive local events are organized, not linked to the car, but to the owners' tastes and lifestyles. Priority seats at operas and theatres are offered, to cultivate the brand's cultural dimension.

The cult objects: licences and boutiques

The luxury brand engenders respect and emotion. As a sacred object, it diffuses its values, its cult. To this end, licensing makes it possible to diffuse cult objects, to make it live elsewhere than on the road, for example. At Harley Davidson, sales of accessories (helmets, clothing, objects of all types, etc) represent a third of all profits. A Porsche Design licence has existed for some time. Ferrari has launched a programme of licences from a line of highly stylized racing (therefore red) clothing, pens, watches (created by Panerai)... all of which makes possible the creation of exclusive boutiques. There is a Ferrari licence with Acer (a Taiwanese PC manufacturer). There are plans for a Ferrari theme park in Abu Dhabi. In all, in 2007, these licences were worth €600 million to Ferrari.

3 Anti-laws of marketing

The two previous chapters have shown that traditional marketing could not readily be applied to luxury, and drew attention to the anthropological, sociological and historical bases of luxury. The purpose behind this was to help understand that luxury is above all a social dynamic. It should also be clear by now that when managing a luxury brand, it is necessary to forget a fair number of laws of marketing, which may very well apply to brands, to premium brands, and even to trading up, but not to luxury.

'Trading up' (see the book under that title by Silverstein and Fiske, 2005) – or persuading a client to choose an item from further up the range, to go 'up-market' – essentially plays on the many excuses people can always find for treating themselves by buying something better and more expensive: a marketing logic is fine here. Trading up is very different from luxury, for it does not have the latter's sociological dimension – its function is not so much social stratification as improving brand profitability.

Not only are traditional marketing techniques not suited to luxury, they can in fact be positively harmful to it. The truth is that traditional marketing is only concerned with the bottom of the luxury pyramid, where they are no longer selling luxury products, but products derived from luxury brands.

One also comes across traditional marketing in brands whose business model has to rely on licensing arrangements and the sale of accessories and perfumes as their sole means of remaining viable.

In the course of this chapter we shall be putting forward 18 management suggestions, which we call 'anti-laws of marketing peculiar to luxury', as they are at the opposite extreme of what marketing doctrine normally preaches – and rightly so – concerning products and brands, even premium ones.

1. Forget about 'positioning', luxury is not comparative

In consumer marketing, at the heart of every brand strategy you will find the concept of positioning, of the 'unique selling proposition' (USP), and 'unique and convincing competitive advantage' (UCCA). Every classic brand has to specify its positioning, and then convey it through its products, its services, its price, its distribution and its communication. Positioning is the difference that creates the preference for a given brand over the one that it has decided to target as a source of new business and whose clients it is going to try to win over. In the war that brought it into conflict with Pepsi Cola in the United States, Coca-Cola was 'The real thing' (its essential distinguishing feature), whereas Pepsi-Cola, introduced in the 1930s, plugged its image as a young people's drink ('The choice of the new generation'), thereby succeeding in boxing Coca-Cola into an image as a product that only parents drank. As we see, the classic brand always seeks to define itself by a key facet, depending on the market context, the main competitor, and the expectations of the target consumers it is aiming to reach.

Nothing is more foreign to this approach than luxury. When it comes to luxury, being unique is what counts, not any comparison with a competitor. Luxury is the expression of a taste, of a creative identity, of the intrinsic passion of a creator; luxury makes the bald statement 'this is what I am', not 'that depends' – which is what positioning implies. What made the Christian Lacroix brand is its image of bright sunshine, full of this designer's bright, vivid colours, suffused with the culture of the Mediterranean; it certainly is not concerned with its positioning with respect to this or that established designer.

It is identity that gives a brand that particularly powerful feeling of uniqueness, a timelessness, and the necessary authenticity that helps give an impression of permanence. Chanel has an identity, but not a positioning. Identity is not divisible, it is not negotiable – it simply is.

Luxury is 'superlative' and not 'comparative'. It prefers to be faithful to an identity rather than be always worrying about where it stands in relation to a competitor. What luxury is afraid of is copying, whereas mass-produced brands fear 'undifferentiation', trivialization. Chapter 6 will present models to define the luxury brand identity.

2. Does your product have enough flaws?

This is a provocative statement. For most people, luxury is the last word in hand-crafted or craftsman-built products. It is true that in surveys into the perception of luxury, consumers from all over the world were interviewed and the consensus was that 'product excellence' is the primary prerequisite of luxury. It would suffice to imagine a bisecting line between two axes – price and functional quality: at the very top right would be luxury. Now, in our view, nothing could be further from reality.

The aim of an upper-premium brand is to deliver a perfect product, to relentlessly pursue perfection. But it would take a touch of madness for it to be counted a luxury. Functionally, a Seiko watch is superior to many luxury watches – it is more accurate (because it's a quartz watch) and shows the time directly and in a perfectly legible manner (because it is displayed on a digital face). If you were to buy some of the famous brands of a luxury watch, you would probably be warned that it loses two minutes every year. The flaw is not only known, it is assumed – one could say that that is both its charm and its guarantee of authenticity. It is the specific and singular nature of their movement that is responsible for that. For luxury watchmakers like adding complications, indeed seek them out in their endless quest of art for art's sake. This is the 'madness' touch that goes beyond perfection and make people collect them.

Let us look at some of the watches that Hermès has to offer, where the time is indicated by just four figures: 12, 3, 6 and 9. So you have to guess the time – as if knowing the time accurately was somehow unimportant, even pleasure-killing and dehumanizing. They are certainly far removed from those state-of-the-art precision chronograph watches, for luxury brands are not interested in being the leader in utilitarian or functional comparisons – primarily they are hedonistic and symbolic.

In the world of luxury, the models and the products must have character or personality. In the world of automobiles, a Ferrari is anything but a perfect car if you like easy, smooth and silent driving; that is why people would do anything to own one. Every model forces its owner to accept its flaws.

Of course, if a luxury product is not a flawless product, the reverse is not true: adding flaws does not turn a regular product into to a luxury product...

3. Don't pander to your customers' wishes

One of the most respected brands in the world is BMW. This ever-growing brand has been successful in creating a cult, a body of owners that are extremely faithful, devoted and committed to their brand. It is in fact, according to the Luxury Institute, one of the 'the most admired car companies in the world'. What are the factors behind BMW's success ?

- A clear brand identity, observed to the letter since 1962, summarized in a slogan never challenged since then, translated into every language – 'Sheer driving pleasure'.
- A stable, family shareholding. Since 1959 the brand has been owned by the Quandt family. It believes in letting things take their time and accepts that it may lose clients in the short term to increase the value.
- A very German enterprise culture, characterized by its engineering and its product cult. Moreover, being descended from pioneers of aviation, there is a tremendous pride in this company.

BMW sells unequalled driving pleasure to people who know how to appreciate it. It has never built cars that were boring to drive. BMW has become an icon of standing and performance; in the 1990s it was the 'official' car of every yuppie or successful young executive eager to show off their success. What is less well known, however, is that despite its success, the brand has remained true to itself thanks to its willingness to resist client demands when these did not correspond to the company's very precise vision as to what made for a true BMW. This does not mean the luxury brand should not care about its clients nor listen to them. However, it should do nothing that threatens its identity.

An example that says a great deal about BMW is that consumers regularly curse each time a new 5 Series car is released, because it is certainly a fact that this model does not give rear passengers enough legroom. According to them, such stubbornness defies reason and good sense. But the makers object that to meet client demands would be to spoil the purity of design of this car, its proportions having been meticulously calculated, as indeed were its aerodynamics! Some may remember the loss of aesthetics that the Jaguar E-type suffered following the addition of two full-size rear seats.

BMW is a good illustration of this principle according to which a luxury brand has to maintain a consistency over time and across its entire range, which guarantees its authenticity, and therefore its attraction, its mystique and its spark. In traditional marketing, the customer is king. Procter & Gamble's corporate identity relies not on one man, or even on one category of product, but on a methodology that puts the customers' desires at the heart of the business: P&G does it by listening to its customers – listening to what they have to say or are trying to say – then transforming these wishes into global, or at least regional, products that are then sold through mass distribution channels. The luxury brand, on the other hand, comes from the mind of its creator, driven by a long-term vision. There are two ways to go bankrupt: not listening to the client, but also listening to them too much.

This relationship with the client is typical of postmodern luxury and dates back to the 19th century. Historically, luxury was the creation of a talented craftsman, using the very rarest materials, who accepted commissions from a client or patron. These craftsmen were known in their day, but their fame did not endure. That is how castles and private mansions were built and furnished. In France, everything changed when at the end of the 18th century craftsmen stopped accepting private commissions after someone came up with the idea of making models, before they too were sold. What we were witnessing at that time was a radical reversal of the relationship between omnipotent client and craftsman. No longer was the craftsman prepared to go cap-in-hand to visit the client; instead, people went to them to see their latest collections, their new creations. The age of the nameless craftsman was now long gone – enter now on stage the creative designer and their retinue, their followers. Not to mention the reputation of their name.

4. Keep non-enthusiasts out

In traditional marketing there is this obsession with poaching clients from other brands: sales growth is management's principal measure of success and of the performance of its managers. This leads companies to come up with new products that will help extend market penetration and thus steal a march on competitive brands. To increase the relevance of the brand – the number of people who would say that the brand was of interest to them – it is necessary to avoid being too exclusive or too different.

When it comes to luxury, trying to make a brand more relevant is to dilute its value, because not only does the brand lose some of its unique features, but also its wider availability erodes the dream potential among the elite, among leaders of opinion. BMW is typical of a brand that is able to grow without cutting back on its rugged features, which are in any event highly exclusive. The Bavarian management has calculated that BMW's target accounts for 20 per cent of the premium segment of the population – only one person in five. This means that 80 per cent are not at all attracted by BMW's values. The brand has preferred to exclude these 80 per cent and base its growth on its true target, those who wholeheartedly share its values. Brand growth is achieved by penetrating new countries, not new customer segments. In order to grow, the BMW Group preferred to buy two other brands which on their own, like BMW, define a segment – Mini and Rolls-Royce; having taken good care to keep Rolls-Royce's identity separate from BMW's.

5. Don't respond to rising demand

The prime objective of traditional marketing is volume growth. It sets its sights at achieving leadership in market share to gain muscle with mass distributors, department stores and superstores, and presents itself as a force to be reckoned with in some of its lines. This ensures wide distribution and broad visibility and provides the justification for a national television advertising campaign. With sufficient volume, the business can work with small margins and still make money. This is the essence of the mass marketing model. Product managers are then judged on just one criterion – growth in annual results. At Ferrero (Kinder, Nutella, Tic Tac) it is not allowed to fall below double figures. The job of each product manager is to increase the penetration be it of Kinder Surprise, be it of Kinder Bueno, and then to push up per capita volume (consumption frequency). If the demand goes up, there have to be supplies to match it – that's the key to this economic model. Not to satisfy rising demand is to annoy the distributor because unhappy customers will not wait and will always hold it against the company. They will take their revenge by gossiping over dinner about their bad experience with the brand. What an absolute scandal having to wait! Sheer mismanagement!

At Ferrari, production is deliberately kept to fewer than 6,000 vehicles a year – rarity value sells. So long, that is, as the customer understands why the product is rare and is prepared to wait. Rarity can be managed just like the relationship with the clientele; so it is not a matter here of poor sales forecasting but of a deliberate strategy of resisting demand in order to be master of it.

6. Dominate the client

Luxury is a consequence of meritocracy. Once the exclusive privilege of the aristocracy, luxury today is what restratifies our so-called classless societies, but on the basis of merit, no longer simply on birth. So everyone is looking for ways to haul themselves up – luxury brands are at the same time a reward and a token of gradual elevation. To preserve this status, the brand must always dominate its client. This is not the same as saying don't respect them: parents dominate their children, but that does not mean that they don't respect them; on the other hand, if they treat them as 'best buddies', making themselves out to be their equals, they lose their aura and profoundly disturb their offspring.

This relationship between parents and their children is very close to that between brand and client.

As a result, a certain distance is preserved that is not supercilious or aloof, but nevertheless maintains an aura of mystery.

Luxury is the domain of culture and taste. Even if many well-off buyers do not actually have the codes themselves, they deduce from the limitless consumption of a luxury brand the fact that it must be coded as a luxury. The luxury brand should be ready to play this role of advisor, educator and socio-logical guide. On this account it simply has to dominate.

7. Make it difficult for clients to buy

The luxury brand is something that has to be earned. The greater the inac-cessibility – whether actual or virtual – the greater the desire. As everyone knows, with luxury there is a built-in time factor: it's the time spent searching, waiting, longing... so far removed from traditional marketing logic, which does everything to facilitate quick access to the product through mass distribution, with its self-service stores, self-checkout systems, the internet, call centres and introductory offers. Luxury has to know how to set up the necessary obstacles to the straining of desire, and keep them in place. People do eventually get to enjoy the luxury after passing through a series of obstacles – financial obstacles, needless to say, but more particularly cultural (they have to know how to appreciate the product, wear it, consume it), logis-tical (find the shops) and time obstacles (wait two years for a Ferrari or a Mikimoto pearl necklace).

Luxury needs to excel in the practice of distributing rarity, so long as there are no real shortages. It's quite natural: just as actual shortages stand in the way of growth, so the absence of rarity leads to the immediate dissipation of desire, and so to the disappearance of the very waiting time that sustains luxury. To create this obstacle to immediate consumption, it should always be necessary to wait for a luxury product – time is a key dimension of luxury, as with all desire for anything even remotely sophisticated. This anti-law has implications concerning the way luxury brands should use the internet (see Chapter 10).

8. Protect clients from non-clients, the big from the small

Modern luxury works on the open–close principle. Too much 'open' is harmful to the brand's social function – Ralph Lauren's success undermined one of the foundations of his success with professionals in Europe: sporting the polo shirt enabled them to be different from Crocodile, the other great casual wear premium brand, from whom Ralph Lauren got his inspiration when he was starting out in the United States. On the other hand, too much 'closed' is too confining and leads to financial suffocation.

In practice that meant that the brand became segregationist and forgot all society's democratic principles. In stores, for example, it is necessary subtly to introduce a measure of social segregation: ground floor for some, first floor for others. Armani set up specialist stores for each of his product lines. Advertising and promotion is for all, but public relations are ultra-carefully targeted, like the CRM for the privileged (personal invitations to meet the designer, the brand perfume nose, or the head wine buyer).

In aviation, these days everything is done to ensure that clients of the new first class never have to meet other passengers, whether from business class or (heaven forbid!) from economy class, and this is not just on boarding, but right from leaving their office until their arrival in the office at their destination – just like being in a private jet. A truly superior private club depends on how successful staff are in preventing 'other clients' from imposing on their own clients.

9. The role of advertising is not to sell

What does Tag Heuer advertising look like? On one side there is the photo of a woman or man, and on the other a shot of a model of watch. No commentary, no blurb about this watch, no sales pitch – just the cryptic line: 'What are you made of?'

Interviewed about his role, the head of BMW in the USA replied that with its customers trading up, and the collective aspiration of the younger drivers, BMW's sales target for the following year had already been 90 per cent met virtually automatically. Did that mean that he would have nothing to do then? His reply was simple, direct, and highly illuminating: 'My job is to make sure that the 18-year-olds in this country decide that, as soon as they have the money, they will be buying a BMW. I have to see to it that when they go to bed at night they are dreaming of BMW.'

Nothing is more alien to traditional marketing than this declaration; in traditional marketing the first thing to be done is to come up with a sales proposal, to have a unique selling proposition – the text is there to make the sales pitch. In luxury, the dream comes first. The explanations of the salesmen are simply post-rationalizations. If you go to a Tag Heuer shop you are handed a thick brochure the size of a book, which says everything there is to say about the Tag Heuer brand, its origins, its finely tuned processes, respectful of a unique design, etc. Then it goes on to talk about the various models, one by one...

If you go to a Porsche dealer they will talk to you about racetracks, about road-holding, about everything that feeds the myth of the hero, after which they will tell you about reliability, etc – by way of post-rationalization. American society being what it is essentially compels people to justify spending dollars by adducing qualities that can be presented publicly by the owner of a luxury item, even if it is the dream that is the major selling point. The purchaser of an impressionist masterpiece could say that it's a good investment.

Of course, advertising as such is not the lever for the BMW dream, merely its ally. Advertising feeds on a sustained myth, mystery, magic, racing, highly people-centred but private shows, product placement, and art – as we saw above, an extremely important element for any luxury brand.

In 2004 BMW asked several great Hollywood directors to each make a film about BMW, not a commercial for screening on different television channels, but a real film lasting several minutes, for which they were given completely free rein. These films were to be broadcast exclusively on the internet. They were an instant hit – these so-called viral films did the rounds of everyone who dreamed about, loved or was interested in BMW. What is more, all this heightened the buzz, gave the brand a fresh and modern look, something that even the most classic brand needs to have.

The dream must always be recreated and sustained, for reality kills the dream. Every time a flesh-and-blood human being buys a luxury product they destroy a little bit of the equity, they increase the product's visibility – and contribute to its vulgarization by putting it in the public eye. The opposite applies when marketing everyday goods: there is an advantage for the market leader, for the dominant market share, and therefore for maximum visibility – it becomes a reassuring purchase.

10. Communicate to those whom you are not targeting

Luxury has two value facets – luxury for oneself and luxury for others. To sustain the latter facet it is essential that there should be many more people that are familiar with the brand than those who could possibly afford to buy it for themselves. In traditional marketing, the keyword is efficiency, but over and above efficiency there has to be a return on investment. In advertising for example, the media plan must concentrate on the target consumers and nothing but the target consumers – every person reached beyond the target is a waste of investment money.

In luxury, if somebody is looking at somebody else and fails to recognize the brand, part of its value is lost. It is essential to spread brand awareness beyond the target group.

11. The presumed price should always seem higher than the actual price

It is a telling fact that advertisements for luxury products often show only the product, without any blurb, and certainly no prices. In the luxury world, price is something not to be mentioned. When you are dining in a top-class restaurant, do you select your dishes on the basis of price? Besides, in many such restaurants the guests' menus do not show prices.

As a general rule, the imagined price should be higher than it really is. It's the opposite in traditional marketing. Renault announced its Logan model as starting at €5,000, but with the full set of options this would bring it up to €7,500. Every seller tries to attract with a low price, a so-called introductory price, then tries to persuade the client to go up-range. EasyJet offers the prospect of round-trip tickets from London to Paris at around $45, but the number of seats available at that price is quickly taken up.

In luxury, when an imagined price is higher than the actual price, that creates value.

This happens:

- When someone is wearing a Cartier Pasha watch, everyone around them more or less knows its price, but tends to overestimate it (on account of its aura of luxury). This increases the wearer's standing.
- When offering someone a luxury gift, the gesture is all the more appreciated for the price being overestimated.
- And lastly, when advertised, the price is that of the top of the range.

12. Luxury sets the price, price does not set luxury

Money is not a good way of categorizing objects or of stratifying them unless it has been culturally coded.

This 'anti-law' means that luxury is a what could be called a 'supply-based marketing'. That is why traditional marketing is in a state of confusion here: it is fully 'demand-based'. In luxury, you first come up with a product, then you see at what price you can sell it; the more it is perceived by the client to be a luxury, the higher the price should be. This is the opposite to what applies in the case of a classic product or trading up, where the marketer tries to find out at what price level there is room for a new product.

There is one key consequence for selling: sales staff in a store help people understand, share the mystery, the spirit of places and objects, and the time invested in each item – which explains the price. Customers will be free to buy later.

13. Raise your prices as time goes on in order to increase demand

In the standard market model, when the price falls, demand rises. With luxury, the relationship is reversed.

In the 1950s, Krug was one of the smallest champagne houses. Its champagne had an excellent reputation, was adored by the great artists and performers of the day, and particularly appreciated in Great Britain. In the late 1950s Moët & Chandon, on finding that Krug was being rationed (the product's objective rarity made that a necessity), launched its new product that was destined to upset the status quo radically. Dom Pérignon was introduced at a price three times higher than that of Krug. In order to speed up the symbolic acceptance of Dom Pérignon, a quantity of it was dispatched to the Queen of England, and in 1961, in the very first film of the James Bond series, Agent 007 drank nothing but Dom Pérignon.

How was Krug to respond to that in order to regain its position at the top of the champagne hierarchy?

- Should it do nothing, believing that the superiority of its product would speak for itself – the truth being in the glass?
- Or, should it imitate Dom Pérignon, and at the same time improve it (a Lexus-type strategy)? This seemed an impossible approach for a house that had been in existence for 160 years, managed by the same family for five generations, and conscious of its mission.

The brilliant stroke – or perhaps one should call it Krug's strategic daring – lay not in producing an exceptional vintage, a very top-of-the-range champagne that would justify the price put on it, but to hoist its prices substantially across the range, starting from the lowest; within 10 years it went up from $19 to $100 a bottle. At the same time, in a move to create a product of great rarity from one small corner of the vineyard, Clos du Mesnil was born.

This champagne takes 10 years to come to fruition, taking into account the time it takes to prepare the land, bring in the harvest and allow for a period of ageing; nowadays, a bottle of Clos du Mesnil fetches a cool €800.

Krug's revival is an excellent illustration of the following anti-law of marketing: when it comes to luxury, price is a mere technical detail. As soon as price becomes an issue again in the classic price–demand relationship, we're no longer dealing with luxury, even if the product bears the name of a luxury brand. Examples abound in every sector: it is by raising prices – and, of course, by reinvesting these additional profits in quality and in advertising – that a brand can stay in the world of luxury.

To live in luxury you have to be above others, not be 'reasonable', in both senses of the word. A reasonable price is a price that appeals to reason, and therefore to comparison. Now, recalling our anti-law no. 1, luxury is 'superlative', not 'comparative'. To be reasonable is also to reduce the object to its tangible dimension and to deny the intangible.

By increasing prices you lose the bad customers, but now you suddenly become dazzlingly attractive to people who would previously not have given you a second glance.

The final point of this policy of systematically raising prices is that it gives the whole company a sense of responsibility. Price is a decisive factor in bringing about a change in mentality; indeed, we see quite profound internal changes in mentality, as every person in the company in their own way is constantly trying to find new ways of creating more value for the customer. It's all a matter of living up to the price.

14. Keep raising the average price of the product range

In traditional marketing, you launch a product at a skimming price, then when competition comes onto the scene, you drop the price. In luxury it is precisely the opposite. A luxury brand must always be seen to be restoring the gap, restratifying, and as such it is acting as a visible agent of meritocracy.

A brand that cannot grow in volume and profitability other than by launching accessible products shows that it is no longer part of the luxury market. For instance, the fact that Mercedes has launched its super top-of-the-range under a different brand name (Maybach) reveals its presumed change of strategy: Mercedes from now on will be the maker of regular and premium automobiles, and the luxury range now goes under the Maybach brand, not Mercedes any more.

This means that, while it may be necessary to have a few introductory products for the benefit of a new clientele, having a luxury brand signifies a permanent shift in vision. Its growth does not rely on running after a less well-heeled clientele but on taking advantage of the global economic growth that is creating thousands of new rich and very rich people throughout the world. These people are looking for a way to reward themselves (through the products) and for a symbol (being the brand) of their accession to the 'Club', having made sure that it is a closed 'Club' – they wouldn't want to mix too much with the wrong kind of people, after all! That is why the average price needs to keep going up – while of course at the same time increasing the value element of the product or service.

15. Do not sell

This isn't arrogance, not at all. The luxury strategy is the very opposite of the volume strategy.

If you pursue the strategy of systematically raising all your prices, as illustrated by Krug, you have to be prepared to lose sales and to lose customers. Most brands don't dare risk it, or else go running after customers; when you get to that point you're no longer talking luxury but mass consumption – which of course can be extremely profitable as everyone knows.

Krug did lose some accounts, some importers, it is true. If not supported by the Rémy Cointreau management in the steps it took, Krug's change in strategy would have been stopped as soon as the first big client dropped away. In luxury, not trying too hard to sell is a fundamental principle in relations with customers, which we shall be looking at in more detail in Chapter 10 on distribution. You tell the customer the story of the product, the facts, but you do not pressure them into making a purchase there and then.

We said a few words earlier about the campaign BMW had conducted on the internet in the USA; a number of the most prominent film directors each made a short-length film around BMW, having been given completely free rein – not a commercial, but free expression. These films were made available on the internet and they very quickly did the rounds in the United States. Commenting on this decision, the marketing director at BMW USA had this to say: 'When it comes to luxury, the best way of reaching the very well-off is to let them come to you.'

16. Keep stars out of your advertising

In traditional marketing, stars of stage and screen are very often used in advertising: there is nothing like a David Beckham for selling sunglasses or shaving cream. Nestlé has also got in on the act, with premium brand

Nespresso calling on the services of George Clooney, and Nescafé recruiting the famous English soccer player Ian Wright. Nestlé, the world's number one in food marketing, knows what it's doing.

Using stars to promote luxury products is extremely dangerous. A luxury brand is courted by the stars, in the same way as those stars are courted by journalists and paparazzi. As we already mentioned when speaking earlier about the luxury brand's typical relationship with its customers, it must respect them, but it also has to dominate them. Even the most famous ones. Calling on the services of a star is tantamount to saying that the brand needs some of this star's status just to survive, and admitting that it has none of its own. For the luxury brand, this is a gross error of strategy, for it turns the relationship on its head. Only brand domination, standing above everything like a god, is acceptable, not simply behaving like any ordinary mortal. If celebrities are used to promote the luxury product, the status of the latter is reduced to that of a mere accessory. Louis Vuitton advertising with Michael Gorbachev, former USSR President avoids this:

- first, the celebrity is not a fashion symbol but a man who changed the world;
- second, his Louis Vuitton is not the hero, but only the witness of an exceptional moment (a strategic negotiation).

17. Cultivate closeness to the arts for initiates

In traditional marketing, the brand seeks to appeal and to create an affective relationship. For that it often uses music, music that is as popular as possible, or at least appreciated by its target audience. The brand follows people's tastes. The luxury brand is a promoter of taste, like art. As we saw earlier, it maintains close links with art. But luxury is not a follower: it is creative, it is bold. That is why it is best for luxury to remain close to the unpopular arts – or rather the non-popular arts – those that are emerging and have yet to appeal to the majority, if they ever will. Louis Vuitton has long been sponsoring concerts of contemporary music, for example bringing the pianist Maurizio Pollini to the Abbaye de Royaumont to perform music by the little-known composer Luigi Nono, rather than by a great such as Mozart or Chopin. Similarly, following the pioneering work done by Cartier, the Fondations d'Art Contemporain are now flourishing in all the great luxury groups. In this way they are making themselves patrons of emerging trends, where they are forming symbiotic relationships that serve their purposes – making luxury-brand objects that are themselves works of contemporary art.

That is why it is so important to develop this curiosity about the here and now among those working in the luxury business and to encourage them to visit art galleries, biennales, and exhibitions of modern art.

18. Don't relocate your factories

Reducing cost prices is vital in the mass consumer markets, and this often means relocating factories.

Luxury management does not apply this strategy. When someone buys a luxury item, they are buying a product steeped in a culture or in a country. Having local roots increases the perceived value of the luxury item. BMW, which is successfully pursuing a luxury strategy, builds all its automobiles in Germany – apart from the entry line: the 3 Series – and is keeping production of the Mini in the United Kingdom. Keeping production of its models and engines in Germany is at the heart of its brand identity: every BMW is an authentic product of German culture – apart from which, producing them in Germany is perfectly viable, there being no difficulty in passing any such additional costs on to the client.

In addition, BMW has a factory in the USA for its current models (3 Series), and also produces some of the 3 Series models in Thailand and elsewhere; these relocated models are no longer true luxury products, but they do serve as access products – products designed to initiate customers into the brand – like the small leather goods at Louis Vuitton: as soon as they can, every purchaser of one of these locally produced 3 Series will want to buy a 'real' BMW 'made in Germany'. We shall be dealing at greater length with these strategies in Chapter 8 on products.

Not relocating factories is as much a question of creativity as of production. When you no longer have a manufacturing workshop near you, creativity takes a nose-dive, because you lose the contact with the raw material and the way of working to be able to sublimate it into a luxury product. Once *prêt-à-porter*'s production facilities were moved abroad, French haute couture gradually went into decline; but, on the other hand, locating manufacture in China is going to lead to the emergence of haute couture in that country, especially as China has a history of luxury clothing – for the emperor's court – going back several thousand years, and of producing very high-quality fabrics, silk in particular.

4 Facets of luxury today

Luxury attracts clients from all over the world, but also entrepreneurs eager to apply a business model that, when successful, is so profitable. It is the latter that we are addressing here.

Everyone knows the keywords of luxury: price, rarity, exclusivity, perfection, history, art, time, dreams, etc. It is important to revisit each of them in depth if we are not to fall either into a mechanical conception of luxury, made up of very high prices and Hollywood celebrities, or into an excessively classical and historical acceptance of luxury. This latter, worshipped in Europe, admittedly has the effect of excluding new pretenders, but conversely also of fixing in time those brands that devote themselves to it, since it prohibits all evolution on their part. It is not a coincidence, for example, if for very wealthy clients the world over, the notion of 'premium' alcohol appears more modern than the classic notion of 'luxury', which is associated too much with images of old alcohol, drunk with a big cigar, by the fireside, a Labrador curled at one's feet, a mode of expression that then immobilizes it. The new wealthy buyers are young and eager for powerful impressions.

New luxury brands, or at least aspirants to that title, will always appear. They will come from emerging countries: India, China, Russia, but also from the USA and Europe. The goal of this chapter aimed at luxury brand executives and those who would like to be so is to pursue the exploration begun in the first historical chapter of what constitutes the specificity of luxury, by examining the exact nature of the links that luxury maintains with the notions that are so spontaneously associated with it (label, rarity, exclusivity, relationship with time, tradition, history, handiwork and complexity) and by revisiting its links to fashion and creation, to art... in today's context.

On the importance of the 'label'

If there is one striking (some would say glaring) aspect of luxury, it is the visible nature of its logos and brands. This remark principally concerns finery, clothing; but as finery is the premier manifestation of luxury, we must approach this public observation as if it reveals an element of the identity of luxury in general.

In fact, we see the Chanel symbol writ large on bags, totes and T-shirts; Burberry's tartan makes it possible to distinguish a wearer from some distance on a Tokyo street. Note however that it is the accessories – more democratically accessible – that exhibit the brand: the masterpieces do so to a much lesser extent. It takes a knowing eye, and therefore the class knowledge and culture, to recognize immediately Chanel's unique touch, its specific look in a suit or a dress. The accessory, being smaller, less expensive, often part of a series and therefore much less marked by the creator's hand (or claw), must compensate for this by exhibiting often the only thing that remains to it, its brand picture, its logo. On a smaller surface, this is clearly visible; it is even designed to be so. As its Greek etymology reminds us, the logo says the brand.

This is normal. Luxury is the symbolic and hedonistic recompense of success, and therefore of the acquisition of power. Through its logos and brands with their high recognition and visibility, it functions like the medals and spoils that the victor receives or that they bring back to share with their own, their clan. This is why luxury must be seen, since one of the sources of recompense is the prestige in the eyes of all, and in particular of peers. By the visibility of the labels – the supports of the brand – is re-updated the function of what was called 'étiquette' at the court of French kings Louis XIII and Louis XIV: an obligation to expenditure and show. Naturally today's victors are no longer princes or military leaders, since the war is economic: they are the economic elites, the bosses, the senior executives of multinational companies, the self-made men or women, the traders, but also the artists and cinema, singing or sports stars.... Luxury is the distinctive sign of their own rarity. As for the logos on the series products, they give additional soul to the products and are an auxiliary means for the consumer to drag themself above their current condition.

In a traditional society, the social order cannot be questioned. This is still the case with castes in India. In monarchical France, luxury was the obligation of power: 'étiquette' was formal rules that regulated visible consumption and expenses, visible to the court, in order to maintain one's position there. Under the *Ancien Régime*, in the context of this 'étiquette', the 'sumptuary laws' were promulgated 'so that none can dress like a gentleman if he is not': it was necessary to regulate appearances (Sapori, 2005, page 39).

'Étiquette', however, fell into abeyance towards the end of the *Ancien Régime*, and with it the sumptuary laws that regulated the usage linked to clothing in society, reminding each to remain within their position, their rank. In the absence of laws, clothing quickly became a field of competition, of rivalry for social recognition, some will say of coquetry and vanity. The merchants and the bourgeois could finally rival the nobles, the class in power. These rules therefore officially disappeared, but not the rivalry or the need to express a scale of recognition of a form of social hierarchy. In our democratic, egalitarian, even presumed classless societies, luxury is linked to meritocracy: it represents the medals thereof. It is, moreover, revealing that we have moved from 'étiquette' to the luxury brand, which is written on ostentatious labels (the French word 'étiquette' is the exact translation of the English word 'label'). This marker conserves in its genes this first function: maintaining rank, and the visibility of rank. This is why it must be highly visible: like a social seal. Admittedly, nowadays a certain fringe clientele asks for more discreet signs from today's brands: but this is to distinguish themselves from buyers of access products, to signal their distance from those who show off their logos.

The French Revolution brought the abolition of privileges, a new ruling class – elected this time – and egalitarian ideology. More importantly, the British Industrial Revolution brought mass production. Automatically, prices could fall if demand was high. It was therefore necessary to stimulate demand. The emerging capitalism created new fortunes, as did the globalization of exchanges linked to colonization. Economic power was no longer an inheritance, a right, but something acquired. Through enrichment linked to work, we could buy better-quality, manufactured products. The imitation of power was the lever for more costly acquisitions, but also for the appearance on the market of imitations of the objects of power: the growing importance of accessories in the so-called luxury market is etymologically 'access via series'. This imitation of power made it possible for anyone to rise above their condition, to accede to pleasures and sensations, finally to become someone, to cease to be just one of 'the people' by imitating 'those people', the ones who really have power. In order to exist, you must be elevated; you must raise yourself up.

This is why the luxury market and its appearances were born: to provide everyone with the means for a provisory, even fictitious elevation, a fleeting pleasure. We can imitate the signs of wealth, without being wealthy: this is the case with clothing in particular, and accessories, if they exhibit the requisite seal, the brand.

The Asiatic countries' penchant for luxury is thus easily explained. These countries have moved from caste to 'class', not so much the sociological concept as the evaluation of yourself and your position relative to others. To have or not to have class, without, however, differentiating yourself to excess.

Luxury: the product and the brand

When we think of luxury, the central unit of analysis is the brand. A brand is 'luxury' when it is perceived as such: a pantheon of so-called luxury brands immediately springs to mind, which illustrate the question far better than a lengthy discourse. In turn a product is 'luxury' as long as it bears the seal of a brand that is itself called 'luxury'. As Teil (2005, p. 13) has remarked, this is circular reasoning, since to the question 'What is a luxury brand?' we often reply that it is a brand that makes luxury products. In luxury, since the product precedes the brand, we should clearly begin with the former: what makes it 'luxurious? By what qualification process does a product accede to this status?

There is a tendency, emanating from public relations and advertising agencies, to consider the product as secondary: it is the qualification of the clients themselves that makes a luxury object. Hence the importance of reaching star clients and to evoke their enthusiastic participation. Reading *The Cult of Luxury: Asia's Love Affair with Luxury* (Chadha and Husband, 2006), you are struck by the emphasis of the authors (both of whom work in an advertising agency) on the role of public relations, celebrities, brand ambassadors, sponsorship and events focused on 'the right people' to give the brand 'glamour' and thus enable the products to benefit from the halo it creates. Almost nothing is said about the products themselves. Now, according to our analysis in Chapter 1, although luxury forms part of a social process of recreation and signification of social distance, it also presupposes an intimate, intense satisfaction, linked to the object itself and its own imaginary and beauty, bought on its merits and for its merits. This satisfaction distinguishes those who are able to appreciate and savour the product deeply, not simply those who are able to buy it, simple followers of others' tastes: taste is what money can't buy.

Conversely, how many small brands, born of passionate young creators tempted by luxury, wonder why their efforts on quality and perfection were never rewarded? There are two answers to their question·

- Luxury is located beyond quality: it is, to borrow an expression from Rémi Krug, 'that which distinguishes the very good from the emotionally moving'. It is not enough to ceaselessly pursue perfection, as the advertising for the car brand Lexus claims. In luxury, it is the emotion that must be sought after at the highest level. It is in the details that we must find the germ of madness necessary to surpass the clinical perfection of Lexus.

● These small brands did not have their 'Kelly bag', which was chosen by the woman who represented the ultimate symbiosis between wealth and glory, beauty and charm, the *Ancien Régime* and the New World, tradition and legend: Grace Kelly, the Hollywood star who became Princess of Monaco.

The popular saying is 'vox populi, vox Dei'. In luxury, it is the reverse. In order to become a grand master of taste, it is certainly necessary to have talent and inspiration, but also the recognition of a clientele whose choices shape the public opinion that will follow them. Under Louis XIV, it was said that to please a countess opened up the region, but to please the Queen opened up France. The Prince of Wales, the future King Edward VII, used to say of Cartier that he was the jeweller of kings and the king of jewellers. The only thing that changed is the countesses and the kings and queens. It is no longer the nobility, but the billionaires' wives, the captains of industry, the great families of the economy, or yet the young, successful CEOs of the new economy, or the cultural stars, foremost among them those of the dream factory that Hollywood is.

It is therefore the union of the two factors above that creates success, not the product alone. It is not insignificant from this viewpoint that an internet site reveals who are the famous buyers of new brands: for the new Swiss luxury watch brand, Richard Mille, born in 1999, whose models are priced above €450,000, they mention Juan Carlos I, the current King of Spain. Many brands in vogue today in Moscow are those that already had access to the court of the Tsars, like the champagne house Veuve Clicquot: although dismissed by the Soviets, the tsars have not lost their cachet in the eyes of the Russians.

The ingredients of the luxury product: complexity and work

The democratization of luxury capitalizes on the desire for the visible logo as a major element of social valorization, to raise the individual from their condition of anonymity among the crowds through growing purchasing power. But we cannot imagine that the elites are satisfied with such motivations: for them, a luxury object must be an object of true luxury. We notice, therefore, as Teil (2005) has rightly highlighted, that luxury passes through a 'double work of qualification':

- authenticating it as a true work of luxury;
- to a true luxury clientele, recognized as such, which is therefore able to understand it.

Here, money is not enough on both sides of this qualification. Simply increasing the layer of silver on a product is not enough for it to qualify in the world of so-called luxury objects. Second, being extremely wealthy is not enough to be a qualifier of luxury. Luxury is about knowing how to spend, rather than having spending power.

Beyond the symbolic value, which is purely social in nature and is analysed in Chapter 1, the value of an object derives from three sources: its usage value, its exchange value and its work value. In terms of luxury, only the third is operational, whereas it is practically non-operational for the majority of current products, where in contrast managers seek to minimize it (delocalization) or to suppress it (automation).

The usage value relates the product to its use, and therefore to a group of functionalities. From this point of view, a Hermès bag could be compared to a Coach bag, and we could establish a hierarchy based on which is the most functional. This comparative approach suits the upper range, but not luxury.

Historically, luxury signals that its purchaser has overcome the constraints of daily life, and has entered into a privileged world where the key to entry is no longer the functional, but the aesthetic, the sensual, the hedonistic, the cultural, the sacred. A Kelly bag is not a better product than a Coach bag, it simply has nothing to do with it; they are not compared, certainly not on the profane fact of usage, reducing all objects to their functions. Luxury is separate, another manifestation of distance.

The exchange value deduces the luxury level from the price level. We often hear talk of the most expensive product. In their time, Jean Patou invented Joy, the most expensive perfume, and Alain Ducasse opened the most expensive restaurant in New York. Other than the fact that an object may be extremely expensive without being luxurious (a rare stamp, a space flight), this approach makes the receiver a being who has not yet been qualified. They do not know without the price, which signifies that they do not have the competence to distinguish for themself.

Interior designers have made their fortunes through this, offering their clients the most expensive of everything as a proof of luxury. The qualitative dimension of luxury is not only accumulative. You do not judge a Cartier jewel by the number of diamonds encrusted on it.

The work value is therefore all that remains: this derives the luxurious character from a series of processes encasing work that qualifies. As Marion observes (2005, p. 293), this approach pays little attention to the client, or to their needs (usage value); it does not present a Ferrari in terms of its ability to enable the client to travel to the office, but as the incarnation of unique, successive know-hows, expressing a unique design, and therefore a sign of a product culture, which can be best shared and explored through its successful expression in the product. There is therefore a wise and mysterious mixture of intangibles (a lineage, a heritage, a single concept of the product drawn from a founder and which must be respected to the letter), added to implementation processes that contain something of the miraculous: the miracle of rare ingredients, mixed with preserved know-how, golden-fingered artisans, according to codes and procedures that are unique to the brand...

The luxury of the product is demonstrated through the guarantee of the means implemented upstream, by an imaginary attached to the production process that speaks of excellence, non-substitutability and rarity. Krug's Le Clos Du Mesnil (€800) comes from a single site with limited area, has been matured over time, and respects the requirements of the Krug house, itself forged over time. Its harvesting and its elaboration derive from knowledge, and each time the cellarmaster produces a miracle. Luxury watches for men are characterized by an incessant search for greater complexity, without complicating the usage of these watches.

This is why luxury needs an expert and passionate sales force. It is necessary to take the time to explain all these qualification processes so that the incomparable value of the object can be appreciated: a value that does not depend on the client, but exists prior to the client.

The luxury of an object is also demonstrated through the renown and taste of the people who have appreciated it: by qualifying these followers, we also qualify the object of their passion, and at the same cause it to benefit from an additional halo of desirability.

Superlative, never comparative

An essential consequence of the manner of qualifying an object as a luxury object is the self-centred nature of this qualification. Luxury never compares itself with others. It has no referent but itself and the extraordinary standards that it has set for itself, and of which each object aspires to be the worthy heir. Hence the notions of heritage, respect for tradition, faithfulness to values and know-how, etc. In order to appreciate the object at its true value, it is necessary to know it: otherwise it is just a piece of merchandise. Can you compare a Porsche and a Ferrari? They are not the same thing, the aficionados will reply; they are two different worlds. To compare them would be to show the degree to which you are uncultured, in the sense that you are incapable of understanding the basis of another's cult. Do you compare religions in terms of the number of daily prayers, the length of religious services, etc? This is why Lexus, the brand of the Toyota group, is not luxury despite its name: its first advertising campaign in the USA claimed that, for the first time, it was possible to buy a cheaper car than a Mercedes E-Class, while in reality buying a more advanced vehicle.

It is important not to underestimate the 'non-comparative' dimension of luxury: it explains its commercialization and communication. These require it to be placed at a distance from all competition:

- Via exclusive distribution where the brand is 100 per cent in charge of the location and can make its identity felt, organizing the sensory and theatrical staging ('living the brand').
- Via a selective distribution where great care is taken that other comparable brands are not present, side by side.
- Through the need for a discourse on the origins (Where does the product come from? Where does its form of design come from?), which in itself requires an exclusive seller through the filial respect for founding, inherited values, a veritable religion internal to the brand that makes it equal to no other, incomparable, and makes the product almost a communion wafer.
- Via advertising communication that loves the almost-empty double page spread, with the goal of creating empty space around the object

Luxury and cultural mediation

A strong brand is one that has been able to create aficionados, eager and proselytizing clients. Money does not buy access to everything. A Pauillac Chateau Mouton Rothschild sparkles with more than its price: it is the product's epic saga, the time it embodies, the know-how, the rituals, the brand legend, its renown, that make the luxury object a concentration of culture. It is still necessary to be able to resonate with the evocation of these facets.

This is why culture is the biggest explanatory factor in the consumption of luxury goods (see Chapter 5). This is what makes it easier for clients who are not among the most wealthy to spend so much money. It increases the understanding of uniqueness and rarity.

In so-called 'new luxury', where the value is often essentially conveyed by the media, and the object in itself holds few mysteries or character without a signature or a *griffe*, this cultural mediation is less operational: it is not needed. Hence clothing, accessories and make-up have become supports for the stretching of luxury brands, even as these objects themselves ceased to be luxury objects per se, but rather mass-prestige, or mass-opulence, also known as mass trading up (Silverstein and Fiske, 2005). Thus the branded fashion clothes have become a porous means for signifying distance. They have become widely accessible to all, even that of creators and couturiers. Every young Chinese manager wants to wear Boss or Armani; it is the new armour of these conquerors of the new world. This is why the distance requires a quantitative dimension: the most expensive objects place the distance beyond the reach of its pursuers. They signal a greater success (Pannekoucke, 2005, p. 67).

The CEO of Yves Saint-Laurent, Pierre Bergé, used to say that it was the obligation of luxury to offer objects and not products, to be a space for enjoyment, not consumption. In fact, the object needs to be learned to be appreciated. It therefore distinguishes those able to appreciate it. Haute cuisine exists only because we have at the same time both great chefs and true lovers of food. Gastronomy implies a penchant for hedonism: haute cuisine is not only the empire of the senses: it claims to be an art, an idea, inspired creation that you either do, or do not partake of.

Some cultural baggage is therefore necessary to appreciate luxury. In fact, the two individual factors that do most to explain the consumption rate of luxury products are firstly cultural capital, and secondly income (see again Chapter 5). It is certainly no accident that Louis Vuitton was successful in Japan. This success is due to numerous causes, but one of them is little-known. In Japan, 'LV' had the obvious legitimacy of being a source of valuable objects in the eyes of the elite. The monogram canvas created in 1892 carried small geometric signs that had no meaning for the average Westerner. In fact, they are Mon signs, linked to Japanese heraldry; in 1892 Europe was in the grip of a Japanizing current, whose aesthetics influenced the design of the canvas. This was immediately decoded by the Japanese eye as a sign of intrinsic value. The Relais & Châteaux chain carries the word 'Châteaux' in its name, directly evoking old, historic buildings. This positions the brand and anchors it in history, although this type of product in fact represents only 20 per cent of its offer.

Luxury and history

Why are there so few Chinese luxury brands today, although there are Chinese fashion brands? The Cultural Revolution cut off the roots, and this eradication made possible the development of an economy with double-digit growth through consumption bulimia and enrichment through work. But from the producer's point of view, what would a Chinese luxury brand look like? It would have to be located above the world of merchandise, be elevated, and be sourced from something timeless, and therefore find its roots, its history. The Chinese have a great history, but to date they have not exhumed it, nor proudly reclaimed it as their own, not in order to replicate the past, but to reclaim an ancient, noble tradition, which would of course be embodied today in contemporary works and objects.

Once China has recovered confidence in itself and its culture, there is no doubt that great Chinese luxury brands will appear, recreating the link with the past; Shanghai Tang is showing the way, via bi-cultural management (Joanne Ooi was born in Singapore, but grew up in Cincinnati, and the company was acquired in 1998 by the Richemont group) and not yet purely Chinese, but how disappointing to find in Shanghai itself only the Western luxury and mass-prestige brands: Boss, Burberry, Prada, Armani... To borrow Chadha and Husband's expression (2006), the new Chinese do not know Mozart or Beethoven, but they know Vuitton and Prada.

There can be no luxury brand without roots, without a history to provide the brand with a non-commercial aspect: it constitutes a fabulous treasure through the mythologization that it enables, by creating a sanctum of uniqueness, of non-comparability, while being the origin of an authentic lineage to which each new product can lay claim.

The European brands, born with history, draw great self-confidence from it, a great uniqueness and a cult of inherited values that translate into products that religiously respect these values. Thus, what fascinates rich Chinese seeking to invest their fortunes are the seven generations of bankers of the Maison Rothschild, even though it does not advertise in their country.

Note that what is important is not simply the history, but the myth that can be created around it, the source of the brand's social idealization. Writing 'Established 1884' does not make you luxury: it makes you old. You must still signal some additional qualities about both objects and people. Madame Cliquot might have remained an inconsolable widow upon her husband's death: in variance to the customs of the day, she assumed the reins of the company and continued delivery of champagnes to the tsar's court. An epic saga was born.

If there is no history, it must be invented. This is what modern American or Italian brands do, since history inverts the relationship with the object and with the client: it is not a case of immediacy, but of lineage, of inheritance. Visiting any Ralph Lauren shop, you are struck by all the black-and-white photos outlining the American way of life of the 1950s. Ralph Lifschitz was a teenager at that time. Moreover, this lifestyle, these characters, these cars, these houses, these pastimes (polo) are themselves highly typified: a pure emanation of the closed world of the WASP (white Anglo-Saxon Protestant), far removed from that of Ralph Lifschitz, but from which he borrowed the mythology in order to create a brand and change his own name. At the beginning of its very new life, Tod's, makers of designer footwear, also flirted with advertising evocations of stars such as Cary Grant, Audrey Hepburn and David Niven, as if they could have worn its shoes. The brand also allowed a rumour to circulate that these unique shoes, these wedge-heeled moccasins, were those of F1 racers, perhaps Juan Manuel Fangio. This is historically impossible, but the beginning of a myth-building history was created.

It is customary to recall that, belonging to a new country, Americans deny the value of two things: history and soil of origin. They have to deny them; it is an economic necessity. How could American entrepreneurs create valuable brands when they are recent and the country has no long history? By devaluing the worth of history, and inventing stories in its place: this is the talent of Hollywood, creator of mythical histories, maker of images that cause the planet to dream. In the same way, new wine-producing countries place the emphasis on the grape variety to devalue the origin of the wine as a criterion of quality, since this would put them at a competitive disadvantage (only France would have had a monopoly on the most famous vineyards).

History gives depth to a brand, and timelessness to its objects. It does not mean imprisonment in the past, but heritage and continuity. The example of Cartier is a revealing one. In 2007, Cartier celebrated its 160th anniversary. At Cartier, every jewel, every watch tells a story, and carries a touch of history:

- The first Panthère jewel dates from 1949: it is true that in Paris, the wild cat had been in fashion since the 1930s. Sarah Bernhardt welcomed visitors to her home while holding a panther on a leash. It became a line, and 25 designers work continually to renew it.
- The Trinity ring was inspired by Jean Cocteau, in 1924: it is regularly reinvented.
- The Love bracelet with its screws dates from 1969.
- Cartier innovated by producing the first watch on a leather wrist strap, a gift for the pioneer of aviation Santos Dumont so that he could check the time without letting go of the controls.
- Tank, one of the most famous Cartier watches, is 90 years old: it was a homage to the Allied tanks in the First World War.

How then can you create luxury if you are a recent brand, and therefore without the history of a brand such as Mellerio dits Meller, the jeweller whose house dates back to 1613, or Krug, which is 160 years old, or the Chanel house born at the beginning of the 20th century (No 5 was launched in 1921)? One thing is certain: the most dynamic brands have, among other things, a patrimonial historical element: a true, authentic history, which gives them hindsight, depth and consistency both internally and in the eyes of clients. At this stage we should however distinguish three types of history, all levers of the imaginary:

- True history, authentic so long as it is capable of engendering modern myth. We have already described how claiming that your business was founded in 1886 is not enough: you need a founding myth, such as that of Veuve Clicquot, regularly updated by the Veuve Clicquot Prize for the female entrepreneur of the year.

- The reappropriation of true historical elements in the service of a recent brand. Thus, the character 'Dom Pérignon' was invented recently (in the 1950s), but through its name has been able to borrow from and enrich a true, myth-building history: that of the monk Pierre Pérignon, who in 1665 accidentally created an effervescent straw wine, which became the wine of the Court at Versailles, and was said to make women more beautiful. Moreover, according to the legend, the form of the champagne glass mirrored the shape of Madame de Pompadour's breast. Other very recent, so-called luxury brands, have made use of historical elements: the Swedish vodka Absolut, or the Dutch Ketel One.
- The creation of a new, contemporary legend (Kapferer, 1990). Gucci hints at a noble origin, linked to a great Renaissance family. Ralph Lauren himself plays at being the modern incarnation of The Great Gatsby, his shops designed like homes giving life to an imaginary of English aristocracy and its accompanying lifestyle. The Italian watch brand Panerai, born in Florence in 1860, draws its slogan from this: 'Inspired by the past, built for the future'. But the history does not always need to be that of the brand itself; it may be the history of its universe of expression. This is the case for new brands: Shanghai Tang takes its inspiration from the Shanghai of the 1920s and 1930s, an era where the demi-monde and unheard-of refinement mixed together, as the brand's website recalls: hence its ripped dresses and its colourful Qi Pao.

Luxury and time

In a very recent advertisement, Hennessy, the world's luxury cognac, highlighted a quotation from Richard Hennessy himself (1724–1800): 'We must let time penetrate what the present cannot.' Luxury embodies time: this is an essential source of its value.

Luxury takes its time; it has time. As its advertising discreetly states, 'A Hermès watch always has time', even though it is often intended for those who live fast. This is what distinguishes luxury from the productivist logic of industry, where efficiency is the criterion of good management. For them, 'time is money' means: work quickly and fast. For luxury, it means the opposite: take the time to offer the very best according to the brand's own conception, nourished and matured over time.

Time is first of all embodied in the ingredients: you need time to reach the maturation of the best woods, the finest ingredients, or the time to go and seek them wherever they may be in the world. Time to allow nature to conduct its miracle, even if synthetic versions would not be detectable to the client, but would nevertheless reduce the object's power to create fascination. The time embodied in the number of years required to qualify as an exceptional artisan (competence): the great alcohols are not an exact science, but the fruit of assemblages, such as those carried out by the makers of a perfume. The time, naturally, of the manufacturing process, painstaking and magical, like that of the maturation of a great cognac or whisky in barrels made of a wood that is itself rare. There is also the time embodied in the brand, in the form of a concentration of transmitted, inherited, respected and venerated values. As noted above, recent brands create a history for themselves, true or false, which makes it possible to incorporate precious time into the products and their meaning.

The time of the luxury brand is embodied in renewed creators. It is significant that Gian Franco Ferré and, later, Karl Lagerfeld, when they comment on their Chanel collections, take a step back and seem, according to their statements, only to rediscover what Coco Chanel would have done in 1920 or 1930. In fact, when they put their names to their own collections, or on other brands (Karl Lagerfeld collections for Fendi or H&M), these two creators design something entirely different from what they do for Chanel: although audacious, even provocative, their collections remain Chanel; they have grasped the soul, the design and the drawing of it. Moreover, when Karl Lagerfeld accepted the artistic directorship of the Chanel brand, he spent a long time immersing himself in the house's archives, with his famous sketchbook, in order to understand properly the semiotic grammar of Chanel, in order to speak its language.

Finally, let us note that time is part of the sale, and the purchase. The two-year wait for a Ferrari falls within this domain. The time that the salesperson will spend with the client does also. The time spent accessing the product: the successive shells that must be opened, in order to have access to the product itself. These successive wrappings are themselves settings and screens: they project the famous brand name, the talented artist, even as they slow down the process of discovery, and will be thrown away immediately afterwards (there is no luxury without waste).

The final dimension of time is that of the time of consumption itself: the great chefs are artists of the moment. This is why the cuisine of great, starred chefs is a ritual that requires time: the guests must take time too, between each course. This intensity of time spent together to which an alcohol may be invited also explains why certain alcoholic drinks qualify as luxury objects and others are disqualified. White rum is certainly linked to moments of joy, but they are too profane, too much in the immediacy of the euphoric effect.

Time is celebrated in luxury: hence brand museums, the hymn to the founders whose soul, and precepts, are respected, the itinerant global exhibitions to recall past splendours (such as the Cartier exhibition of *haute joaillerie*), the systematic republication of old models, the durable sales of the oldest models – Chanel No 5, Nina Ricci's L'Air du Temps – the time that accumulates forges uniqueness, mythology, and therefore value, if it can be mixed with modernity, with what resonates with today's clients.

The search for a dose of timelessness in luxury also concerns the products themselves. At the time of the first collection by Christian Lacroix, an impatient Bernard Arnault asked the creator where his 'timeless' elements were (*Télérama*, 15 August 2007).

In order to conclude our discussion of this facet, it is one of the more significant paradoxes of luxury that it must maintain both timelessness and trendiness at the same time: of course the two approaches go together, compensating for the failures of too much timelessness (boredom) and too much ephemerality (superficiality, the fashion that falls out of fashion): hence the importance of limited lines, special editions, all by allocation...

It becomes all the more necessary to implement this trendy facet when the luxury brand is obliged to be enrolled within a 'tradition'. Once the word 'tradition' has been used, there is a risk that it will evoke mummification, imprisonment within the past. This is the case if the brand does not offer the necessary ruptures and distances that characterize luxury. It becomes self-repetition and no longer forms relationships with today's world.

Tradition is not *passéisme*

Chivas Brothers created the luxury whisky brand Royal Salute: its first product, the RS 21, was the tribute to the new Queen Elizabeth II, in honour of her coronation in June 1953. The name 'Royal Salute' derives from this time. As for the age of the whisky, 21 years, it is linked to the 21 cannons fired by the Royal Navy on that day. The strength of Royal Salute is that it knew how to create a bridge between that now-distant event and young, successful entrepreneurs around the world, particularly in Asia: the brand is for them the sign of supreme respect, both for the Queen and for themselves. It is a brand of power. All its communications activities continually stimulate this facet: for example by creating meetings for Chinese CEOs where they could meet the former British Prime Minister John Major, who had come to Shanghai to carry out an exclusive conference on the state of the world. The luxury brand is also thus intimately linked to the Chinese Businessman of the Year Awards, which distinguish the conquerors of this new world.

History and tradition only have value through relevance today, and communication plays an important role in this equilibrium. Advertising for the watch brand De Witt places a simple phrase beneath the photo of its watch face: 'De Witt, the manufacturer of the 21st century'. The slogan of Patek Philippe advertising is, 'Begin your own tradition': this shows a father and son, both very modern. Blancpain describes itself as 'a tradition of innovation, since 1735'.

In the same way as the modern upper-range brand boasts of a technological leap forward, and runs after 'best product' rosettes, so the luxury brand boasts of its lineage, and places itself in the context of a tradition. The word 'tradition' does not mean dangerous petrification; it means respect for the values and manners that have carried it through time. This is also why there is no luxury without a dose of manual labour.

Luxury is made by hand

The advertising for the Aston Martin DBS states that it is 'handmade in England'. However, the acme of luxury is not to be entirely handmade. Who today would wish for a car built by hand? It is the sign of artisanship. Luxury is not artisanship; it is on the side of art. India has the best luxury artisans. This is the legacy of the maharajahs, those vastly wealthy princes who maintained corporations of gold-fingered artisans for their orders and purchases. The Indian government wonders why India, despite its artisans, has not emerged in the global luxury market. The answer is that is has not yet reached the post-artisan stage (organization of production and distribution, democratization of products). It has not produced true artists capable of inverting the relationship with the ultra-rich clients of its country and elsewhere, and of creating not only a recognized creative offer, but also an aura through the glamour of its famous, media-friendly clients. The luxury revolution, its genuine emergence as a market, comes from the fact that the executor becomes the prescriber. Indian artisans have remained workers, admittedly highly qualified, but who have not been able to achieve ascendancy over their clients, as did the couturiers who became famous and created their own court in France in the 19th century, like artists.

This being said, every luxury object should have some part, even small but spectacular, that is handmade. This is the dimension that makes it stand out from the series, from the world without surprises of the factory. As Patek Philippe's text for its modern design watch, Nautilus, says: '265 individually hand-finished components'. The imaginary picture of the artisan, which is not far from the artist, is also one of the embodiments of the notion of tradition, even in the productions of our time.

Like the grille of a Rolls-Royce, much of the fitting-out of a Swan or Wally boat is done by hand. This must remain true even at a larger scale: at Nina Ricci, the *baudruchage* of each bottle of L'Air du Temps perfume was done by hand. The plaque on each bottle of Royal Salute 50 whisky is hand-engraved by a goldsmith. This handiwork is the sign of a cult: that of attention to detail. It adds a strong impression of rarity and preciousness.

Real or virtual rarity?

Rarity is central in the identity of luxury. Since wealth, in the modern world, signifies the quality and success of exceptional people, what could be more natural than to offer them rare goods and services, on a par with their means and their discrimination? The extreme example of this is the single piece for the ultra-rich (see Chapter 5). They no longer know how to spend their money: the term 'outside the range' was invented to designate those single pieces that they will yearn for: submarines, planes, haute couture dresses – if not paintings by the great masters. All luxury speaks of rarity: rarity of ingredients, artisans, know-how, and the ultimate rarity, the brand and the values it respects.

The 'luxury market', however, is born from the abandonment of rarity. The global sales success of so-called luxury brands attests to the fact that rarity is no longer part of the definition of luxury for the major groups that make up this market: LVMH, PPR, Richemont, Pernod-Ricard, etc. There are two major reasons for this:

- There are more and more rich people, and very rich people. Thus the demand for Ferraris has never been higher: to the American, South American and European markets can now be added those of Russia and China, where the liberated entrepreneurial class and show business create billionaires. Ferrari could therefore double its production, maintained today in an objective (industrial restrictions at Maranello) but also a subjective rarity (mastery of what luxury means). Can they respond to the goldmine that Asia represents, while maintaining objective rarity?
- In Asian countries, the importance of social integration is such that everyone is ready to pay high prices to buy 'instant class'. Japan was the first to demonstrate that it was possible to sell at a high price and in high numbers. This is why all the Western luxury brands have rushed to install themselves in Asian shopping malls and department stores, where the crowds file past the windows to learn of an international lifestyle, and to buy a sign of it, an object to mark that they too belong to this universe that gives rank. The fact that Japanese 'office ladies' all carry the same Louis Vuitton handbag does not worry them; on the contrary. In Japan luxury is a luxury of integration: too much rarity would therefore destroy the brand's value.

The business model of major capitalist luxury groups is to sell for mass consumption products that are labelled by a luxury brand but are no longer themselves luxury, hoping that this edifice will survive, and that the halo of luxury will be continually regenerated through communication and exceptional products. It is necessary to maintain a very high brand status to support this large-scale use of the brand capital.

Particular treatment is reserved for the economic, show business or cultural elites: rare products, in all facets of their slow design process, expressing all the know-how of the luxury brand. This elite consumption is mediatized by public relations, and cascades down to the mass of (predominantly female) readers: since the brand is made sacred by the media exposure of the stars, its objects are desirable, and the affordably priced versions are runaway successes, especially if one such fashionable star has been spotted wearing one in a photo deliberately released in the female press. The world has become obsessed by celebrities, and by wanting to be like them: what do these living demigods buy, drink or wear? To borrow the famous phrase: 'what is ordinary for extraordinary people has a tendency to become what is extraordinary for ordinary people'. Thus a genuine market is born: the luxury brand no longer restricts itself to selling in small amounts for high prices, like Patek Philippe, but in large amounts for lower prices, like Tag Heuer. In order better to understand luxury, it is therefore necessary to take the notion of rarity to a deeper level, going beyond the classical notion of a small number.

In reality, there is more than one rarity. Objective, physical rarity is necessary at a certain stage of building a profitable luxury brand, but not at all stages – quite the reverse. Otherwise, there are no sales and no profits: accessories are the least rare version of the edifice, but that does not mean that they do not deliver considerable net margins, since these objects incorporate very little objective rarity and are therefore relatively cheap to manufacture. What will increase their cost is a rarity that we may describe as virtual, with which they must be imbued. Asked about his role, Bernard Fornas, the CEO of Cartier International, replied that: 'I have to manage the desirability of this house, it is necessary to maintain the ratio of availability to rarity' (*Air France Magazine*, August 2007). For availability, Cartier created the concept of the 'Must' in 1973. The *haute joaillerie* is there to signify and to create rarity as a counterweight to this.

We should therefore distinguish between two major types of rarity: on the one hand physical rarity, the best-known type, that of ingredients or processes, and on the other hand a virtual rarity or impression of rarity, signified, created and maintained by the communication itself. The first is that of true luxury.

Our HEC colleague, Bernard Catry, distinguishes five types of rarity, from the physical to the virtual, and links these levels to their capacity for opening the floodgates of volume, but also to the types of managerial know-how critical for the so-called 'luxury' company.

First, the rarity of the ingredients by definition limits the sales volume. Here the buyer is the key person, through their ability to secure supplies of the rarest ingredients. Dormeuil, the specialist in luxury draperies, unearths rare and exceptional materials, addressed both to the cream of the tailoring profession and specialists of male high luxury fashion. In 2008 it was the Royal Qiviuk, where it was necessary to pay €1,840 per metre of fabric to wear a suit made of this fabric: it came from the inner fur of the musk ox, an animal living in the far north of Canada. Its short, fragile fibres are collected by hand by the Inuits. They are mixed with Super 200s wool and cashmere.

Cosmetics are fond of rarities emerging from research, which play the role of technological rarities. A brand such as La Prairie is known for its 'Caviar Luxe' cream, selling at €328 per 50 ml. In 2007 this brand also launched a serum with pure 24 carat gold, already used in medicine as an anti-inflammatory, priced €514 per 30 ml.

Second, technical rarity: it creates an impression of rarity through the ultimate demand for perfection. In *Newsweek* of December 2007, the advertising catchline for the Rolex Oyster Perpetual model, is 'Pure Rolex': it talks of its exclusive foundry, which creates new and exclusive alloys of absolute purity. Likewise Richard Mille boasts of its technological alchemy on its website: 'metallic alloys, ceramics, carbon nanofibres, silicon: a watch like this does not contain any standard parts'. The Black Centurion payment card, from American Express, also plays with this strand: it is made from anodized titanium. Likewise all the new upper-range vodkas introduced in the USA since 1998 have launched a pursuit after purity, each adding another distillation for even more transparency and purification, like a mystical quest for a purifying grail. Grey Goose, a luxury vodka made in France and sold at a higher price than all the others ($37 per litre), is distilled four times, reaching a kind of purified essence, cleansed of all impurities, which makes for a kind of quasi-rarity at the imaginary level. It boasts of being the 'World's best tasting vodka', a title received from an Institute in Chicago. Everything about it therefore says rarity, but reality permits volume: it has the strongest growth in its segment and sells 4 million cases per year. Saying that it takes 10 years to train an artisan capable of working on the mechanism of a Cartier watch evokes rarity, but does not give away the number of artisans.

Third, the rarity of the production itself. This is the logic of self-limitation of demand, of limited series, announced on the sly to the elite for pre-orders and to wind the spring of desire through the emulation of those who will display the product before everyone else, in this intra-class rivalry to signal pre-eminence. Ferrari limits its production, hence the waiting lists that increase desire.

Fourth, the rarity of distribution also creates an impression of rarity. Lacoste is seen as a luxury brand in China, because the brand, which has only recently opened there, is only present in the best department stores, and in a few own-brand boutiques in Beijing and Shanghai. The reverse is true in Japan, where the brand, which has long been entrusted to a local licensee, was distributed in neighbourhoods and shops that scarcely evoke luxury. Montagut represents the extreme in rarity of distribution: this brand of sweaters with Fils Lumière made its reputation in China by buying huge advertising posters – which were very cheap at the time – when it could not be sold in China, and its distribution was therefore non-existent. By creating recognition without distribution, Montagut created the dream of what people could not buy.

Fifth and finally, informational rarity capitalizes on the rarity not of the objects, but of the famous people who wear them, or who frequent such-and-such a hotel, spa or restaurant. The constant feed of scoops, false rumours, false secrets, etc is also aimed at increasing the virtual rarity through the dissemination of things that we should not have known about. Exclusivities disseminated through the press have the same effect. Informational rarity is also built through the use of the word rare itself in product labelling, and the names of products themselves (Lancôme's Rare cream). Rumour has it that only 10 Brazilians have an Amex Black Centurion card: this type of rumour also increases the perceived rarity. Table 4.1 sets out the five types of rarities.

In modern luxury, it is therefore necessary to know how to distribute rarity without rarity. Rarity is managed, or even simulated. After the Gulf crisis of 1991, champagne entered a crisis: falling consumption, increasing stocks. Consequently, throughout LVMH the order of the day was to push the volumes. As we saw in Chapter 3, in luxury prices must constantly move upwards, which is contradictory with a volume strategy. If Moët raised its prices 10 per cent, its volumes would immediately fall by 10 per cent to 20 per cent: Moët is not a luxury brand. Dom Pérignon, a luxury brand, also under pressure from the logic of stock reduction, decided to put all the major accounts on allocation. When these accounts were preparing, during the annual renegotiations, to complain of business slumps and exaggerated prices, Dom Pérignon wrong-footed them by telling them that in any case

Table 4.1 The five types of rarity

Natural	Type of rarity driver	Compatibility with volume
↓	1. Ingredients, components limited capacity, rare human expertise eg: diamonds, rings, fur	Little
	2. Techno-rarity, innovations, new products and features	Average
	3. Limited editions, custom-made orders, one-to-one relationships	Average
	4. Distribution-based rarity	Good
	5. Information-based rarity, marketing, brand, secrecy	Very good: no physical limit
Virtual		

Source: B Catry (2006)

there would not be more for everybody: each major distributor was therefore offered a contractual volume lower than the year's sales, and told to think themselves lucky, in addition to a 20 per cent rise in prices, conditions and restrictions. Dom Perignon thus succeeded in achieving the systematic rise in prices, without loss of volume.

Luxury and exclusivity

The luxury product is exclusive in two ways: 'I am the only person to own one', and 'This excludes the other'. It makes the owner someone special.

For Veblen, the Norwegian economist (1899), luxury is that which is socially most desirable, since it places you at the summit of the hierarchy. This is one of the drivers of what are known as Veblen goods: those for which demand increases as the price increases. What is expensive will as a consequence be even more expensive tomorrow. This is why billionaires like art: the possession of a painting excludes all others. The same is true of privileged villa sites at St Tropez or Gstaad. To be there or not to be there; only the chosen few can be. Hence the rising prices in art and fine furniture, which will be endless: there are in fact more and more rich people in the world, entering into the cycle of pecuniary rivalry.

As with rarity, the luxury market could only grow by becoming less exclusive. If an object is out of reach, we cannot desire it. Except for the ultra-rich. As Gabriel Tarde noted as early as 1890, while barriers exist, making exclusivity official, the consumption or lifestyle of others cannot be desired. It is only by making it accessible – through price and through the lifting of any legal restrictions on its acquisition, such as the sumptuary laws – that the mechanism of the desire for that possessed by the other can be set in motion.

The brand must do everything possible to appear exclusive, even if exclusivity never appears as a factor in surveys regarding what is most appealing about luxury. Very few people will in fact admit that they buy something because it is exclusive. In the interviewees' responses, it must firstly be very beautiful, of very high quality, with a magical element, from a prestigious brand, etc.

Several comments should be made at this point. Exclusivity is not the premier factor in valuation, but its absence is a factor in devaluation: it harks back to the marketing of common objects. On the other hand, everything depends on the survey sample: the elites value exclusivity, the masses do not. The luxury market has grown, by allowing the public at large to have access to some luxury products. Now almost everyone in Western countries or in Japan can afford a little bit of luxury, combined to their liking, whether in their interior decoration, in their day-to-day clothing or among the panoply of beauty creams.

The difficulty for the emergent luxury brand is to know when to open up, to be less exclusive, in order to become profitable. In order to open up, it is necessary to have already created an inaccessibility that is a source of desire. From his first lunch with Bernard Arnault, Christian Lacroix told him that he wanted to work on affordable *prêt-à-porter*. That year, the year of the first haute couture collection by the young prodigy under his own name (he had previously designed for Jean Patou), *Elle*, the women's magazine, asked him how people could dress in the Lacroix style on a tight budget. Arnault declared that he had lost face when he came across the article (*Télérama*, 15 August 2007). For him, it was clearly too soon. What would have been acceptable to launch a 'creator' of classical fashion, was not so for a young luxury brand that needed first to become consecrated as such.

The need for exclusivity and public honour explains why luxury today increasingly nests within the service sector. Therefore, all around the world, we are witnessing the renewal of first class air travel, which had disappeared for a time in favour of frenetic competition between the airlines on business class, to turn it into the haven of peace and serenity so necessary to the major international manager (see also page 261).

The example of the airline clearly demonstrates the paradigm we witnessed in the first chapter, namely that the need for luxury is broadened by democratization, the so-called classless society. There has never been such variance between the prices of different seats within a single aeroplane as there is today. Admittedly this is due to the need to provide a few seats at very low prices to retain clients attracted by the 'low-cost' airlines such as Ryanair and easyJet. At the other extreme, however, the offer is also becoming more sophisticated, either by the creation of 'trading up' segmentations from economy class, such as the Economy Premium class introduced by Virgin Airways for those paying the full fare, or at the top end of business class such as Iberia's Business Plus or British Airways' Club World, and finally the 'Must' of comfort, the new first classes. Luxury is the watchword of first class, comfort that of business class, and for the shrewd there is economy class. The decoration of the first-class cabin, like any luxury clothing, is entrusted to famous designers such as Terence Conran for British Airways. Revealingly, the difference between first and business class is seen less in the products: some business classes also now offer proper beds.

Let us look again at our anti-law number 8: 'Protect... the big from the small': the first pleasure of a traveller in first class is to be truly a person apart – both literally and figuratively. The Senior Executive Vice-President of Singapore Airlines, considered the world's best airline, Mr Bey Soo Khiang, gives a succinct summary of the key to first class: 'First class must offer absolute exclusivity, a golden segregation... the first class passenger must enjoy the luxury of being totally separate from the other traveller flows. To pay for first class is like an entrance ticket to an exclusive club.' Everything, therefore, must be done to reinforce the feeling of difference – let us call it superiority – from other passengers, in particular those in business class. This begins with a personalized transfer in a branded limousine from your office in the city centre to the airport, a part of the terminal exclusively reserved for such passengers... Thai Airways and British Airways also offer access to a private spa. One company also has the passenger driven to the foot of the aeroplane's boarding steps in a Mercedes: this treatment, once reserved for presidents, is accessible to those who expect and appreciate these honours, which reward their extraordinary success.

To conclude the section on exclusivity, let us tackle the subject of the ultra-rich, who can therefore buy everything; the fact of remaining among their 'own kind', among people of the same social status, is very important: they do not mix.

Selective clubs and public honour

In a world where, as we have seen, the codes of luxury are imitated by the mass-market brands, it is important to recreate and resignify the distance. Luxury is the metaphorical equivalent of the rows of gold stripes on military sleeves: they indicate the wearer's rank, and therefore the honours that are due them, for their prowess and success, and with the prestige of rank luxury confers exclusive services: a chauffeur, access to clubs reserved for the higher ranks, the homage in public places where we are proud to see them there. In the civilian world, watches and cars are the male stripes, of which everyone knows the price and the meaning. Women's handbags show the cultural, professional and income level of the owner. Luxury functions as a fence: it expresses and recreates hierarchical difference. In addition to the fact that it cannot be ruled by the marketing of demand – which always sells more – it must therefore be difficult to access, socially speaking. Hence the fact that luxury brands are clubs. This should be taken in the literal sense: they organize their clients into selective clubs. Luxury is the enemy of equality.

Swan yachts set their owners up in a private club. Initially, the Black Centurion card from American Express was only offered by invitation. Nowadays you must prove that you are worthy of the club: spending at least $250,000 per year (the ticket) and paying an entrance club of $5,000 the first year, and $2,500 thereafter. This is how you become 'America's most exclusive charge card'. This appellation is a direct homage to the victories and successes of its holder: a centurion of modern times.

The feeling of exclusivity is also stimulated by private places and clubs: whether the traditional Polo in Paris, where you must be sponsored and the waiting time is around five years, or the restaurants and clubs of Dashanzi, a north-eastern neighbourhood of Beijing, abandoned factories turned into artists' lofts but also into incredibly fashionable, selective premises and ultra-private clubs mixing ultra-modernity with references to the past, where the now-wealthy Chinese, young entrepreneurs and successful artists mix. It is about finding yourself among your peers, away from others, to signal this distance.

Remember how the car brand Lexus has used this typical trait of luxury. At Flushing Meadows, the New York home of the US Open tennis tournament, the brand has conspicuously reserved two car parks for the exclusive use of Lexus drivers. There is also, moreover, a valet service, and finally you are accompanied into the stadium itself. In Australia, Lexus has created the Club Encore giving priority access to the city's operas, restaurants and, naturally, the closest car park.

Luxury and fashion: an essential difference

Even if the luxury brand needs to be modern and uses fashion as a source of this necessary aura, let us remember here that these are two completely different approaches (see Chapter 1). The entrepreneur must choose between the two, since their business models are far too different from each other. Veblen had already emphasized that fashion had no meaning when social structure was immutable: fashion assumes social rivalry. Luxury and fashion are both instruments of individual differentiation, but nowadays only luxury relates to a latent social hierarchy, and luxury is solely responsible for latent rehierarchization: fashion has spread as a tool of clannishness throughout society. Therefore, there is more than one fashion; there are enough fashions for everyone to differentiate themselves and to integrate themselves into their group, their tribe, even at low prices.

Luxury and art

Luxury and art maintain a constant and intimate relationship (see Chapter 1). What would be Absolut Vodka without the picture of the bottle created by Andy Warhol, the Pope of Pop Art, in 1985, at the Swedish brand's inception? Chanel produces an itinerant exhibition on contemporary art in seven world capitals. For this purpose, the luxury brand has asked the fashionable female architect Zaha Hadid to create an original, itinerant structure, 'Mobile Art', a futuristic capsule where contemporary art will be exhibited in relation to the brand and its quilted bag in all the world's capitals. This clearly highlights the structural proximity that luxury brands have always had with art, in particular contemporary art, since they too are desirous to be included in the disruptive, the beautiful, and the timeless, the sources of the trends that will make up the beautiful of tomorrow.

Today, following the pioneer Cartier and his Fondation pour l'Art Contemporain, all the major luxury groups are now encouraging all types of arts, through their foundations (the Gucci Foundation in Venice, the Louis Vuitton Foundation in Paris...). What are the drivers, motivations and work-ings of this intimate link?

First of all, luxury for billionaires means being able to buy the very rarest and to possess it for reasons of exclusive enjoyment. The systematic price rises in art at the moment indicate that the world is growing richer, and that this movement brings with it a pressure of demand for the most unique, refined, beautiful, timeless, and famous art.

Billionaires themselves have a desire to leave their imprint behind. Hence the foundations and the patronage: princes and kings have always encouraged artists through sumptuary orders. The prodigality of their patronage attested to their power and made it possible for the work, once completed, to be seen by all, especially when it related to paintings or the decoration of buildings, most often religious, hymns to the greatness of God, or royal or public buildings. Many of the artists of the Renaissance had reason to be grateful to these patrons: in addition to money, they were bringing them fame. Nowadays the patron also acts as a consecrating agent on the work and the artist: the patron is the 'gatekeeper'. With them, the doors are opened to the aristocracy of their rank; in order to avoid standing out, they will follow the patron's choice.

The predilection of luxury billionaires for art has is founded on identity: it perpetuates the idea that the function of luxury is the aestheticization of society, the overtaking of the material by the spiritual, elevation through beauty and art. In short, the accumulation of material wealth should encourage and offer elevation through the intangibles – here the arts – to all. In addition, the mythology of luxury must be maintained: it requires temples. We are talking here of the founding legend: that of the artisan (art-isan), the iconic figure in the imaginary of luxury manufacturing. The more luxury brands are built on houses whose growth is achieved through industrialization and long series, the more this luxury industry will venerate the unique, authentic piece. It trans-mits this myth-building veneration to the media via art.

The emergence of the luxury market through its democratization, and therefore de facto the logic of series, makes the upkeep of the myth of arti-sanal, manual, coded production, respectful of tradition, more indispensable than ever. The reference to the pure artist, and the financial support, are a way of being included in this consecrating lineage, without ever speaking about the reality of the artisans.

Historically, art was essentially religious: the great and good of this world ordered works to embellish and build sacred buildings, to the glory of God. Art accompanied the religious rituals: there was no religious object that was not in itself a work of art, an expression of the utmost refinement that the arts and sciences of the time would allow. Of this reference, a sacred dimension to art remains, through the elevation of souls with which it was associated.

But if art in its modern conception has become profane, it remains a sign of culture, of the capacity to appreciate the intangibles, and not only to possess them through the effect of accumulated wealth. Luxury brands wish to create this vertical dimension. Moreover, while production in series has given rise to the luxury market, art is the market of the single work: the flirting between luxury and art also sustains this mythology.

Art also makes it possible to nurture the specific relationship between luxury and time, which differentiates it from fashion. Luxury nurtures the myth that it is timeless: just as fashion – as required by the economic system – organizes obsolescence on a massive and annual scale with the help of women's magazines, so luxury aims at timelessness. A Ferrari gains value over time; part of the Maranello workshop in Italy is dedicated to maintaining the 38,000 Ferraris of all ages sold worldwide. Art, by its essence, aims at eternity: the work will survive the creator and, over time, his epoch. This is how luxury attempts to signal that it is not simply merchandise.

Luxury and charity

Bill Gates's image had never been as good as when he created his vastly endowed foundation. This is American culture: the citizen destiny is within his grasp, through hard work, luck and God's help. Once their fortunes are made, the magnates partially redistribute them: to their university, to their town, to foundations, etc.

The same is true with luxury: there are now innumerable charity dinners and foundations. A place at the Royal Salute charity dinner costs $10,000. Mont Blanc finances UNICEF.

In fact, luxury also gives a great deal. Is this through shame, or from the desire to redeem itself, since luxury has always been the target of censure through the visibility of the inequalities that it reveals? Or is it in fact the symbolic application of moral precepts that are incumbent on the rich?

PART 2

Luxury brands need specific management

5 Customer attitudes vis-à-vis luxury

Who are today's luxury clients? What characterizes them, at either the socio-professional or sociocultural level? How many types of relationship to luxury are there?

What is the size of the market?

Capgemini and Merrill Lynch have identified the profile of those who make up the luxury market, the best potential clients: they are called HNWIs, or 'High Net Worth Individuals' worldwide. These are people with more than $1 million in assets, excluding their principal residence: there were 8.7 million of them in 2005 and 9.5 in 2006, or an increase of 8.3 per cent. Among these, 3.3 million live in North America, 2.9 million in Europe and 2.6 million in Asia. The rate of growth in the number of HNWIs is 21.2 per cent in Singapore, 20 per cent in India, 16 per cent in Indonesia, 15.5 per cent in Russia, 15.4 per cent in the United Arab Emirates, 14.1 per cent in South Korea, etc.

The number of the very rich falls to 85,400 when the threshold is raised: owning more than $30 million. This is typically the clientele of investment banks and private banking, either local or offshore. As 61 per cent of HNWIs are over 56 years of age and as everywhere the consumption of the 50–64 age bracket in numbers of luxury brands bought is markedly inferior to those in the 35–49 age bracket, and that of those over 65 is even less (Dubois and Laurent, 1994), it might be assumed that the expansion of the luxury market is not occurring among HNWIs over 56.

More recent data leads us, however, to recognize that the gap being created between these HNWIs and the rest of the occasional luxury clients, nicknamed 'day trippers' or 'excursionists', primarily buyers of accessories or of products that are mere brand extensions at accessible prices. In fact, according to the American publisher Forbes, the Cost of Living Extremely Well index is moving ever further away from the index of current prices (see Table 5.1).

These figures show that the financial resources necessary to live a life of luxury become extremely large and out of all measure with incomes in line with the current cost of living. This is important, since if they run after the day tripper clients too much, who are admittedly numerous but only buy occasionally, luxury brands may be discredited among the HNWIs, where the true potential luxury market lies. For them, only brands that have managed to maintain their distance will be strongly attractive.

To be rich or to be modern?

For RISC, an institute that has been following the purchases and motivations of luxury clients for more than 15 years, the luxury clientele is defined less by its sociodemographic profile than by its behaviours, its purchases of products from so-called 'luxury' brands. RISC evaluates the core of the luxury clientele throughout the world at 80 million people: 32 million in Europe, 36 million in the USA and 12 million in China. Interestingly, two competing factors may explain the rate of luxury purchases in one person: the income level, of course, but also the person's 'modernity', that is their openness to change, to external influences. According to the data published by RISC, clients with smaller incomes still purchase luxury when they have a modern orientation. Conversely, someone who is extremely rich but not modern, a

Table 5.1 Comparing the cost of living and the cost of living extremely well

	1976	1983	1994	2000	2007
Cost of Living Extremely Well Index	100	200	400	500	772
Cost of Living: Consumer Price Index	100	160	250	300	385

Source: Forbes 2007

hoarder who may invest their fortune in furniture and art, may be less of a luxury client.

Let us examine the data from global surveys (Dubois and Duquesne, 1990) on 12 million frequent purchasers of luxury in Europe (see Table 5.2):

- higher incomes account for 61 per cent of luxury's 'heavy users', but 39 per cent of multiple purchasers are not among the most wealthy;
- sociocultural modernity (mobility, openness to change) plays an equal role alongside money, since 60 per cent of the heavy users are socioculturally 'advanced'.

Let us look now at Table 5.3, which relates to the penetration rate of luxury. The percentage in each sociocultural case indicates the proportion of frequent luxury purchasers in this type of population segment. We have summarized the analysis of the overall European population into four segments: rich versus non-rich, and 'advanced' versus 'more conservative' on a sociocultural level. We can see how much the 'modernity' of the individual promotes the acquisition of luxury objects. According to Dubois, 'to move into modernity is to double the probability of acquiring luxury products among the rich – moving from 5.4 per cent to 11.3 per cent – and from 2 per cent to 5 per cent among the less rich'.

What does the analysis of these sociodemographic factors teach us? Are they linked to the propensity to buy luxury objects or products from luxury brands?

- Income is the principal explanatory factor of this consumption. The higher your income, the more you buy. The propensity to buy luxury, however, may be strong in people who do not have very high incomes, provided that they are 'modern'. Conversely, very high incomes without this sociocultural mentality give rise to fewer luxury purchases. Level of education is the

Table 5.2 Population structure of luxury heavy users

Rich 61%	25%	36%
Not rich 39%	15%	24%
	Conservative	Advanced

Table 5.3 Penetration of luxury into each segment

Rich	5.4%	11.3%
Not rich	2%	5%
	Conservative	Advanced

second explanatory factor: a higher level of study increases the propensity to buy luxury. There is a cultural dimension to luxury.

- Age is also linked to the propensity to buy luxury, but the relation is not a linear one: it has the form of a bell curve, with the peak being reached among the 35–49 age group, at least on the basis of European data on 12,500 clients.

Heavy users and day trippers (also called excursionists)

Up until 2000, the luxury market had grown worldwide based on what we call 'luxury day trippers' or 'excursionists'. These people are less wealthy but are advanced in sociocultural terms, and therefore allow themselves to occasionally purchase an object from a luxury brand, motivated by self-indulgence or hedonism or to celebrate a person or a moment. This announced the democratization of luxury. Today, it is no longer the case: the principal volume of the market is made up of those who buy frequently. Why this reversal? From the beginning of the 2000s, the Western middle classes have been worried about the future, and less optimistic: progress is no longer automatically associated with happiness. They fear that their children will have a less pleasant life than their own. This puts a brake on their occasional consumption of products perceived as luxury. It is true that in the West, individuals are ten times richer than the Chinese, for example. But their income is stagnating, their discretionary purchases are reduced by rising property prices, energy, service and health costs, etc. Paradoxically, therefore, they feel themselves to be 'poor'. In contrast, young Chinese who see their income perceptibly increasing are much more optimistic: they feel rich. In China, there is no brake on the economic rise of new population layers, unlike India where the caste system blocks the mechanism of climbing the social hierarchy through economic success. Hence the luxury market in India is much less dynamic than in China.

Significantly, the group that makes up the bulk of the luxury market, wealthy purchasers (20 per cent of the population), for their part have maintained their optimism: they are even, according to RISC, moving further away from the middle classes, who in their worries for the future are moving closer to the less affluent categories. This polarization of the market has been accentuated year upon year since 2001. Having kept their aspirations, but now conscious of a certain precariousness, the middle class has given rise to what is called 'masstige', a neologism used to designate a hybrid of admittedly prestigious names, but covering products at accessible prices. The demands of masstige are well known: boosting the image of the mid-range to capture this demand for trading up, with the traditional mid-range being abandoned, either in favour of much less expensive, low-cost type products, or for products that offer rather more in terms of image and perceived quality. L'Oréal Paris is the typical brand of masstige clients: it imitates the codes of prestige brands while communicating to the masses, for example on television – its non-selective distribution network requires this. Italian brands, such as Armani, also know how to capture this demand for trading up: they offer a wide range of prices, adapted to the client and the circumstances of use.

The four luxury clienteles

Beyond the sociodemographic and sociocultural variables, what is it about luxury that is so seductive? Why do clients indulge themselves in luxury? What intimate benefits do they gain from it? The statistical analysis of the responses by an international sample of young managers with high disposable income, asked about the characteristics that define luxury in their view, make it possible to identify four concepts of luxury (see Table 5.4). Moreover, since each interviewee named the brand or brands most representative of luxury in their eyes, we can discern the prototypes of each concept of luxury, of what luxury means to them (Kapferer, 1998):

- The first type of luxury, according to this international sample of affluent young executives with high purchasing power, is the closest to the average hierarchy emerging from our studies: it gives prominence to the beauty of the object and the excellence and uniqueness of the product, more so than all the other types. The brand most representative of this type of luxury is Rolls-Royce, but it also includes Cartier and Hermès.
- The second concept of luxury exalts creativity, the sensuality of the products; its luxury 'prototype' is for example Jean-Paul Gaultier.
- The third vision of luxury values timelessness and international reputation more than any other facets; its symbols are Porsche, with its immutable design, Vuitton and Dunhill. These are the institutions of the safe choice, of the certainty of not making a mistake.
- Finally, the fourth type values the feeling of rarity attached to the possession and consumption of the brand: in their eyes, the prototype of the brand purchased by the select few is Chivas or Mercedes, possession of which clearly signifies that you have 'arrived'. The presence of Mercedes as a symbol of this fourth type of luxury testifies to the brand's problems at that time. Only a few years ago, its only potential market was among those looking for the luxury, not of an intimate and sensory pleasure, but above all of a status, the badge of belonging in an affluent class and reaping the benefits of this in terms of prestige, impression and attraction, even seduction.

Table 5.4   Consumers' four concepts of luxury

	Authenticity of the experience	Creative niche luxury	Safe values and prestige	Outstanding badges
What defines luxury:				
Beauty of an object	**97%**	63%	86%	44%
Excellence of the products	**88%**	3%	9%	38%
Magic	76%	50%	**88%**	75%
Uniqueness	**59%**	10%	3%	6%
Tradition and know-how	26%	40%	40%	38%
Creativity	35 %	**100%**	38%	6%
Sensuality of the products	26 %	**83%**	21%	6%
Feeling of exceptionality	23%	23%	31%	31%
Never out of fashion	21%	27%	**78%**	19%
International reputation	15%	27%	**78%**	19%
Produced by a craftsperson	12%	30%	9%	3%
Long history	6%	7%	16%	13%
Genius creator	6%	7%	10%	13%
Belonging to a minority	6%	3%	2%	**63%**
Very few purchasers	0%	3%	2%	**69%**
At the cutting edge of fashion	0%	17%	36%	31%
Typical brands of this luxury according to interviewees:				
	Rolls Royce Cartier Hermes	JP Gaultier	Vuitton Porsche	Chivas Mercedes

Source: J N Kapferer (1998)

This fourth type has a quantitative approach to luxury: they buy the most expensive items to mark their success and share this pleasure.

In China, India, Brazil or Russia, it is the very expensive and status-loaded Mercedes S-, M- or E-Class that sell. These are de facto inaccessible cars.

A strong axis of segmentation: relationship with the product or with the logo?

The four types of clients described above may be situated in relation to one another along a key dimension: one that opposes sensitivity to the logo to sensitivity to the product, the search for emblematic brands rather than that for small masterpieces.

This dimension plays an important role in structuring and differentiating clients, and even countries, regarding the relationship to the logo. It is no accident that luxury brands exhibit their logos. The logo is the semiotic version of 'étiquette', or the code of correct dress at the Royal Court (see page 77). This external manifestation may vary according to circumstances, from more to less visible, knowing that luxury needs a certain minimal visibility, even if only discreet, to signal that absolute separation to which it bears witness.

The fourth of the above groups is very 'pro-logo': they consume the sign. They need known and recognized badges to distinguish themselves from others, to transmit their success. It is significant that a Mercedes advertisement in 2007 talked about 'the car that has succeeded... like you'. The third type is also moved by strong signs, visible and recognized logos: they enjoy the magic of the great names and become sure of themselves through these known brands, incontrovertible institutions of luxury worldwide, in the same way that we feel more at ease when we put on a dinner jacket. In contrast, type one clients see themselves as connoisseurs, aesthetes, capable of appreciating what is exceptional in a product: they like the authentic and are sensitive to the intangibles, the intensity of a rare, shared moment. As for type two clients, they are more concerned with showing their individuality, through choices that set them apart, above the rest, through the originality of the creator.

A second axis of differentiation: authentic does not always mean historical

Luxury clients expect that luxury will compress time. The four concepts of luxury are conscious of the 'tradition and know-how' expressed today. Taking it further, two of these groups, three and four, expect the brand to have 'a long history'. In fact, even if it is recent, luxury always compresses time. Luxury is long term. Even if the sales are written in short-term plans, the luxury brand has time for itself, much more than a fashion brand. Nevertheless, as we have seen (Chapter 3), the brand's temporal dimension characterizes European luxury more than American luxury.

For Europeans and many Asian fans, there is not authenticity without temporal compression. A brand that has a true history draws an absolute prestige from it, which does not mean that it communicates only in a *passéiste*, traditional form. Hennessy knows how to play with ultra-modernity, even if its logo is a medallion representing the historical figure of Mr Hennessy. The same is true of Veuve Clicquot. However, young people and most Americans do not have the same relationship with time: the authentic, for them, does not require vintage or historicity. It is enough to tell exciting stories, to make us dream, to give status through the people who testify to the brand's rank. Having said this, the product must be adjudged to be without equal. Moreover, in this culture, it is customary to subject the product to tests and comparisons, which brings luxury closer to premium, since performances will be compared. Thus, for Robert Parker, whatever the history linked to a classic *grand cru*, it must be scored like any other wine.

An examination of luxury brand strategies clearly shows these two brand construction models. The first is based on product quality taken to the extreme, the cult of product and heritage, History with a capital H, of which the brand is the modern embodiment. The second is American in origin, and lacking such a history of its own, does not hesitate to invent one. These New World brands have also grasped the importance of the store in creating an atmosphere and a genuine impression, and of making the brand's values palpable there. America invented Disney and Hollywood – both producers of the imaginary.

A third axis of differentiation: individualization or integration?

Finally, the four groups identified above differ according to a third, classic axis: individuation on the one hand, and integration on the other. For the former, luxury is used to show that they are different: some will not buy a known champagne brand, but will be in search of new, creative, audacious brands. For others, this individuation is achieved through visible excess: Crystal Roederer to make it plain that they do not buy Dom Pérignon.

On the other side of the individual vs social axis, we find the desire to fade into a universe or a world. This may be done discreetly, almost intimately; you need a certain level of culture to appreciate Krug and know the legend. This desire to integrate is also the desire that promotes the great names of luxury, known and safe – conduits of social propriety and distinction.

Luxury by country

These three axes make it place to situate countries according to their relationship to luxury. If France can boast of having given birth to modern luxury, the luxury market, for its part, can hardly count on the French. In fact, in this country, a principle of non-ostentation reigns, where wealth must be hidden: we buy Peugeots, not Jaguars. France is brought up on a vision of intimate luxury, for the connoisseur, where history, know-how and detail are consumed, before enjoying the object on its own terms. For the French, luxury is pleasure: hence haute cuisine. Italy is inspired by art. The United States wrote into its constitution that the pursuit of happiness was a duty and a right: in short, you become happier through consumption rather than through pleasure. You progress through life through more comfort, more performance, and more efficiency. A country of builders, here everything must have a functional alibi. A diamond is forever, so in addition to professing love, it is also a good investment. A Porsche is beautiful, but with its high reliability also has a good resale value. A Nautor Swan yacht has exceptional navigation qualities. It is always necessary to be able to talk of the superiority that the luxury object confers.

The emerging countries of luxury (Russia, China, etc) are very different. Like the USA they are countries where you can climb the rungs of society through economic success. Having done so, you then wish to benefit your clan through it and make it widely known. It is a more hedonistic, sensual relationship with luxury, where the signs of value must be strong, known and recognised: you drink the special cuvées of the great names of champagne, as if at a historical potlatch. Luxury is in the present tense, the intense and emotional sharing of a renowned brand. You exist through luxury.

An examination of Figure 5.1 should not, however, deceive the reader or the manager. The first mistake relates to the deep function of luxury: remember that luxury is not premium. Luxury is there to recreate the distance, the gap, to signify the inequality in riches, status and culture. It would be a mistake to limit this key function to only one of the four quadrants: in reality each of them – our four types above – seeks to mark the distance, in its own way. For creators or managers of luxury brands, there are therefore several ways of offering this manifestation of absolute distance. Krug and Dom Pérignon do not play in the same quadrant. We would have to invent four luxury champagne brands.

With time and growth, however, the four quadrants should not be seen as exclusive. If a brand begins its existence in one particular quadrant, it will necessarily have to express itself in the other quadrants later: otherwise it risks seeming frozen, anchored in a single model of representation of luxury. Moreover, with the desire to renew its clientele comes the need to separate the modes of expression according to the different clienteles, and according to the range levels – all this for a single brand. Cartier does not communicate in the same way on *haute joaillerie* and on its 'Must'. Chivas, likewise, does not do so on 12, 18 or 25.

Why are the major emerging countries so avid for luxury?

Nothing speaks more clearly than etymology. The word 'luxury' derives from Latin *luxus*. How, therefore, do the Chinese transcribe it? Through

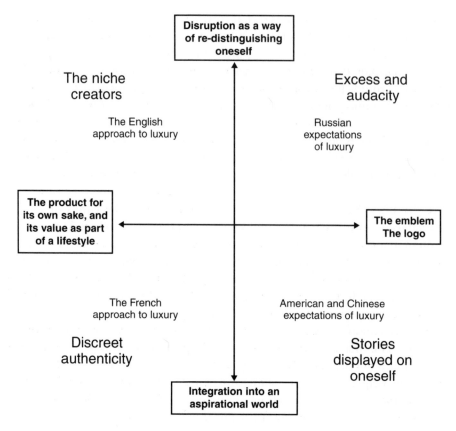

Figure 5.1   Four ways of distinguishing oneself

two characters (*she chi*): the first means 'important people', the second means 'much'. As we can see, luxury in China relates to VIPs: through luxury you become someone important, or simply someone. You acquire an immediate distinction. China is the country where the number of dollar billionaires shows the highest growth: they will desire distinctions in line with their success.

In a society of nouveau riche, very rich, such as India, since business is an Indian talent, it is necessary to make a great show of your power: after private helicopters come yachts paid for in cash. There is a genuine bidding war of personal recognition, first in relation to your peers and neighbours. Second, there is a great deal of money that needs to be got rid of, illegal money. This gives rise to a 'high roller' state of mind. In New Delhi, on any given evening there are innumerable private firework displays, signs of parties where hundreds of millions of dollars are spent. Still in New Delhi, three whole months before the opening of the showroom of the Bentley representative, 18 Bentleys had been sold, even while the streets of New Delhi are still strewn with potholes.

The paradox is that the normal daily expenditures, of €10, are subject to reasoning, even meanness, but excess takes hold when it is a question of flaunting your status before your neighbours and spending a million dollars. For these people, Dior is not enough.

Currently, in countries where an entirely new moneyed class is emerging, the Western brands are somewhat mixed up: a Spanish *prêt-à-porter* brand such as Mango will be seen at the same level as Boss, or even Bulgari or Davidoff. In a recent survey by RISC (*Time*, 4 October 2007) Chinese luxury clients cited first Chanel (42 per cent), Rolex (36 per cent) and Lacoste (33 per cent) as luxury prototypes. In India, the same RISC survey elicited the names of Park Avenue, Wills Lifestyle, Rolex and Omega. The first two are local brands: the first is a sari brand, the second a textile extension of a cigarette brand (Wills) that is well known but expensive by Indian standards – at the level of Marlboro. This is why the salespeople of Western luxury houses in India are half-salespeople, half-PR agents: they must spend much of their time explaining and educating as to why the price is so high. An expensive product is not necessarily a luxury product (see Chapter 1): it requires a cultural trans-formation to turn it into a vehicle of social distinction and stratification. In order to appreciate it you need the keys of this culture, and therefore an education. To date in the moneyed classes of India, 30 per cent of the people have acquired this culture, and 70 per cent only wish to signal that they have arrived. This is characteristic of emerging countries, such as China and Russia.

The mistake here is not to integrate the long term associated with luxury: of course these purchasers are 'recognition seekers' prioritizing the visibility of the logo and the large institutional brands based on a patrimony, a heritage recognized at the international level, even if they do not under-stand it. Others, reproducing the ancient logic of the potlatch, want to be 'high rollers' and empty whole cases of Cognac Louis XIII, Remy Martin's *nec plus ultra*, during large parties: they are living luxury in a hedonistic, social manner, leaning towards provocation, disruption, and always aimed at making an impression.

But the brand that offers nothing more is setting itself up for a difficult tomorrow: of course it must be able to accompany these exceptional parties, or even organize them itself – a new trade for luxury brands, as Courchevel and Porto Fino well know – but the luxury brand has a foundation, a heritage, and a patrimony that luxury clients in these countries will discover later; when they are tired and eager to redifferentiate themselves they will prioritize the object and its intrinsic pleasure, its epic story, its history, more than its logo alone.

Differences in the concept of luxury in the USA, Japan and France?

In a comparative study of what the notion of luxury evokes by country, our colleague at the HEC, Dubois, used similar samples of luxury clients in the USA, in Japan and France (Figure 5.2). The interviewees had to declare whether the item in question was associated with luxury, or not. As the list below shows, the profile of evocations of the word 'luxury' is very close between these three worlds, but with significant differences nevertheless:

- All associate luxury with high price: luxury must be expensive.
- Superior quality is in second place.
- We note that Japan places prestige much higher than either of the other countries, at a level above both quality and price, in fact: the brand must be prestigious.
- In contrast, Japan does not consider being exceptional, nor the fact of being bought by a minority, as criteria of luxury, unlike the other two countries. It is true that the sample of luxury purchasers may be mostly comprised of day trippers who clearly do not want to distinguish themselves, but to do as others do. It is estimated (Chadha and Husband, 2006) that 60 per cent of women in Tokyo aged between 20 and 30 own a Vuitton product: the power of the pressure to conform in Asia. In the USA, exclusivity and status must not be sold through obstruction of access, but as an affirmation of one's own individuality and status.
- Finally, note the importance of the 'art' and, to a lesser extent, 'fashion' aspect in the perception of luxury in Japan, unlike the other countries. However, these are average figures per country and we have seen above that national averages may aggregate very different profiles within a single country.

These data makes it possible to understand why in Japan Lexus is not perceived as a luxury brand: it lacks the necessary dimension of prestige. This local brand has no pedigree, no history, no culture: it is only the upper end of Toyota's range. In the USA, pedigree is important, but less so than in the other two countries: when you have no heritage, 'meritage' may suffice. American society is open, inclusive, meritocratic: what holds true for people also holds true for brands. Here the absence of history is not insurmountable, as it is in Europe.

In the expectation that the China curve will soon be added to this graph, let us recognize that Japan and China function differently in their relationship to wealth. The Japanese are more discreet in their visualization of wealth, the

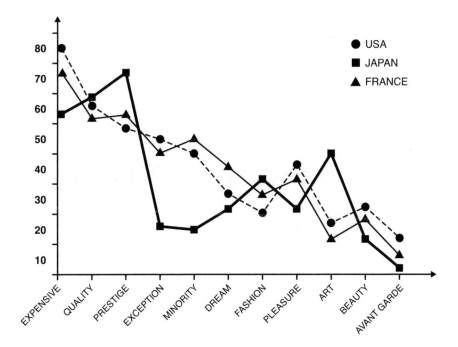

Figure 5.2   What luxury evokes

Chinese more demonstrative. In general, Asia is becoming the great luxury market, thanks to the power of demographics and the rate of growth of its economies. It is significant that we associate the success of Louis Vuitton with Japan. Likewise the revitalization of Burberry came through success in Asia, where the weight of sales increased from 18 per cent in 2000 to 28 per cent in 2006. In Japan, Burberry was voted in 2004 'the most fashionable brand' by young Japanese women aged between 20 and 30.

What explains the attachment that Asian consumers feel for luxury? Above all, the exceptional economic growth and the size of the potential market (linked to the emergence of a sizeable middle class). Through loss of culture, and denial of their own history, certain countries have no other standard by which to measure the value of things other than their price and reputation. Money becomes the standard of all things. Moreover, it testifies not to your heritage, but to the fact of your own success. It is a measure of your merit. We would add that luxury is the medal of this merit. The old Marxist class struggle is replaced by the individual struggle for class. For lack of culture, international luxury brands have become the language of immediate distinction (cf. page 30).

6 Developing brand equity

Can we imagine luxury without brands? The brand is an integral part of the luxury product, but not of the concepts of luxury, which are abstract.

There is no luxury without brands

Luxury objects are objects of luxury brands. Only diamonds are luxury objects appreciated without brand. What counts is their size and purity. For everything else, there is no luxury without brands: even an emerald is 'from Colombia', a ruby 'from Burma', a caviar 'from Iran'. The luxury brand goes beyond the object: it is constructed from the reputation made from its objects and its service within the social micro-groups favoured by the elites. A recognized signature of all that is beautiful and exceptional in the product and the service, the luxury brand is thereby weighted with a particular significance: it relates back to a latent social and cultural stratification and makes the wearer or purchaser someone apart – even if they are not alone in possessing the object. In this way, it fulfils the essential recognition function of luxury: recreating the distance, the things that distinguish it from the premium brand. This, of course, is hidden beneath other expressed motivations, such as hedonism linked to the aesthetics of the product or the subtle taste of a special cuvée of champagne accompanied by knowledge of the epic story of its manufacture. In order to create separation, it is still necessary for the signalling of this separation to be recognized by others, by those who count: everyone else, in the case of Ferrari, or a select few for Patek Philippe.

The brand is therefore the social visa, the 'star-maker', both of the product and the person. To be expensive is not enough to qualify as luxury: it must also be inscribed with a cultural hallmark accepted as a social stratifier. This hallmark is the brand, when the brand itself has a reputation with the cultural, political and financial powers. This is what distinguishes it from quality artisanship: an authentic Connemara Irish pullover, an English Morgan car, are clearly rare objects, full of history, made by hand, sources of pleasure, steeped in authenticity, but they are not factors of social stratification. They build the purchaser's identity but do not create vertical distance. They have not been raised to the level of objects of distinction by those who have the casting vote (Bourdieu, 1970).

A luxury brand is a brand first, and luxury second; this is another fundamental difference between luxury and artisanship. It explains why India as yet has no luxury brands, despite having an ancient artisanship of extremely high quality. A lack of infrastructure (no roads and a faulty electricity grid) means that industry cannot develop. Moreover, the understanding of what a brand is has yet to be promoted. What does this mean?

- The artisan creator of luxury saris in New Delhi certainly offers choice, but in a single size each sleeve and neckline are slightly different: not all size 36s are rigorously identical. To make a luxury brand is to make a brand, and therefore to assure the purchaser that a 36 is indeed a 36, and that all the size 36s of a particular garment are the same. The luxury side is attached to the multisensory nature of the product (appearance, touch, smell, etc) and the narration that accompanies it (on the materials, the finishing, the cut).
- In India, when you buy a diamond brooch, admittedly they will deliver it to you, but in a plastic bag: the idea of investing in sumptuous jewel cases, packaging that contributes to showing off the object's beauty, by slowing discovery and increasing the waiting time, remains unknown.
- The concept of a brand is not yet fully understood: the importance of its very visible signal, which attests to the creator, the 'house', and therefore everything that makes a product more than a product or the name of an artisan, but rather the expression of a concept of the world and an authentic talent recognized socially by the elites.

A luxury brand is a real and living person

It was founded by a person, often the person whose name it bears, and contributes in some way to that person's survival after death (Coco Chanel, Hilton Hotels, Guerlain). You can provide it with a more or less mythical ancestor (Dom Pérignon, Dom Ruinart, Veuve Clicquot), whose history is then rewritten: in that case, the brand functions in the same way as the founding myths and heroes of a society (Homer, the *Bhagavad Gita*, etc).

Its universe is as rich and complex as the personality of a human being. Like any human being, it does not appear from nowhere: unlike ordinary brands, you cannot 'launch' it, but it is built progressively, weaving together its reputation and its network of enlightened supporters over time. The creator therefore precedes the brand.

A luxury brand has roots

Like a living being, the brand has ancestors, a history, cultural and geographical roots. It is anchored, not invented. Hence the importance, as already discussed, of knowing its country of origin, from which vision or culture it derives. It is a pity for the Lacoste brand that many people in the world still do not know that Wimbledon champion René Lacoste was French, and even fewer that the brand was born in 1933, a sign of the durability of the value it offers. A country is a context, a culture, an art of living. This does not mean that the luxury brand's communications should be aimed at the past: quite the opposite. Nothing is closer to contemporary art than luxury brands.

The luxury brand must radiate

For a luxury brand to fulfil its ontological function (recreating the social distance, the gap) it is necessary for it to be known beyond its real clientele: it must radiate, in the literal and figurative sense. This is a key difference from the traditional brand, which is concentrated on its real target, that of the potential purchasers, only. The luxury brand is a social indicator, it recreates distance. In order to do so, the hierarchic nature of the brand must also be known beyond its pure clientele.

The goal of Rolex's advertising is not to sell Rolexes, but to make those who have the means to buy a Rolex happy that others, who do not have the means to do so, know what Rolex means. Depending on the brand's style and strategy, the extent of its reach beyond the actual target may vary.

- Institutional international luxury is a global Esperanto of class (Dom Pérignon, Dior, BMW, Chanel, Rolex, Cartier...), it is like wearing a dinner jacket: everyone in the world can decode its social meaning and its price. This type of luxury goes so far as to be displayed in the street, in the literal sense.
- What is known as 'discreet' or bespoke luxury aims at people who only wish to impress those in the know. Their reach is narrower: Patek Philippe, Krug, Swan...

No life cycle for the luxury brand

A luxury brand lives differently

To begin with, there is no 'birth' to speak of. In any case, there is no date of birth (or of launch), since a luxury brand is not created *ex nihilo* in a moment, nor does it spring fully armed from Zeus' forehead. A luxury brand is progressively elaborated, as it discovers a clientele (recall here one of the fundamental characteristics of luxury: its strictly personal side). Admittedly Coco Chanel (or rather Gabrielle Chasnel) was born in 1883, and the perfume No 5 was born in 1921: these dates are well known. But when was the Chanel brand born? You might rather say that it was progressively brought to life between these two dates, and nothing more.

The life cycle is not linear

A luxury brand rarely has a quiet life: we have seen that it must constantly reinvent itself, recreate the separation: this is not always easy, and according to sociological evolution and economic circumstance, or errors of brand management, the interest of the clientele can vary markedly. The closer the brand is to fashion and to accessories, the stronger the tremors (Gucci), but this affects all sectors (Aston Martin, Maserati).

Sometimes an entire category must redefine itself in order to survive as luxury, as was the case some decades ago for furriers: Revillon died, unable to find other territory, but Fendi is still here, through fine leather goods and textiles. We can even make a correlation between the 'level of luxury' of the brand and its capacity to survive when faced with a crisis in the trade. When the cigarette lighter lost its status, ST Dupont was able to change its trade and move into pens, and remain an effective luxury brand, while Flaminaire, a mid-range brand, died from an inability to transfer its image to other products. Likewise, under attack from the quartz movement in watchmaking, Timex died, but all the great Swiss watchmakers have done better than survive.

There is no such thing as final death

Gabrielle Chasnel died in 1971, but Coco Chanel is still living. If the Chanel brand never died, other brands have been considered dead (Bugatti). And yet, like the phoenix, a luxury brand can always rise from the ashes. To do so, it is necessary to understand to whom (potential clients and non-clients) the 'dream aspect' of the brand 'talks', or could still talk, and to make that aspect live again. Many investors are continually relaunching old names, which, like the fire beneath the ash, are still able to feed the flame of desire. This is true of Balenciaga, Lanvin, Nina Ricci, but also Bugatti, Aston Martin and Maserati.

A legitimacy created from authority, class and creation, more than from expertise

A key point, and one that is specific to luxury: the luxury brand is subsequent to the product, since it is built progressively. Then it slowly abstracts itself from the first product which made it known, and survives long after the product has gone: provided that an extremely well-managed strategy is in place, the brand territory may be enormously enlarged without damage to the brand. Gucci started its life in leather goods but has extended far beyond.

Think of Chanel and her 'total look' – comprising couture, fine leather goods, shoes, perfume, watches and jewellery, and so on. Nowadays nobody expects Chanel to restrict itself to a single expertise, its original expertise in couture.

Conversely, in normal mass consumption goods, the brand territory is more restricted, linked to a category or single benefit expertise.

The financial value of luxury brands

Luxury is the extremity of the intangible ladder. This translates into financial evaluations of luxury names (see Table 6.1).

The key to their profitability is the extreme concentration of intangibles that they embody. The luxury brands are in fact, of all brands, those to which the greatest part of 'intangibles earnings' is attached, what the company Millward Brown calls 'brand contribution', that is, the percentage of profit that can be imputed to the brand alone and its power to attract.

It is this, the intangibles, nurtured by the creativity of the objects, their heritage and the distinction of the points of sale that explain the difference

Table 6.1   Luxury brand valuations

#	Brand	Parent	Brand Valuation ($ billions)
1	Louis Vuitton	LVMH	25.7
2	Hermes	Hermes International	9.6
3	Gucci	PPR	9.3
4	Cartier	Cie Fin. Richemont	9.3
5	Chanel	Chanel Sa	8.7
6	Rolex	Montres Rolex S.A.	6.3
7	Hennessy	LVMH	5.4
8	Armani	Armani	5.1
9	Moet & Chandon	LVMH	4.9
10	Fendi	LVMH	4.7

Source: Millward Brown 2008 (including data from BRANDZ, Datamonitor and Bloomberg)

between the cost price and the sales price. Moreover, economic growth, in India, China or Brazil, ensures strong financial prospects for those luxury brands that know how to remain so.

The core of the luxury brand: its identity

In traditional marketing, the brand is defined by its positioning: it aims to be the brand that offers the greatest (the promise or the client benefit) to a certain type of person (the target) in relation to certain competitors (the source of business, the enemy to which you want to be compared). This positioning constitutes the cornerstone of brand management (Kapferer, 2008): it is the lasting angle of attack on the market to take an increasing share of it. This also concerns premium brands.

In luxury, we should not talk about positioning. The luxury brand cultivates its uniqueness; it prefers to be faithful to an identity rather than constantly worry about superiority over an opponent (its competitive advantage). Even if the client makes the comparison, the brand is not managed by seeking to compare itself to others – like an artist. Do you think that Gauguin sought to compare himself to his contemporaries? Each painted in their own way, according to personal touch.

A brand can only be built through coherence. To achieve this you must know who you are and stick to it. While the creator is at the helm, they are the benchmark, the source of disruptive creations that mark their style and taste. When the creative person is gone, it is necessary to codify the brand identity in order to make it last through time. One of the authors of this book regularly intervenes at this key moment: it is a question of clarifying the identity, in order to make it an internal guide, without turning it into a straitjacket.

Identity expresses the tangible and intangible specificities of the brand, those that make the brand what it is, without which it would be something other. Identity is not something that can be bolted on: it is nurtured from the brand's roots, its heritage, everything that gives it its unique authority and legitimacy in a specific territory of values and benefits. It translates its DNA, the genes of the brand. It also integrates its know-how and semiotic invariables: by which tangible, palpable elements is it recognized, both in the products and in the shops, in the staging or the advertising and communications? The brand is also an intangible: what do you say when you are not talking about products? More than anything else, the luxury brand is an epic tale, carried by its stories: storytelling is its mode of expression.

The identity of the luxury brand thus contributes to building the identity of its clients themselves. This is why the brand must be analysed as a holistic whole: it is a cultural prism for reading the world, for creation. The identity prism (Kapferer, 2008) breaks down the symbolic dimension of brands into their essential facets, while linking them together (Figure 6.1).

The summit of the identity prism is that which defines the constructed source, or at least the representation thereof: what are its physical and personality traits?

First, the physical aspect of the brand is the facet that makes it possible to define the family resemblance necessary within the brand: what are the codes,

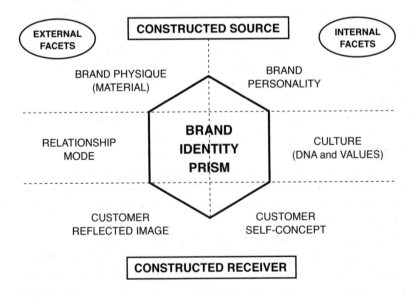

Figure 6.1   Luxury brand identity prism

signs, gestures, postures, colours, traits that make up this resemblance? Thus, at a fashion show, we should be able to recognize the Chanel touch, even without the double-C brand: the softness and the silky look of the jersey, the classic design, the quality of the often innovative textiles. The more the products have a symbolic, social and cultural function, the more importance attaches to the non-verbal imagery. This is why the luxury brand needs a semiotic grammar of its own, in order to express itself in its own way: the camellia, the quilting, the collars at Chanel, for example (Floch, 2004). The physical facet of the brand identity also comprises those iconic products or features that currently underpin its representation: at Yves Saint Laurent it is black, the dinner jacket, and other attributes of masculine clothing adapted to women's style, the perfect cut.

Second, the brand has a personality, when it itself is not a personality. In luxury the brand is often a real living person, a creator: it has a strong personality with character traits. The brand inherits these or constructs them. The brand's personality expresses an anthropomorphic vision of the brand, particularly relevant in the world of luxury, which emanates from the creation emanating from a person. How do we describe the brand personality? Through the same character traits as a person (on this subject see Kapferer, 2008). Thus Yves Saint Laurent gave his brand his impertinent, provocative, seductive and inaccessible character.

The next two facets of the brand identity prism relate to the constructed recipient. We will insist on that word 'constructed': in fact, the brand through its communication does not describe its target, it offers a representation of idealized clients, among whom they may or may not belong. This does not necessarily mean that people are shown in the communication, of course, but that we think of them in the way that the brand expresses itself.

Third, any luxury brand is a reflection of self offered to others. This is why everyone is capable of describing a luxury brand through the image that they have of its clients (this is what we call 'the reflection', the 'external mirror' of the brand), even if we never see clients in luxury advertising. This is how it works at Porsche: the advertising never shows the driver (unlike Audi, Volkswagen's premium brand). Porsche wishes to leave the client to the imagination, to allow the establishment of a direct affective relationship between the client and the brand, and not disrupt it with the interposition of a third person, however well known. Chanel offers the reflection of an elegant woman, seductive, sophisticated, and yet who loves to attract attention. At Yves Saint Laurent, the reflection is of a woman in command of herself, femme fatale, in competition with men, seductive and inaccessible.

It is often through the reflection that the brand fragments in its representations. Ralph Lauren is characterized by many different product lines, all highly targeted: but each of these targets manifestly belongs to the same family, and adheres to a core of highly recognizable values.

Fourth, the brand is a 'mentalization' – a facet of Kapferer's identity prism, generally translated as a 'consumer's self-concept'. We should talk here of the internal mirror, which may be different from the external mirror (the reflection). How does the typical client construct themself via the brand? For example, the mental picture constructed by the Black Centurion Card is to have reached, by your own efforts, a level where you need deny yourself nothing, and where you should be in a position to access everything.

Each luxury brand offers a self-concept to its followers: this is less a question of luxury in relation to others (the reflection) but of 'my intimate relationship with luxury'. Thus the mentalization of the woman who is a follower of Yves Saint Laurent is: 'I don't need a logo to affirm me or to gain power: I feel sexy and seductive.' At Chanel it would be: 'I am exceptional because I wear Chanel, elegant, classic and modern.' At Ralph Lauren: 'I have access to American distinction, made up of power and class.'

The two intermediary facets of the brand identity prism are relationship and culture.

Fifth, it is through the 'culture' facet that the luxury brand creates a cult and develops proselytes. This is the soil of its deepest values, which it venerates and respects more than anything, religiously. For us, this is the essential facet of the identity of a luxury brand. Too often we define the values of the brand on the surface, through encompassing and international words such as romance, classicism, elegance, Italianate, or yet the values of the upper bourgeoisie for Chanel. In order to properly manage the brand over time, however, it is necessary to dig deeper. What is the brand's DNA, which nurtures its renewed and reinvented inspiration? Thus, Ralph Lauren chose polo as its symbol: besides being an aristocratic sport, one of the few that remain today, what is the symbolic significance of polo? What does 'being Italian' mean? Beyond the simplistic stereotype, how does Prada's innate Italianness differ from that of Ferragamo or Gucci?

In order to know its cultural underpinnings, we must closely examine all of the brand's identity signs. For example, who are the three women on the Nina Ricci logo? What is their hidden meaning? You do not answer these questions by interviewing clients in Mumbai or Buenos Aires or Paris. The identity is the source of the creative act over time: we should therefore ask ourselves what Mr Ricci saw in this well-known symbol, whose roots go back to the pre-Grecian mythology, to agrarian pagan cultures: these three Graces are fairies. What therefore is the value system of the only brand in the world symbolized by the three fairies of mythology? Is not the essence of Nina Ricci to be the initiation into femininity?

Sixth, as for the 'relationship' facet of any brand, it defines the nature of the relationship installed between the brand and its recipients. Thus Chanel liberated women, and Yves Saint Laurent gave them power: it lifts them up and causes them to be affirmed.

It is the conjunction of all six facets that defines identity and singularity, and also weaves the fabric of emotional connections with clients, to the point that some of them become proselytes, ambassadors, or in any case devotees. To create fanatics or ambassadors in each country, it is necessary to attach them to the deeper meaning of the brand, and to its creative manifestations (rather than solely the pride of exhibiting the sign or the logo). Through its identity, rich, sourced from history or legend, the brand lends memory and culture to its products and knits intimate relations with its followers.

The identity prism of a luxury brand should never be ordinary. It captures the fine detail of its uniqueness and appeal. It is also, however, a management tool: as such it should be useful, a lever of coherence, without which there is no brand (luxury or non-luxury). Finally, it is a springboard for creativity in the service of the brand. Figure 6.2 gives an example of an identity prism for Ralph Lauren.

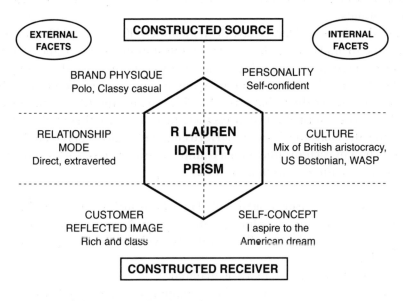

Figure 6.2   Ralph Lauren identity prism

Building coherence:
central and peripheral identity traits

There is no brand; there are only expressions of the brand. The clients do not know the identity prisms; they simply live the brand products and experiences that we offer them. Clients therefore go from the experience to the essence. This is why a brand perception is only built up through coherence. In luxury, however, in order to grow it is necessary to innovate, to surprise, not to repeat yourself endlessly, even while remaining faithful to your identity. This dilemma of diversity and coherence is particularly acute in luxury, since without inspiration here there is no aspiration. How, then, can the necessary brand coherence be ensured over time and in all its products and communications? Through respect for the core of its identity prism.

In order to do so, it is necessary to consult the identity prism and identify the facets that are central and those that are peripheral. By central, we mean that without them the brand is no longer the brand: thus they must be few in number. The other facets may be more or less present according to circumstance.

This distinction between central and peripheral facets of identity comes from the psychology of representations (Abric, 2003; Michel, 2004). Take the analogy of a family: not all traits are equal in their capacity to distinguish members of the family, or to estimate whether someone belongs to the family or not. Is it height, face, nose, or a way of acting or speaking? The same is true of brands.

Once these essential facets have been identified (Kapferer, 2008, p.188) it is necessary to make sure that every manifestation of the brand strongly expresses these distinctive values in its own way. Let us take the example of Chivas. Its central values are energy, glamour and luxury; therefore each of the three global products that carry the Chivas name (the 12-year, the 18-year and the 25-year) must always express these three values, either in the product, the bottle, the label, the cases, the advertising, the social events created for the introduction of each product into a country... nevertheless, each product will interpret these three traits in its own way:

- Chivas 12 will create a picture of 'The Chivas life', made up of fishing in Alaska or the hunt to photograph tigers in Assam, which is more the 'energy' part of the brand's central core, without forgetting the glamour and luxury.
- Chivas 18 stakes much more on glamour.
- Chivas 25, incredibly rare, will be communicated more exclusively in the manner of the cult of the luxurious product.

This is not a question of curbing the creation of each product but of ensuring that in addition it builds the same brand. Each of the brand's creations has its own tonality, but the melody is the same.

Two modes of luxury brand building

Building a brand, let us remember, is building a unique, strong perception. In luxury, it must also be inspired and aspirational. An examination of luxury brand strategies reveals two main models of brand building:

- The first is based on the creation of value, product quality taken to the extreme, with a cult of the product and heritage. This model is nurtured at a symbolic level by History with a capital H, of which the brand is the modern emanation. It also pays regular allegiance to the spiritual legacy of its founder, who is embodied in a new creator – passing over their own personality – to reincarnate the original spirit of the brand.
- The second mode is American in origin: lacking such a history of its own, it does not hesitate to invent one. Mr Ralph Lifshitz became Ralph Lauren, taking on his Great Gatsby-like traits and character, a direct descendant of the ultra-chic Bostonian high society. These New World brands also grasped the importance of the store in creating an atmosphere and a genuine impression, and of making the brand's values palpable there. America invented Disney and Hollywood – both producers of the imaginary. This brand gives high priority to the experiential.

Today, these two models are converging. Recently Ralph Lauren created Purple Label and Black Label, two clothing lines aimed at a demanding European clientele and more formal situations, made in Italy from sought-after fabrics. In the same way, all the European luxury brands have grasped the role of the theatrical at the point of sale, or of consumption. The way in which Hennessy create microbars to sit down, converse and consume is evidence of this. Figure 6.3 illustrates the two modes of brand building.

Building and preserving the dream

Companies regularly measure their brand capital, or 'brand equity' (Kapferer, 2008). In order to do so, they ask at least four questions: awareness of the brand, level of consideration ('Would you buy it next time you make a purchase in this category?'), behaviour ('Have you already bought it?') and finally its ability to create fanatics and active proselytes.

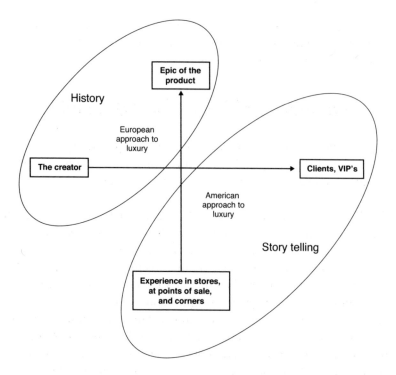

Figure 6.3   The two modes of luxury brand building

With luxury it is different. Here, we do not talk of consideration, but of dreams. The fundamental paradox of luxury, however, the one that must be resolved daily, is that purchase destroys the dream.

Luxury is access to a dream. Let us recall the dimensions of this dream. One is the social dimension: luxury confers immediate class – or is thought to do so. Luxury refers back to the implicit hierarchy of society, even if this is denied for ideological reasons. All men may be created equal in a democracy, but in a meritocracy, they do not all finish equal: their work, their talent and their relationships cause some to succeed, to gain access to success and glory, and therefore money, by which success is measured nowadays – but not others. The other dimension of this dream relates to the sensorial compression that the luxury object offers. The object is a source of intrinsic pleasure due to its multi-sensory nature taken to the extreme, and the epic tale of its gestation. This distances it from the purely functional world of constraints, of price–quality ratios, and usage value.

The notion of a dream must be taken literally. Moreover it can be measured, and makes it possible to mark out the progression of a brand dream. This also makes it possible to identify what are the determining factors of dreams in the world of luxury. This is how what is known as the luxury dream formula was established (Dubois and Paternault, 1995). It is simple:

The dream equation: Dream = –8.6 + 0.58 Awareness – 0.59 Purchase

The dream is measured by means of a question such as: 'Imagine that you won the choice of a handsome present in a competition, which are the five brands (from a list) that would give you the greatest pleasure?' This formulation removes the price barrier, since a dream is by definition the negation of the obstacles to the attainment of accepted or rejected desires. The statistical analysis of the interviewees' responses to these three questions reveals that the dream is a function of the difference between brand awareness and the rate of owners of the brand. Here again we find the fundamental notion of luxury as separation (social separation and separation on quality, excellence and price). The luxury dream is boosted by the distance between those who know and those who can.

The operational consequences of this dream equation are considerable and should be reiterated.

First, without awareness there is no dream. The brand needs to be known in order to begin to provoke the desire driver. Too many young creators will never cross the threshold of access to the dream, for lack of awareness. This is why the creator must be media-savvy. It is also why luxury brands are quick to produce perfumes. There is no perfume without media advertising, an immediate lever of wider recognition. More: the first perfume expresses the brand identity: all of Thierry Mugler is in Angel, and all of Van Cleef is in First.

Second, if awareness is high, then it is the distance between the number of people who recognize it and the number of wearers of the brand that creates the dream. This key factor only concerns luxury. Thus Americans dream of Nike, or Adidas, as our studies show: these brands cause them to dream because of the athletes with whom they can identify by wearing trainers every day. Here, however, for Nike and Adidas, the product diffusion does not work against the dream: they are not luxury brands. Moreover, Nike or Adidas's product lines are very fragmented, almost clannish.

For luxury brands, however, the perceived diffusion kills the dream through the loss of exclusivity and therefore the loss of the social driver of luxury, and of the impulsion of the desire of others. It is therefore necessary to reduce diffusion, and increase the obstacles to accessing the brand. This is done through a large rise in price: this divides the true luxury clients from the false, those who are looking for meaning from those who consume the sign of this brand today and of another brand tomorrow, as fashion dictates. This is also done through a reduction of distribution, increased selectivity, exclusivities offered to clients... Finally, in the communication, it is necessary to make the difference between a brand for more people and a brand for everyone.

Figure 6.4 illustrates the ways of creating the dream according to the level of brand awareness and penetration. They can be described as the search for equilibrium between a brand that is too closed and a brand that is too open.

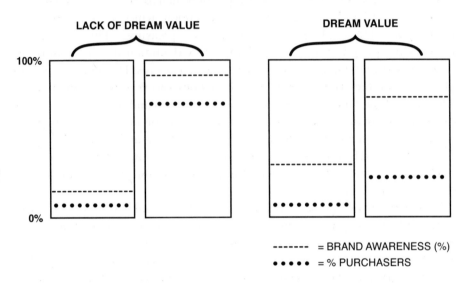

Figure 6.4   Managing the luxury dream equilibrium

Product roles and luxury brand architecture

Luxury brand management implies a balance between four poles: the reference to the past, the pursuit of status and prestige, the modernity that gives it vibrancy, emotion and creativity, plus some accessibility (Figure 6.5).

Certain of these poles are opposed: past and current creation, brand growth bringing public exposure in opposition to the quest for distinction. Managing the balance needs permanent monitoring; to do this, some general rules are set out below.

Luxury often talks about icons

As the luxury brand expresses an almost religious respect for strong and authentic values, it is the source of a 'culture' and of a cult for some. Like any cult, it needs officiators, grand masters, sacred places and cult objects. The icon is a holy image. By analogy, the luxury brand has one or two iconic products that symbolize, and prefigure its values. The icon is present over the long

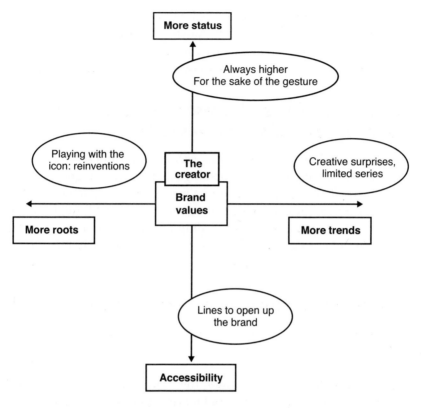

Figure 6.5   Luxury brand architecture: poles and product roles

term, and therefore appears early in the brand's life, hence its leftwards position on the mapping above, on the side of the roots. Thus the painting of Absolut Vodka by Andy Warhol clearly shows that the bottle is the brand's icon. Chanel No 5 is Chanel's iconic product, as is the cut invented by Madame Chanel, which expressed her vision of woman, also a radical change at the time.

The iconic product is venerated. It is significant that at Chanel, in order to grow and renew itself, all the perfumes have had variants and descendants: for example, after Allure came Allure Sensuelle. Chanel No 5 never does this. There is only one Chanel No 5. This does not mean that the icon is fixed or mummified. Imperceptibly, but regularly, the Chanel house modifies the design of bottle and label every 10 years. Of course it retains its shape and simplicity, recognizable among a thousand others, but it is kept in touch with its era by small, delicate touches. The communication around the iconic product also evolves. The icon is not necessarily the best-selling product, as No 5 is for Chanel, but it remains a definite value.

The luxury brand maintains its past: it draws from it its strength, its serenity and its confidence in the durability of its values. This is why it organizes demonstrations that revive the memory of its founder. Who was 'Mademoiselle Chanel'? The Chanel website allows us to visit her very private apartments.

The luxury brand must also resonate today, be a key emitter of trends and tomorrow's tastes

This is why, regularly, it must surprise us with products and acts that place it in a modern context, even if it is not pursuing an objective of higher sales. Thus Chanel surprises us by staging a genuine Chanel surfboard, or a Chanel snowboard. This is not a question of stretching the brand, which might decide to licence the sale of surfing or snowboarding products under its label, but to signify the brand's presence and interest for this particular form of sport, which marks a generational rupture.

The luxury brand must have access products

We will discuss this in more depth in Chapter 8 on products, but they aim at two different objectives:

* conquer new clients for the brand, the 'future faithful', who will subsequently buy more sophisticated and more expensive products;
* meet the demand of those who may be called luxury 'day trippers', all those clients who occasionally buy luxury, but not a specific brand.

If it does not extend the number of its loyalists, the luxury brand does not create a religion: it remains a sect. If it is accessible only to its loyalists, it can even become an obscure, even threatening sect – the opposite of what is required to become a positive social marker. The church doors must be open to all who wish to enter, as long as they behave themselves. This is why, while targeting a restricted clientele, the luxury brand manifests itself in the broadest of mass media, allows itself to be seen and visually consumed by all.

The luxury brand must continually raise its status and prestige

Particularly if its business model is based on profits made from low-priced ranges, the luxury brand is threatened by the loss of exclusivity, which erodes its prestige among the ruling classes and elites. We will see later on, in Chapter 10 on distribution and Chapter 11 on communication, the key role played in this field by these two aspects of the marketing mix. Currently, in China, Lacoste is perceived as a prestige brand: its entry into the market is recent and was very selective regarding its points of sale. It is also main sponsor of the brand-new Shanghai Tennis Masters. Moreover, the Asian journalists who count are invited to the New York Fashion Week, where the Lacoste collections for the following year are paraded among all the great names of fashion and luxury.

It is therefore necessary for the luxury brand permanently to outdo itself in terms of star products, the function of which is to remind all and sundry of its supremacy, its status among the elites, among the media that count, the sources of prestige. Whereas the world only talks about speed limits, radars, points lost from your driving licence, Porsche regularly launches a car in a limited series, or at a price that amounts to the same thing, outdoing all the competition in terms of brake horsepower, power, pure speed, etc. In this quest for the absolute, which characterizes the brand, there are no limits. This nurtures the dream and the supremacy.

Managing the dream through communication

We will dedicate an entire chapter (Chapter 11) to this very important subject.

Defending the brand against counterfeiting

Counterfeiting is a parasite endemic to luxury, whose economic basis is simple: as we have already seen, a luxury product has a functional side and a dream side, and the client pays for both; it is therefore possible, by counterfeiting the product, to cheat on both aspects.

From the moment that the product becomes a luxury product, and therefore carries a significant weight of dreams, an enormous field opens up to counterfeiting, through the conjoined effect of two mechanisms:

- All the investment made in the dream, particularly in distribution and communication, often translates in visual terms as only a simple logo on the product, often particularly cheap to imitate (Chanel's 'double C' on a T-shirt, or 'LV' on a canvas bag).
- By also communicating to people who are not part of its target, in order to create social stratification, a brand automatically creates an in-draught to the counterfeiting of the only obvious aspects, such as a logo, or a characteristic shape (Oyster by Rolex).

That said, counterfeiting is only possible if the brand has reached a significant awareness threshold (characteristic and universally recognized logo – LV; or shape – Rolex), and is highly desirable; we may even say that if there are no counterfeits of a brand, apart from those few cases where it is technically impossible (cars for example), it is because the brand is not luxury: when the Richemont group acquired Lancel, it aimed to quickly turn it into a luxury brand. The absence of counterfeits, which would appear to be good news for a group containing a brand like Cartier, one of the most heavily counterfeited in the world, convinced Richemont that the way would be long and costly if they wished to achieve this.

The existence of counterfeits (up to a certain limit) is therefore a proof of the health of the luxury brand, in the same way that pain is a proof that we are alive! As Jeanne Lanvin used to say, 'counterfeiting is Vice's homage to Virtue'.

Who are the clients of counterfeits?

It is necessary to separate the client who buys a counterfeit, and the one who wears it, since it is not always the same person.

We can distinguish three categories of client:

- Those who desire the brand in order to be part of the 'club', but do not want to pay the price, either because they cannot afford it (fake Vuitton in Africa), or because they think that the price is not justified by quality (Vuitton bag considered as just a plastic bag with a logo), or finally because they believe that nobody will see that they are wearing a fake (Rolex with a quartz mechanism... and weighed down with lead).
- Those who buy as a present, thinking to deceive the recipient. It even happens that a man buys two products: a fake for the wife and a genuine article for the mistress...
- Those who buy a fake believing that it is genuine. Such a case, much more frequent than we might think, is generally the consequence of poorly controlled distribution.

The key point, for a brand, is not to treat the wearer or carrier of a fake automatically as an enemy, but as a potential customer: if they are wearing the counterfeited product, it is because they like the brand, and maybe believes that it is a real one (especially if it is a gift). Another point: for economical reasons, many consumers of fakes could not buy genuine products now, but may be good customer later, when they become more affluent. Finally, if the tangible added value of a product is too weak (a simple T-shirt with a logo), counterfeiting merely penalizes this abuse.

Even as a client who wears a fake must be treated with tact, so the producers of counterfeits should be given no quarter. In fact, not only are they perfectly well aware of what they are doing, but they often belong to powerful criminal networks, who traffic not only counterfeits, but also drugs and arms. Counterfeiting presents fewer risks for the organized networks that now operate in this domain: the prison sentence for transporting a suitcase full of fake Lacoste has nothing in common with that for someone who traffics drugs. Moreover, since this counterfeiting does not present any physical danger for the consumer (unlike medicines), and the client dream is often caricatured as ridiculous snobbery, it is often difficult for a copied brand to obtain genuine support from the authorities in their struggle against counterfeiting.

Counterfeiting as a way to diagnose the health of the strategy of the brand

In addition to the fact that the existence of fakes proves the strength of the dream for the brand, it is also a way to check the quality of the strategy of the brand, in production and in distribution.

The distribution network is too selective

The existence of counterfeits is often a sign indicating that distribution is too selective, and that it is necessary to open up more points of sale: the clients that do not have easy access to the real product cannot differentiate between genuine and fake, and/or the value (monetary or symbolic) of the product is not enough to justify the journey to the existing shops.

In contrast, the complete absence of counterfeiting in a country may signify the complete absence of desire for the brand, and the futility of opening a sales point: first it is necessary to create desire by investing in communication.

The distribution is too large or uncontrolled

In this case, it happens that fakes are sold with real products. Some years ago, Louis Vuitton discovered in Japan a subtle strategy, linked to counterfeiting. Through 'tourists', local Japanese retailers were buying genuine products in Paris and displayed them in the shop, but sold fakes without the client realizing: the retailer explained that they could not sell the product shown in the window, since it has been damaged by the light, and brought out another (this one fake) from stock.

The production is poorly controlled

If a luxury brand subcontracts part of its production, the temptation for the subcontractor to produce more and to discreetly sell off merchandise is very strong. The product may be a real one, but sold outside the brand's circuits, in which case only the brand is the loser, or a product of inferior quality, but presenting all the external appearances of the genuine article, in which case both the client and the brand are hurt.

Drawback of licensing

Since licences are expensive, it is tempting for the licensee to use the brand for products other than those specified in the contract, or to sell products of a lower quality.

Counterfeiting and the internet

We have mentioned elsewhere the dangerous role of the internet in the sale of counterfeits: as soon as a brand agrees to sell products on the internet, a big door is opened for counterfeiting. Online, 23 per cent of spam is for counterfeits, often renamed 'replicas'. On eBay, many sellers are in fact selling counterfeits: this is why the brands, having signed the VERO protocol, can have offers removed from the site if their provenance cannot be confirmed.

Always defend your rights and communicate frequently

In countries that do not recognize, or only partially recognize, intellectual property, it is difficult to lay claim to your rights: it is necessary to continually pursue counterfeiters through the courts and to make this known in the press, if only to reassure clients. This is what Cartier has done successfully for a long time, with the spectacular, televised crushing of fake watches by a bulldozer.

In June 2008, eBay lost against LVMH and was ordered to pay €38.6 million: too many luxury products sold through eBay are counterfeit.

7 Luxury brand stretching

Every day we hear of luxury brands moving out of their original sphere and extending their reputation to other sectors: Baccarat is to put its name to a range of hyper-luxury resort-hotels; Bulgari and Armani have already done so. Ferrari inscribes watches and a PC manufactured by the Taiwanese brand Acer. The Richemont group is to produce Ralph Lauren's luxury watch, and so on.

In parallel, premium brands are entering the luxury world. Vertu is the luxury mobile brand of Nokia, and the mobile telephone now also uses *griffes*: Samsung is offering an Armani phone, LG a Prada one.

In fact, the luxury market is made up of brands that have, for the most part, grown through moving out of their original sphere. Fendi is a former furrier. Former dealers in fine leather moved into footwear and then into *prêt-à-porter* (Gucci, Ferragamo); a great name in the jeweller's craft (Cartier) now puts its name to pens, famous watches and fine leather goods. Ralph Lauren sells *prêt-à-porter*, but also decoration, furniture, household linen, even paint (interior decoration). The creator of glass and crystal objects, Lalique, now sells jewellery. Some brands have moved classically from haute couture to *prêt-à-porter* and then into accessories (Chanel, Dior, etc); others have followed the opposite trajectory: Hermès, Louis Vuitton. What are the origins of this propensity to extend elsewhere?

The origins of stretching

Until the beginning of the 20th century (see Chapter 1), luxury flourished in a world segregated and structured by regulated professions, like lawyers and doctors today, and guilds, such as the goldsmiths. A well-known artisan ('supplier to His Majesty') or a famous company (Saint-Gobain, makers of mirrors) were linked in a unique fashion to a trade, sometimes even to a single product (the Gobelin tapestries). This structure lasted until the Belle Époque, when Hermès was a saddler, Vuitton was a luggage and trunk maker, Christofle a goldsmith, but began to experience profound change after the First World War. The big luxury houses began to manufacture or to put their name to things that they had not originally known how to make. One of the forerunner trades, both then and now, was the couturiers: from 1858, the great couturier Charles Worth would give his best clients gifts of his perfume Je Reviens, which would not be truly commercialized until 1932, eleven years after Coco Chanel had launched her No 5. It was the first true structured and openly admitted 'brand stretching'. This brand stretching strategy has developed considerably in luxury since the end of the Second World War, in parallel with the explosion of the market.

In fact, luxury has been transformed by the practice of brand stretching. Remember that the luxury market was born from the economic and legal opportunities that more people were given to access luxury products, without the products themselves seeking to become more accessible, except by means of extension within their own original trade, such as the luggage-maker Vuitton becoming a seller of fine leather goods (the handbag as the everyday luggage of the female urbanite) or a technically close trade if their original trade was a cul-de-sac, such as the saddler Hermès becoming a fine leather goods dealer.

Much later, when they had become 'brands', many sought to stretch their brand in order to increase the commercial repercussions of their fame. We could call this the adolescent phase of the luxury market, where many brands are attempting incursions in all directions.

In mass-consumption or even industrial marketing, stretching has also become the norm. Marlboro cigarettes also put their name to a range of men's casual clothing (Marlboro Classics). Yahama produces both motorcycles and musical instruments. There are rules on stretching (Kapferer, 2008): each brand is characterized by know-how, a territory of competence, which defines a zone of legitimacy for its stretchings and limits them to variants that seem to derive from the same know-how.

In order for these to be legitimate, there must be a 'fit', a coherence between the original trade as it is perceived by the public, and the proposed stretch. Brand stretching in luxury has a particularity in that it does not seem to have limits. This is to be expected; the luxury brand is a transmitter of taste and distinction moved by a creative passion and standards higher than the usual, exercised with a total control over manufacture and distribution. If the first-circle stretching must respect the brand's field of competence, the growth will increasingly rest on the immaterial aspect of the luxury brand. This is not in short supply.

Luxury stretching: a practice that has changed the sector

Stretching has allowed luxury houses to grow more quickly, without being limited to organic internal growth, or finding themselves prisoners of the regression of their original trade (Hermès and the disappearance of horse-drawn carriages). Many have departed from luxury altogether, launching themselves into the licensing system, which then places products that are not luxury on the market.

What has generally accelerated this evolution is the financial aspect:

- on the one hand, building a luxury brand is a long and costly exercise; the need for money can lead to a rapid stretching through licences;
- on the other hand, the value of a luxury brand is such that pressure from shareholders to 'leverage' that value on other products, in order to improve the sacrosanct 'return on equity', is very strong, particularly when the brand is no longer in the hands of its founding family.

In these luxury brand stretching strategies, it is necessary to separate what is brand stretching in luxury (Hermès and silk), which is generally legitimate, and what is stretching beyond luxury, which is often very dangerous.

Why has this expansion model proved so seductive? Because it does not require financial capital, only strong brand capital: creative renown and the ability to maintain it. Licences are also accelerators of growth: they flesh out the brand and enable it to grow rapidly, without the need to invest, or to take time to acquire all the necessary know-how:

- perfume brings mass market awareness thanks to the launch advertising;

- accessories bring profitability (hence their importance in the order of stretching) and visibility (a bag is seen) and modernity (through fashion);
- cosmetics, spas, bring intimacy, physical contact with the client.

All these stretchings together make it possible to create boutiques where the client, who came to buy one product, will leave with an entire panoply, or in any case with several products, which increases the average income from each visit to the store at the same time as increasing the reasons to return there.

At a time when luxury brands, like religions, are building their modern cathedrals or pyramids (their megastores) on the most expensive main streets of each world capital, the importance of a broad, and maximally profitable, range is vital. Stretching is also risk-balancing: having remained a specialist in fur, Revillon suffered when this market fell, unlike Fendi, which had moved out of this specialization.

Two models for extension: vertical or horizontal?

An examination of luxury brand stretching reveals two approaches:

- either the brand seeks greater accessibility in price and therefore brings its absolute price down, through accessories, in order to seduce the broad clientele of luxury 'day trippers' or 'excursionists';
- or the brand stretches out horizontally, without changing its relative price level, parading its lifestyle in other areas of the client's life.

The first model is known as vertical stretching: it may move downwards, like many haute couture brands, but also upwards, as for example in the creation of a couture line made in Italy by the American Ralph Lauren, or in the trading-up model of all credit cards like American Express, which launched the luxury card: Black Centurion.

The second model orbits around a centre, the brand's spirit, often in the form of the eponymous, still living creator. All the extensions of the brand are differentiated expressions of the brand's values, as expressed by the creator or the creator's successor. Beyond brand stretching, these two ways of working are in fact business models, two ways of making money in the short but also in the long term: the pyramid or the galaxy (Figure 7.1). A major difference between these two models is that in the pyramid it must be possible to display all the products in one place, known as the shop, which demonstrates the coherence of the brand, whereas the galaxy is made up of different universes whose coherence is ensured by the creator themself.

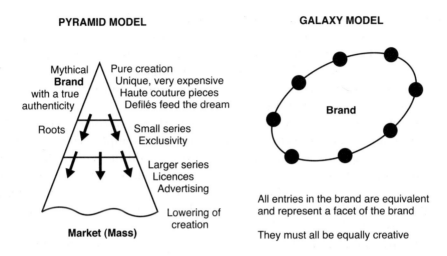

Figure 7.1   Two types of luxury brand expansion

The pyramid

The luxury brands emerging from haute couture position themselves on the pyramid, occupying (or not) several levels according to their strategy and their financial results (see also Chapter 13). Some take the position of remaining at the upper levels even in their accessories.

Chanel stays at the upper level. Its bags are expensive, as are the accessories. The exception to this rule is the brand's presence in optics distribution, admittedly selective but nevertheless mass (Optic 2000 for example).

Most of brands emerging from 'haute couture' keep to the summit of the pyramid, but the business is made mainly on very accessible products: this is the case with Dior. Finally, we find the case of houses that have abandoned haute couture but attempt to preserve the memory and the myth of it by revitalizing a *prêt-à-porter* business: a house such as Thierry Mugler, now bought by Clarins, once had a haute couture business and still capitalizes on this memory to sell perfumes with great success (Angel).

Italian houses such as Armani have followed this pyramid model, but – until recently – without haute couture at the summit. Thus we found Giorgio Armani, then Armani Collezione, then Emporio Armani for the young, and then beneath these the very casual Armani eXchange, or Armani Jeans. These lines correspond to the price strata, the targets, the degrees of exclusivity of the boutiques, each line having its own boutiques, in order to avoid mixing the clientele (remember that the luxury brand is segregationist: it must protect its clients from its non-clients). With each of these lines, we find accessories:

leather, shoes, watches. Beneath them there exist even more diffuse lines in multi-brand shops (glasses, cosmetics, perfumes). The system is therefore highly stratified, but united by the aura, the style and the name of the creator (Armani), whose personality is transmitted through the media and the world of art. Recently, Armani added the missing summit to its pyramid: haute couture in Paris (Armani Privé).

In a pyramid model, sub-brands names are chosen to compensate for the lower creativity or the legitimacy handicap. For example, Saint Laurent's second line is known as Rive Gauche, in order to add the halo of distinction that the words 'Rive Gauche' carry. Likewise, Chanel cosmetics are known as Chanel Precision, Dior's as Dior Science, since there is no obvious legitimacy in passing from the mastery of needle and thread to that of the molecules that preserve eternal beauty.

This pyramid model is tempting for many brands and their financial owners: it offers a rapid increase in turnover and profits through lines that have low cost of production through industrialization, but priced upper-range, since they benefit from the prestige halo of the luxury brand. Hence the profitability of these so-called accessible lines: the average gross margin on bags and perfumes of this type of 'luxury' is typically around 75 per cent. This source of short-term profits is attractive to the stock market.

However, this carries the risk of the impoverishment at the bottom of the pyramid on the three essential elements of luxury: creativity, excellence and selectivity. This trading down quickly becomes a descent into hell, through destruction of the brand value. Luxury is a dream, but the dream has a fragile equilibrium. Democratization reduces the distance – and luxury is meant to create distance. Mainstream clients may not express this need: the elites do.

This is why strong luxury brands do not follow this model. They have a long-term vision and seek to preserve their reputation. They develop a very short range for these lines, made of products that are all creative, made in short series, and distributed exclusively in the brand's own boutiques. Above all, they control production: this is the case for Chanel, which acquired six artisan houses on the road to disappearance, in order to preserve their unique know-how (for example an artisan in bird feathers) (see also page 235).

The galaxy

This model is represented by Ralph Lauren: it has been nicknamed the 'galaxy' model (Sicard, 2006). Ralph Lauren in fact sells everything: *prêt-à-porter*, accessories, perfumes, and cosmetics, but also furniture and paintings, not to mention the cafes and restaurants under its name. Every Ralph Lauren product is a legitimate entry into the brand universe. Its lifestyle adapts itself to the times of day or of the week, according to the occasions and situations of use. For greater clarity, Ralph Lauren segments into highly coherent sub-brands, each offering a complete selection linked to each usage, moment or occasion: the Polo line is casual sportswear; Purple Label corresponds to more formal occasions.

Here, therefore, there are no very creative, superior products and other, non-creative, inferior products.

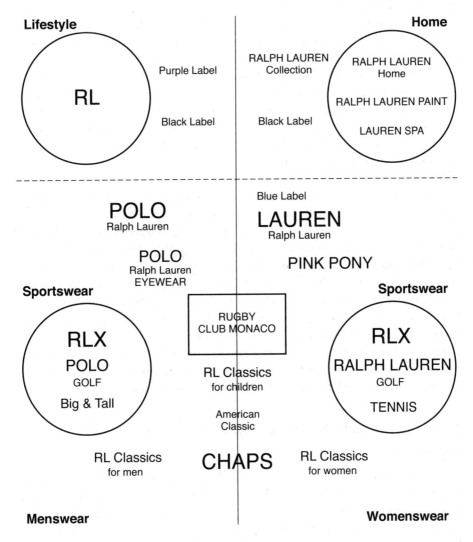

Figure 7.2   Expansion by sub-brands: Ralph Lauren galaxy

In the galaxy-type model, the sub-brands are all equal: they are all variants on a single concept at the centre of the galaxy, differing according to the moments and occasions or gender (women's and men's lines).

Typology of brand stretchings

How can we classify stretching?

In luxury, the most important parameter is that of price: there are extensions into much higher price zones, and in contrast the search for new clients through a more accessible price. In Europe, the fiefdom of the great couturiers, Ralph Lauren essentially communicates regarding its couture line, named Purple Label for women and Black Label for men. These products in sought-after fabrics, in a highly refined style, made in Italy, aim to draw the brand upwards, to bring it closer to couture. On the side of downward stretching, even Mellerio dits Meller, the illustrious house that has been lodging at Rue de la Paix for 400 years, supplier to crowned heads, has access products – at around €1,000. Like Tiffany, it uses the engagement ring as an opportunity to penetrate into this house.

The second parameter enabling us to classify these stretchings is the distance from the original core product: when Baccarat makes small crystal jewels, it remains within its core of legitimacy. The same is true for Lalique or Swarovski. It is less so for Christofle, a brand of tableware. What link is there between cars and IT, between a Ferrari and a PC? Admittedly, there are Ferrari fanatics who would like to have the colour of their cult brand and the sound of the motor when they open their laptop, plus a certain level of performance, but these are metaphors for the mechanical power of the Scuderia's engines. We should therefore talk about stretching beyond legitimacy, closer to pure branding, or even badging.

The third parameter is the maintenance of the level of luxury. Certain cases of brand stretching are not luxury products, nor yet premium. What remains of Chanel in a Chanel T-shirt, even the most expensive one?

How far can brand stretching go? The notion of brand legitimacy

In traditional marketing, the legitimacy of an example of brand stretching is linked either to recognized know-how, or to respect for the intangible concept of the brand. Provided that stretching forms part of the brand's perceived competence, or foregoes the concept of it in other areas, it is legitimate. In luxury, there are very specialized trades (jewellery, saddler, luggage-making, fine leather goods), rather than recognized transversal competences. And yet transversal stretching is practised almost without restriction. On what bases is the brand therefore legitimate?

We should begin with the sociological definition of luxury: the two eternal sectors are habitat (therefore the palace – Versailles, Chambord – and its decor – Baccarat) and dress, which is subdivided into clothes (haute couture) and finery (jewellery); it is these that legitimize the others, not the other way around. This is why dealers in fine leather goods like Hermès or Vuitton have no legitimacy in haute couture, hence their very relative success: in fact, they are seeking an updating and energizing of their brand through fashion.

Certain brands are more at ease with their original know-how than with their cultural universe. Through a desire for coherence and prudence, the first extensions are called similar: they remain within the trade. Lalique diverted its know-how with crystal and its art deco style onto vases, tables, objects, costume jewellery, cufflinks. Stretching, however, can go beyond physical similarity, exploiting the brand's imaginary quality in its own way. The first perfume from Van Cleef and Arpels was called 'First', since it was the first time that a jeweller had created a perfume. This name strengthened also the desired pre-eminence of this house on the Place Vendôme.

There are other forms of legitimacy for brand stretching in luxury: history is one of them. It is significant, for example, that Baccarat references its history in order to launch jewellery, an approach that has existed from the very beginning. On another level, the stretching of the Baccarat name to luxury resort-hotels derives from a coherence linked to the 'dream life' according to this 'house': crystal – the brand's identity material – is the imaginary lever of a superior lifestyle, made up of great receptions in prestigious palaces. The Baccarat name may then signify an intimate, rare, pure and precious excellence, beyond the classic great names of luxury hoteliers. This stretching into the hotel business makes use of and reincarnates the cultural facet of the brand's identity.

This is not true for Armani cafes, or Ralph Lauren restaurants. Giorgio Armani or Ralph Lauren are living human beings: their approach is mimetic. 'You want to imitate me? Absolutely: do it by taking everything you want from my world' – something that the two Louis (Vuitton and Cartier) cannot do, since they are no longer living.

As for Pierre Cardin, although the character is still as fascinating and has a very good image internationally, its problem arises from the fact that it has stretched its universe of products so far that we can no longer perceive the link or the distinctive power. Cardin divides out its licences by territory and by product. This is no longer a galaxy (which, let us remember, is a group of stars gravitationally arranged around a black hole that ensures their coherence), but has become a nebula (an inconsistent and unstructured group), which will eventually dissipate.

Having said this, the Cardin system still works very well in economic terms, thanks to the creator's exceptional talent, but nowadays on purely populist targets. In France, for example, it is the premier brand of men's shirts, or belts. At Galeries Lafayette, the Cardin stand (shirts, ties and belts) has the highest turnover per square metre. It is therefore a popular reference in both senses of the word. In China, too, the public wish to buy Cardin, but not at a high price.

Leading a brand stretch

This approach comprises four steps. The first is that of strategic diagnosis. Stretching is not an end in itself. Before going ahead, it is necessary to ask yourself what your idea of the brand is in the long term. This is known as the 'big plan'. Successive stretches are then comparable to steps that must be climbed in order to reach the top of the staircase. For each of these, you must also ask yourself what it borrows from the brand, and most importantly, what it gives back, and what are the principal objectives (awareness, conquest, loyalty, etc).

The second step is researching extensions based on the brand's sources of legitimacy (trade, materials, history, culture, lifestyle) and its resources.

The third step is coherence with the identity, and the level of luxury that it belongs to. This is why, prior to any brand stretch, you should carry out a brand core analysis to understand the deeper meaning of the brand, clarifying its identity prism and in particular the cultural facet of it. This identity core, which must be respected, is too often buried or unknown. What is the deeper identity of the Nina Ricci brand, for example, the identity hidden behind the three Fates of its visual symbol or the blurred features of the famous photos by David Hamilton, which accompanied the brand for so long?

This fundamental questioning is the necessary preamble to any brand stretching, since it makes it possible to answer two important questions:

- Is the new category compatible with the essence of the brand?
- If so, can we impress our brand upon it, that is, can we differentiate ourselves strongly and creatively, in the manner of our brand?

To return to Nina Ricci: is a stretch into the category of tableware coherent with the essence of the brand? Knowing that at a deep level Nina Ricci symbolizes accession to femininity helps to eliminate the extension to tableware.

The brand must breathe its own spirit into the extension. However, it is not sufficient to place a few Thierry Mugler-type stars, or Christian Lacroix-type suns, on glasses or plates to transform them creatively according to the two brands. This would be merely badging, like Maserati, which launched a line of jackets.

The idea of respect for brand identity is an essential one: for commercial reasons there is too much of a tendency to want to soften the edges of the brands, hoping thereby to reach more clients and increase sales. This is a mistake. A brand must remain a brand. If Paloma Picasso is the vivid, red brand with a strong Hispanic connection, there is no point in launching less-heady perfumes under its name in order to attract an Asian clientele. Better to concentrate on South America, or Texas and Florida.

The fourth step of the extension process is risk evaluation. In luxury more than anywhere else, everything is in the realization: therefore the SWOT (strengths, weaknesses, opportunities, threats) analysis will be done on this. Each extension may succeed or fail. What is more serious, in luxury, is that it is easy to borrow brand capital without recreating any in return. Finally, extension is often accompanied by reduced control over creativity, manufacturing, distribution and communication; thus you are leaving the luxury business model behind.

An example of stretching: Mont Blanc

Mont Blanc is a typical case of a brand that was able to use its extensions dextrously, without deviating from its identity, in order to give itself means to grow and above all to survive. We can see the four steps above demonstrated here.

At the diagnosis and objectives level, was there in fact a future for a brand that only produced pens? These are admittedly precious, but they are the fruits of a tradition where the written word was art, at the very moment that the great managers the world over write only e-mails on their Blackberry. Stretching should make it possible to increase the attractiveness and the noto-riety of the brand via communication on other products. It should also increase its value among women, and finally increase the frequency of visits. In particular, through the extension of the products, it should finally be possible to develop their own, exclusive distribution. Mont Blanc would finally have shops, of an attractive size, and profitable on a range of products. They create gift, impulse and repeat buying opportunities.

The function of these stretches was to allow a genuine second economic wind for the brand. The stretching process was pursued over three steps:

- understanding of the brand identity, and in particular its intangible dimension;
- the exploration of possibilities, both on the manufacturing and the market potential levels;
- verification of the coherence of the projected realization with luxury and with the facets of the brand's identity prism.

The preamble to brand stretching is an intimate acquaintance with its identity. What is Mont Blanc? What are the key facets of its identity? It was necessary to identify them in order to preserve them, injecting them into the as-yet-unrealized extensions.

For such a purpose, it is useless to interview clients first. The truth of a brand is within itself: it is a trait that strongly differentiates luxury from traditional marketing. Before interviewing clients the world over, it is necessary to carry out brand archaeology. If a brand identity exists, it is manifested over time, and in particular in the products or acts or personalities that founded the brand's international success. It is to them that you must turn: what does this star on the top of the Meisterstück pen mean, why is the colour black a distinctive sign of the brand's physical persona? Why the pen? What is the significance of the name of Mont Blanc, and why is taking out your Mont Blanc more than taking out a pen?

The approach followed to explore legitimate extension routes began with the identity as expressed by Meisterstück, the iconic pen. For this it was necessary to deconstruct the brand's iconic product in order to reveal the facets of the brand identity. A pen is a revealing object: small in size, it is personal, intimate, something a man carries close to his heart, on the inside, in a jacket pocket. It expresses the owner's personality in the truest sense, given that it is the tool that he brings out at the moment of signature. A symbol of the written, the cultural facet of its identity prism harks back to the humanities, to literature, to classical art. Black in colour, and white by name, like a dinner jacket, Mont Blanc is distinguished and formal. Finally, Mont Blanc is a mountain, which may be located in France, but is equally associated with Switzerland, also a country of luxury for watches.

The extensions of a luxury brand must be conceived in a concentric manner (Figure 7.3):

- The first circle begins with the brand's prototype product (the pen) and gravitates around it. In the first circle of Mont Blanc we find a man's other personal objects that gravitate around writing: leather briefcases, file holders, office notepads. Mont Blanc offers a complete range, a universe for the office.
- The second circle moves further away from the first, but must nevertheless express all the key facets of the Mont Blanc identity. The second circle is that of small, intimate, personal objects: cufflinks, wallets, leather cases for the iPod, the iPhone or the Blackberry.
- As we move still further away, certain facets of the brand may be less present, but in any case are never gainsaid. The third circle is that of watches and jewellery for men and women.
- The fourth, and most intangible, is that of perfumes.

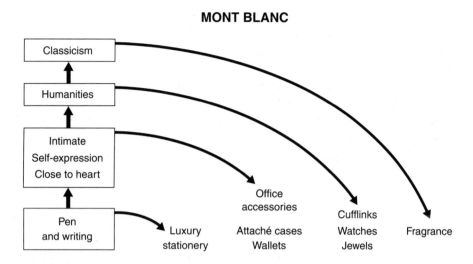

Figure 7.3   From close to remote extensions

The virtue of these extensions is their strong coherence around a clearly identified identity with its semantic invariants, its strong recognition codes (the
star, the colour black). As for communication on these extensions, it generally
calls on celebrities from the world of arts and the cinema, whose personality
reinforces the identity of the brand. Let us add that in capitalist terms, the first
circle – that of the intimate know-how of any brand – should be closed to
external investors: it has to stay secret.

Stretching: brand coherence, but also the creative and unexpected

The brand is built up through coherence. Everything that is a sign of the
brand must express the brand, even if the logo is not visible. Coherence,
however, should not mean repetition or uniformity. In the world of luxury,
surprise is part of the fun.

Non-coherence is not incoherence. Non-coherence is sometimes a virtue.
Clarins is a good example of this. This brand surprised people by launching a
range of intensely red lipsticks, with an advertising campaign where the face
of a black model contrasted with the bright red. For this very soft, relational
brand, accustomed to the white or cream-coloured codes of cosmetics, this was
truly disruptive.

Clarins' entry into this category was a consequence of the need to remain on
the ground floor of Japanese, Korean and Chinese department stores. In

order to do so, it was necessary to keep on increasing sales. Since the growth of cosmetics was not enough, it was necessary to offer other products on the same stand, products that would not cannibalize the existing ones but would increase the average spend or would attract a new clientele.

Strict coherence would have insisted that Clarins also talked about protection regarding this line of make-up products, and launched the range by promoting its non-allergenic qualities. This was tried, but the motivations of make-up clients are far removed from worrying about taking care of themselves: here everything is play and seduction.

The dilemma was therefore simple: either to remain highly coherent in terms of the brand, and thereby handicap the success of the extension, or to accept a lower degree of coherence but seduce young Asian women... without waiting for their first wrinkles to appear.

This example of Clarins, a premium brand, does not entirely address the specific situation of luxury brands. In fact, in luxury, there is no need for a product promise: it is taken as read; only the universe remains. Of course we expect a form of qualitative excellence in all products, but what forms the essence of the luxury brand is its universe, its stylistic and imaginary territory.

Let us examine a case of incontrovertible success: the Angel perfume from Mugler. Angel followed a genuine luxury perfume strategy, the same one that No 5 and L'air du Temps had followed in their day, and which is exceptional today.

The Clarins group is small compared to the giants of L'Oréal, Procter, etc. In order to launch the first Thierry Mugler perfume, they knew they would only be able to afford a modest advertising budget. Angel was therefore the result of a series of voluntary risks and strong bumps, in order to involve a small group of enthusiasts from the very beginning:

- The product has a great intrinsic value: the scent is expensive to produce.
- It was a genuine creation: thanks to original molecules, it was possible to create a completely new olfactive family: the 'Oriental gourmands'. In fact, the scent was highly innovative, sugared, built with the creator himself. Tests revealed that it was highly polarizing: people either loved it or hated it. A large company, naturally risk-averse, would have suppressed it. The directors of Clarins kept it.
- The bottle is superb, with the star, a universal archetype, closely linked to the stellar imaginary quality of Mugler himself.
- The name and the advertising are loaded with all the imaginary quality of Thierry Mugler, a mixture of romanticism and intergalactic symbolism, which creates a dream.
- The initial distribution was highly restricted, comprising only those retailers who could subscribe to the high minimum volume requirements

set by Clarins; as a consequence they were obliged to push the product vigorously, to become its zealous ambassadors.

- A symbolic act has strong emotional resonance: 'the source'. Aiming at the young, Angel made it possible to refill the bottle once empty, rather than throwing it away, which is an ecologically friendly gesture; hence the creation of a 'fountain' at point of sale. Angel is on the side of the planet. Its philosophy translates into acts.
- A high price: more expensive than Chanel No 5.
- For the first time in perfume packaging, a little note was inserted inviting the client to share their feelings about the product and to give an address: this made it possible to create a database of followers and to directly maintain the flame in the client. Luxury is also about making the direct, personal connection with the client.

Success rewarded the strategy: Angel became the best-selling perfume in France and remained so, ahead of No 5, and the second best-selling in Europe, with little advertising expenditure.

Stretching of a luxury brand should therefore be a direct emanation of the brand universe. But what is a brand universe?

- First, it is its stylistic invariants, everything that makes it recognizable without reading the name: the size of the gems that says Mellerio dits Meller, the 'invisible setting' of Van Cleef & Arpels, the Issey Miyake pleat or the typical fluidity of Chanel tailoring, the quilting on the Chanel bag... It is therefore a perceptible universe that can be recognized by other means than through the glimpse of a logo: the brand shop is a multi-sensory vision of the brand.
- Second, it is everything that is not tangible: the brand's imaginary power, the life that goes with it, its underlying myths, its system of values, its Muses, its symbols. Think of the cosmic at Thierry Mugler, the solar at Christian Lacroix, or WASP Bostonian aristocracy at Ralph Lauren.

Two major implications follow from this:

- In order to practice stretching, the brand must already have defined its own 'dream life'. Defining itself as 'chic, relaxed sportswear' is not helpful enough in specifying the imaginary quality that is offered to clients the world over. This is why the country of origin plays such a role in luxury: it provides roots, and offers a degree of imaginary quality of its own. Something chic and relaxed that is 'Made in Paris' does not suggest the same imaginary quality as 'Made on the Riviera'. In the first case, the Japanese will imagine the dream life of the Parisian bourgeoisie and French nobles. In the second, it will be Portofino, the Rivas and the stars of Cinecitta.

- Since the 'know-how' dimension of stretching is overlooked in relation to the intangible dimension (a luxury brand rarely means a mere product promise), it is necessary to multiply the semantic invariants. All Mugler perfumes retain his highly typified stylistic inspiration (the interstellar universe) and elements of code such as the star. It is also significant in this respect that all Hermès products are signed with the equestrian symbol that harks back to the history and the initial know-how (the saddler) and the imagined social status of those who could afford Hermès saddles.

Should extensions have a name?

Let us return to the example of luxury cosmetics or make-up. Taking into account the size of this market, and of the continually renewed desire to buy increasingly expensive products, as the eternal quest for beauty demands, it is easy to understand the attraction of this very profitable market for luxury brands from elsewhere. However, they are not necessarily very legitimate there.

Why would a dress brand put its name to anti-wrinkle creams? With no competence in this highly scientific market, the connection can only be created through the luxury brand's intangibles: it can signal nothing but excellence, unless it wishes to derogate from its rank; the label requires it. Moreover, luxury is the art of the beautiful: it elevates everything it touches, both products and persons. Nevertheless, each category of extension has its own rules: cosmetics are a Faustian promise of eternal beauty to women who are living longer and longer. This is a major challenge: it is the domain of science, which is being asked to roll back the effects of time. For any woman, it is a risky, intimate purchase: the skin may react badly to certain molecules. Not all creams are called equal in their effects. You do not trust your face to an unknown cream.

This is why Chanel certainly has an advantage, linked to the supremacy of its haute couture, and the confidence of the women of the world (in both senses of the phrase), its legitimacy to evoke the beautiful. A workshop, however, is not a pharmaceutical laboratory. The laboratory that underlies Chanel's cosmetics does not appear anywhere, in order to avoid destroying the dream. It is necessary, however, to reassure clients: hence the creation of daughter brands for the category in general, whose name expresses a guarantee (Chanel Precision) or a know-how that the brand lacks (Dior Science).

Let us note in this respect the strategy employed by Sanofi Beauté in care products issuing from Sanofi research: a highly effective molecule (slimming for example) always has strong secondary effects; it is therefore a medicine. An active, but less effective molecule will have far fewer side-effects; it can therefore be used as the basis for a cosmetic care product (the 'Sanofi concept' line), or the luxury product, highly finished in terms of smell, touch, pleasure of use, and introduced into the Yves Saint Laurent perfume range, at the time a subsidiary of Sanofi. For this line, the name of Sanofi was put in small letters ('Sanofi research products').

The risk factors of brand stretching

Brand stretching was the key to the expansion of most big luxury brands. Admittedly, there are some brands that have remained single-specialists: Patek Philippe, Riva, Wally, Krug, Oberoi, but they are generally small.

Stretching can bring success, but it means departing from the original know-how, from the legitimacy of your trade, of what first sealed your renown as a respected artisan, in order to seek another kind of renown as an artist. It does therefore entail taking several risks.

The principal risk with stretching is that it undermines the essence of luxury itself: the recreation of distance. Most often, brand stretching is the consequence of a business model that leads to earning money lower down the pyramid because it is not being earned higher up. Moreover, the brands that rarely practise stretching are those whose business model requires them to earn money higher up. These are true luxury brands.

What are the factors that expose them to this risk too much, and how can they be avoided?

First, the risk of lowering the brand's creativity, if not lowering its quality, is the great challenge of brand stretching, whose short-term financial attraction is clear, the lower you go.

Is this risk unavoidable? No. The quality of the execution, respect for the fundamentals of luxury, and therefore creative control are decisive factors. Chanel and Armani demonstrate this. In a luxury brand, even the so-called accessible products must 'speak' and be objects of pride for both the seller and the buyer. This can lead to a decision not to descend below a particular price level. This is what Chanel does: the Chanel pyramid begins very high up indeed but does not descend far. It does not have several price lines in accessories, but only one: the highest. Chanel bags, the simple summer totes, are priced above €1,000. In contrast, Armani has a succession of lines, from the most expensive to the most accessible: Armani Privé, Giorgio Armani, Armani Collezione (with online sales), down to the young Emporio Armani, or the casual A/X and Armani jeans. However, four points need to be made regarding Armani:

- Even the latter lines remain expensive for their segments.
- They all remain creative: you could even say that they are more creative than the more expensive lines, which represent the sartorial philosophy of Armani himself, made up of soft fabrics, innovative textile research, simplicity, purity of line and discretion that seduces even a puritan America, since it is very well suited to the world of business.
- Each has its own exclusive distribution: there are Emporio Armani shops, Armani Collezione shops, etc.
- Going onto the Armani website, you are struck by its coherence: each line has its own variation on the common spirit, that of the eponymous creator.

Second, the risk of loss of control over the brand, linked to the internal organization within the brand itself. The licence must be controllable. Licensees are independent companies: their principal goal is not to build up the brand, or to invest in its long-term development. In order to control a licensee, you need the ability to do so with a talented management, experienced with figures, but also with an intimate sense of the brand. You also must not be too dependent on the money brought by the licence. Faced with big groups like L'Oréal, or Coty or Procter & Gamble, you need more than managers; you need guarantors of the luxury brand, who understand when the brand's essence is no longer being respected, even if the product is selling well.

Third, relocations lead to a qualitative risk. Everything still depends on the mode of organization: at Devanlay, the historic licensee that produces the textile lines of the Lacoste brand, local production in France of the iconic Lacoste shirt, voted by Americans 'the best polo shirt in the world', represents less than 5 per cent of the whole. However, Devanlay controls around 90 per cent of the total production, through its own factories, on all continents. The Lacoste shirt is in fact the 'prototype' of the brand: it summarizes all of its tangible and intangible virtues. There is no question of delegating its fate to anyone else.

Fourth, risk also attaches to the concomitant stretching of distribution. There is a big difference between the brands that sell their extensions only in their own shops or megastores or corners, and those that, due to the production and distribution licences, find themselves engaged in a distributional stretching. Of course, contracts stipulate that the distribution of the products under licence should be carried out with care to the selection of the points of sale in order not to damage the prestige of the brand. But if a local manager is asked to choose the multi-brand points of sale that in their view are selective, they will have a very different point of view from that of an international manager concerned with overall coherence.

On the other hand, the licensee must remain profitable despite the payment of a licence fee: the licensee makes a few upper range products, but could be tempted by volume and rotation, and therefore tempted to select points of sale with high traffic. Conflicts of interest can thus arise. We are familiar with the court case between Calvin Klein and its jeans licensee, Warnaco. The famous designer accused the licensee of selling its jeans to Costco, a giant of mass distribution. He received the riposte that in any case, the designer had barely any actual control over the Warnaco creations any more.

It is true that most market studies show that consumers do not associate luxury with rarity (Danziger, 2005). In fact, there would be hardly any luxury market today without the relative democratization of luxury. Nevertheless, these studies are deceptive: they focus on mass-market clients, even if they are wealthy ones. These clients are followers: it is not they who crown the brand and make it a luxury brand. Those people always keep one eye on the growth of diffusion, and therefore the loss of the distancing function of the luxury brand.

Fifth, another risk of brand stretching is the fragmentation of the advertising representation, and therefore of the brand's discourse. There are innumerable Ralph Lauren advertisements, due to its many daughter brands and extensions. However, they all seem very Ralph Lauren, because they tell the same story.

When you entrust the creation and distribution of your perfumes to a mass-consumption products company, you also entrust the advertising strategy. The distinctive competence of L'Oréal and Procter & Gamble lies in their know-how in terms of the repetitive launches of new products, based on demand marketing. Based on the brand's identity facets, demand marketing first establishes the potential market by measuring the number of clients to whom these facets are attractive, by means of quantitative surveys. Then it divides this potential market into 'client types' and constructs perfumes based on celebrities worshipped by each of these client types.

The problem is that there are so many brands in this universe that they must necessarily share a few of the same identity facets, and therefore the same targets. For example, both Boss and Ralph Lauren express the values of 'success' and 'ambition'. Beginning with stereotypes (who are the preferred international actors of each client type?) ends in communications aimed at these segments, without any intimate link with the depths of the brand, leading to a strong impression of interchangeability between the advertisements of all the perfumes constructed in this way. Moreover, when you put together all the communication of all the perfumes of a same brand, arising from different stereotypes, you do not get the impression of a unified clientele, of a true community, but rather of a patchwork of personalities that manifestly have nothing in common. This is the very opposite of identity.

Sixth and finally, stretching creates a service risk, when licensees are manufacturers and distributors. For clients, any point of sale bearing the brand name is the brand. They therefore expect to be recognized there, particularly if they are major clients. This creates a level of requirement in terms of decoration, personnel and recognition that you cannot be sure will be adhered to. If the clients themselves are disappointed, this knocks the brand off its pedestal. In addition to the brand capital, stretching also therefore delegates the client capital.

Controlling the boomerang effect of extension

One of the brand's sources of value is its reflection. This facet of the brand identity prism shows the idealized portrait of the typical client (see page 123). The luxury brand must give an element of distinction to both the products and the purchasers. Stretching, however, extends the brand's social sphere of consumption and therefore entails taking risks with the reflection. It is through extensions – badged and accessible – that crises of reflection arise. In Britain, the rejuvenation of Burberry has led to London pubs and clubs refusing entry to those wearing it: in fact Burberry products have become the uniform of so-called 'chavs' (a derogatory term used to describe members of a particular socioeconomic group). In the USA, the 'preppy' Tommy Hilfiger brand has itself been diverted in the same way.

The question can also be asked of Louis Vuitton. Will clients continue to dream of a brand that is the darling of Japanese 'office ladies', and famous for the queues of Asian tourists outside its Champs-Elysées shop at opening time? The answer is clear: it is 'yes', as long as LV, through its traditional monogrammed trunks and suitcases, continues to be a common supplier to extraordinary people, and sells the products and bags that it manufactures only in its own shops. It is extension in textile and fashion that could lead to fragility, or distribution outside its shops (internet)... or both at once!

The next question is therefore the long-term consequences for the brand and the degree of control over its extensions, in particular those that move towards a wider audience. As a result of having lost control and allowed its extensions to be sold in mass distribution circuits, Calvin Klein is no longer perceived as a luxury brand in the USA. The manufacturing and distribution licence is in fact a delegation of brand equity. Nothing is more precious than maintaining the prestige tied to the brand: it is nurtured on myth, exclusivity, virtual and actual rarity, glamour, everything but diffusion. Otherwise, the brand will engage on the fatal path 'from class to mass'.

The problem is that this erosion is not initially visible: periodic surveys of luxury clients do not pick up on it, since 95 per cent of them are non-wealthy people, making up the majority of what the late Professor Dubois at HEC called 'luxury day trippers', buying a product here or there from various brands.

These are the people found in classical market research. This audience, however, is made up of followers. It does not have the power to name and consecrate luxury brands. It is the elites, the celebrities, the men and women of power, the artists, and the leaders of opinion who have this power. It is among these latter that the loss of status gives rise to immediate changes in behaviour.

These opinion leaders are not available to interview through the usual methods of surveying institutes, but they are reachable. It is among these people that one must regularly sound out the present and the future of the luxury brand.

8 Qualifying a product as luxury

In luxury, everything begins with the product. Here we will take the term 'product' in the broader sense: it could mean a concrete product, like a watch, a cultural good such as a concert, a service such as a night in a hotel, or a product–service combination such as Vertu by Nokia, etc. What does a product need to become intrinsically the object that stimulates dreams among the greats of this world, a source of intimate pleasure and the aspiration of others?

No product without service

In luxury, the 'product' always comprises one (or more) objects and a service; a luxury service should become material in an object, a souvenir (a present when leaving a reception) or transactional object (which embodies the service, such as a mobile telephone embodies the actual service, which is remote communication), and a luxury object is always accompanied by a service, or is even the expression of it. Going even further, this means that a luxury product becomes a complete, holistic 'experience', lived in a multi-sensory manner over time by the client.

For example, the packer Louis Vuitton was not originally a suitcase-maker, but came to the client's home to wrap possessions so that they could be transported without suffering too much damage. Then he invented the flat, waterproof suitcase (until that time suitcases had been rounded and were not waterproof), making it easier to handle and to stack, important functions for the new transportation of his time, the Belle Époque: the railway and the packet steamer. He therefore became a luggage-maker, opened a manufacturing workshop, and became hugely successful as the maker of a product: the steamer trunk; but the service was always maintained for the important clients. Until the closure of the Avenue Marceau shop, they were able to leave their belongings in their trunk or suitcase. Likewise, luxury hotels keep certain personal effects and objects, whether furnished or not, at clients' request, so that, as soon as they arrive, their room becomes their home.

The relative importance of these two components, object and service, may vary widely according to the market (essentially object in personal accessories, essentially service in leisure, both to the same degree in a restaurant), but the point of commonality is that it is this object–service pairing that is the luxury 'product' that the client pays for in a clear and perfectly conscious manner; the other components of the marketing mix are an environment that is not accounted for as such.

Of course there are areas of overlap, in particular in terms of distribution: service at a restaurant is paid for and therefore forms part of the product; service in a shop is free and is therefore not part of the product. Another key aspect: the product must be strongly humanized, that is, the object must have been made 'by hand', the service must be rendered by a human being, and the client must have a genuine interlocutor.

In order for a luxury product to succeed, it is important to master three concepts: the separation of the dream aspect from the functional aspect, the holistic understanding of the competitive universe, and management of the time relationship.

The luxury product and the dream

The most discriminating aspect of the luxury product is its relation to the dream:

- The basic product corresponds to a need. The need must be met as quickly as possible (you are thirsty or you need to go to the hospital). The role of the basic product is to do this at the lowest cost compatible with a minimal quality level: a glass of tap water or a common transport vehicle will do the job. Once the need is met, the product is abandoned (you turn off the tap, you step off the bus).

- The branded product corresponds to a desire, a wish. We are thirsty, and we desire a Leffe beer, preferably on tap; we wish to own a car, and desire a Volkswagen Polo. Desire is artificial and does not need to be immediately sated (in emergencies we drink water or take the bus). It lasts for a while, but not too long (we give up the idea of buying a car, since it costs too much) and is substitutable (we buy a Renault Logan, since it is cheaper than a Polo). It must therefore be systematically maintained, and this is the role of advertising, which simultaneously maintains the desire for the product (beer) and for a brand (Leffe).
- The luxury product corresponds to a dream. Dreams are an integral part of human beings: 'We are such stuff as dreams are made on', said Shakespeare. They do not necessarily need to be satisfied: sometimes, their existence alone makes us happy. They are outside time, and often last forever (the dream of travel is not extinguished by taking this or that journey). Dreams are beyond need or desire; the role of the luxury product is to respond not to the individual's needs or desires, but to their dreams.

We have seen above that the luxury product always comprises a functional side and a symbolic side (dreams for the user, prestige for others). In the conception of the luxury product, the most fundamental and the most difficult thing is to separate the functionality aspect (the product's use justifies its purchase, even in luxury!) from that of the dream that it carries. This distinction is difficult to make since, if functionality is objective and measurable, and therefore easy to define, dreams are individual and subjective, and therefore particularly difficult to manage. A single product may lead to very different luxury objects, according to the differing dreams of potential clients. Therefore it is possible to create new products in an existing market, without necessarily entering into head-on competition with existing products, without necessarily cannibalizing them, taking a part of their market share. The market is not totally elastic, but one of the particularities of the luxury universe is that a new product proposition is always possible: unlike the universe of consumer goods, it is never saturated.

Let us take the book as an example, with the alternatives 'luxury' book or paperback. As the functional part of the book is the written text, the paperback is a perfect answer to the problem for a modest price; having bought the book in paperback form, you will not buy it again in the same format.

However, there is a very large and diversified luxury book market, corresponding to dreams of various kinds:

- Valorizing yourself in the eyes of visitors by displaying your culture: how many encyclopedias or prestigious, leather-bound titles sit enthroned on living-room shelves, and have never been opened?

- Living in the past (luxurious reprints).
- Being one of the privileged (numbered editions).
- The very sensual pleasure of touching a book (Bible paper, leather binding) from La Pléiade.

Very different dreams inscribe themselves onto the same function, reading a book; very different luxury strategies are therefore possible, with corresponding, very different products. Moreover, people may buy the same book in different formats: owning a paperback copy of La Fontaine's fables would not prevent you from owning one or more illustrated editions.

Another enlightening example is that of the 'live show', compared to the recorded show. The function of 'enjoying a Verdi opera' is perfectly satisfied by viewing the DVD of *La Traviata* filmed by Zeffirelli on a high-quality home cinema network. Going to see a performance of the same opera at La Scala in Milan or the Opéra Palais Garnier in Paris adds a considerable amount of hedonistic experience and dream to the pleasure of listening to it. The development of home cinema has not emptied the opera houses, since the additional cost in money and time of visiting them is compensated by other elements:

- luxury for yourself (exceptional architecture, the beauty of the staircases and corridors, gilding and statues, the grandeur of the hall, the velvet on the seats, and then the excitement of hearing the voices live and having the actors present);
- luxury for others (to be seen at the opera, and to see famous personalities there).

Rationally, in terms of functional value, you may choose to view at home the recordings of the best interpretations, while a live performance of the opera may not be up to standard. As for comfort, you are better placed at home than in a seat at the opera house. And yet everyone fights for a place at the opera, impelled by the experiential and the dream.

Functionality and dreams do not follow the same economic models

Not only do the functional part and the dream part not obey the same economic models, but they obey opposing logics:

- The functional part obeys an industrial logic of cost reduction, economies of scale and of decreasing returns on investment.

As a consequence, very rapidly, investing in production to reduce costs becomes illusory, since it would be necessary to increase the volumes sold in a way that is incompatible with a true luxury strategy in order to make significant profit return.

- The intangible part is either separate from cost logic (individual dream) or obeys the economic logics of networks and increasing returns (social stratification).

As a consequence, investing heavily in communication and distribution is unprofitable as long as you are too small, but once a critical mass has been reached, investment in communication, to increase awareness and recharge the dream, is marginally more profitable than investment on the product to reduce its cost; until this critical mass of clients has been reached, the brand must be content with inexpensive means for making itself known... hence the initial importance of 'word of mouth' (including the internet) in luxury.

The conclusion is that initially it is necessary to expend all your energies and resources on fine-tuning the product and in conquering a first core of clients who will be the brand's advocates; once critical mass has been attained, it is then better to stabilize the offer and no longer invest heavily in the product, but reorientate your financial investments towards distribution and communication.

It is typically in this way that the great luxury brands in the field of fine leather goods, such as Hermès or Louis Vuitton were developed: in the beginning, an artisan-creator and a small shop, often in an inconspicuous location. Then, once success has been attained, after decades of work dedicated to the product and the satisfaction of the first few clients, and once profitability had been reached, they move on to the stage of opening a second point of sale, then a whole network of shops, all sustained by a massive communications effort, which swallows up almost all the company's resources. This change of direction, which is accompanied by a revolution in priorities and a change in the company's economic model, is particularly tricky to manage.

The luxury product is not a perfect product, but an affecting product

There is often a contradiction between the functional aspect of the product and what makes it luxury: think of the discomfort, noise and the wasted potential speed of a Ferrari, or the extreme difficulty of maintaining certain luxury fabrics. These practical faults are in fact qualities in the eyes of their true clients (ah, the pleasure of stopping at every dip in the road to see if the

Ferrari will be able to make it across!), and is an integral part of their dream ('you have to suffer for beauty').

For many luxury niches, in particular that of luxury cars, hedonism takes precedence over functionality, in contrast to the upper range or premium (see Chapter 2).

Another very important aspect of the luxury product is its holistic nature. The functional part may be sensually one-dimensional, but the dream part must satisfy all the senses; in a great restaurant, the food must be excellent, but the plates must be beautiful, as must the table and the room as a whole, the table-cloth must be agreeable to the touch and the ambient noise must be pleasant.

Now let us turn to the more concrete aspects of product management.

Luxury product and competitive universe

In consumer goods, competition is clearly defined: it is one product against another product with the same function (competition is between Renault and Volkswagen, between Coke and Pepsi, etc). The case of luxury products is completely different. Of course, there is competition between Louis Vuitton and Hermès for a handbag, and between Chanel and Yves Saint Laurent for a dress or a perfume, but in fact the field of competition is much wider: it is that of the dream and the gift.

Seen from this angle, a Hermès bag is not only in competition with a Chanel or a Vuitton bag, but also with a weekend in a fancy hotel for a birthday present; likewise, a bottle of Veuve Clicquot champagne is not only in competition with a bottle of Taittinger, but also with a floral arrangement from Quinquaud or a Pierre Hermé cake for a party among friends.

This explains, moreover, why luxury houses group together, by trade (champagne) or by sector (Colbert Committee), for joint advertising or events: before they can compete against one another, they first need to enlarge their common potential client base in the face of other offers. We can go even further: luxury competition is sometimes 'nothing at all': the client would rather buy nothing rather than buy a product that does not correspond to their dream, or simply a product other than the one from the brand the client dreams of. Which moreover explains the phenomenon of waiting lists, so common and so well tolerated in luxury, because, since the product is not indispensable, waiting is not a problem, and because having ordered a product you dream of is to already have part of the dream… when the wait does not increase the pleasure. On this last point, the luxury product must be earned, whether through an initiation (which takes time), or through a certain difficulty of access (of which the waiting list is part). We will discuss this point again later, in the section on distribution.

Luxury product and time

Luxury's relationship to time is one of its essential characteristics. As much as fashion is fleeting and constantly renewed, so luxury and its objects have time in themselves and for themselves. The 'dream aspect' of the luxury product is intimately connected to this relationship to time, and by this means we can succeed in pricing the product. Remember anti-law number 12: 'Luxury sets the price'. This price remains to be deciphered: a dream may have no price, but the luxury product does. Remember here that, even if the client buys the dream, they still need to rationalize it to justify the purchase, *ex ante*, but also *ex post facto*.

There are a few ground rules, the simplest and most obvious being to take into account the occasion of use and the frequency of use; the 'cost per hour of use' is always implicitly calculated by the client. This attitude is particularly explicit in the USA, but the fact that it is more implicit in Europe does not make it any less important. Nowadays the problem of haute couture or *haute joaillierie* is that their products will be used very rarely, since the occasions for wearing them are becoming rarer. This was the problem for tableware a few decades ago: lifestyles have changed, and so have tastes.

Occasion of use and perception of value

If it is easy to quantify the frequency of use, it is more difficult to quantify the occasion of use. The product must not only be used, but must be seen to be used: a piece of luxury furniture in the depths of a cellar, even if it is filled with various belongings, is not being used as a luxury object but as a piece of furniture; time spent in the cellar does not count!

Consequently, an occasion of use will have more value as it gives more public or social value to its user. This explains why a woman may spend a great deal of money on a handbag or a man on a watch: these are products that may be carried all day long, and are visible to all; social stratification is deployed to the maximum in these cases.

Lasting a lifetime… and beyond

When a product is durable, the answer is simple: you must seek out the longest possible lifespan. The ideal is eternity (for *haute joaillierie*), but a century for a Louis Vuitton case or 20 years (at least) for a Hermès or Louis Vuitton handbag are impressive lifespans, which in themselves justify the price. This imposes constraints on the materials, but also, and much more so, on the style, which must have a touch of timelessness about it. More specifically, the luxury product must remain both current and be timeless. How can we resolve this difficulty? Through two aspects: painstaking design and materials that age well.

In fact, a luxury product sees its value increase over time, like a great wine. Fashion is perishable, but haute couture models are displayed in museums and exhibitions. There is a genuine market for second-hand Chanel dresses.

Prolonging the ecstasy of a privileged moment

If this 'long-term' relationship is easy to understand and to manage for durable products, it entails specificities when the product is used only once. In these cases, it is necessary somehow to prolong significantly the pleasure of the consumption or the single use of the product; to do this, two principal product strategies are possible, one managing the 'after' and the other the 'before', knowing that the ideal is to combine the two.

Management of the 'after' via the product

- First there are the objects that will be retained after use, in memory of the event: for these, there is no particular problem in justifying the price of the dream: how many women keep their wedding dress for the rest of their lives, and even leave it to their daughters?
- If the object itself cannot be reused in its entirety, it is necessary to design at least one part to last longer: how many empty perfume bottles clutter up bathrooms; how many empty bottles of great wines are stored in cellars, with their labels lovingly preserved, or turned into lampstands? Seeing them again recalls the pleasure of tasting, as Proust's madeleine caused him to relive part of his childhood. It is at this level that the holistic nature of the luxury product comes into its own: since all the senses were awakened during consumption, the memory remains strong and can easily be recalled.
- If this is not the case, it is still necessary to find a way to make the memory live on; the simplest and most practical is to offer the client a souvenir-object; thus, for example, all travellers on Concorde were given a small metal object for daily and visible use (ashtray, bottle opener in the shape of a Concorde) which many of them would leave negligently lying around on the coffee table. Luxury services must overcome the stumbling-block of their intangible nature: a meal in a great restaurant is a great moment that, once finished, cannot be transported or shown. It must nevertheless leave a durable trace: hence the importance of the staging, with the great chefs as the artists of the instant.

Enjoying the wait

Management of the 'before' is more complex to manage via the product. The client must be able to buy it, but put off consumption for as long as possible, while enjoying possession of it.

The most classic case is that of great wines, which are allowed to age in the cellar, always putting off the moment of consumption (they are 'improving'), until it is definitively rejected (the wine is now too valuable, or there is a fear that it may have gone off). How many bottles, jealously guarded for decades by our parents, have we finally opened to find nothing but an unpleasant plonk?

Another, similar case is that of great cognacs lovingly transported home by Japanese travellers, which will never be drunk but will sit enthroned in the living-room; in this case the aesthetics of the bottle are more important than the quality of the cognac, since the luxury is not in drinking it, but in contemplating it while telling themselves that they can drink it if they wish to.

Adapting to its time

Let us move on to a completely different aspect of time management for a luxury product: that of adapting to society. We have seen the importance of qualifying the occasion of use to justify the price of the dream. It may be the case, and often is the case, that the evolution of society means that the occasion for use of a luxury product is inexorably constrained: we have examined the case of Christofle's massive silverware, but we could also take the example of Hermès saddler; they have remained luxury products but their market, to which they are prisoner, has progressively shrunk.

There are, however, cases where a luxury product can change its goal: let us take the example of the Louis Vuitton trunk, which is a particularly enlightening one.

During the belle époque, travelling was reserved for persons of prestige; moreover, intercontinental voyages lasted a long time, particularly by sea, and clothing was very sophisticated. A trunk was therefore both a utilitarian object, since outfits had to be perfectly protected in transit, and a luxury object, which would be used a great deal and would be very visible, whether in cars, ocean liners, or on arrival or departure from hotels. It was therefore worth investing large sums of money in a trunk: as the occasions for use were highly qualitative, and the hours of use were numerous, it was not especially unreasonable.

Nowadays, other than those people whose trade is to travel constantly and carry exceptional outfits (singers, for example), this is over and done with: we travel fast and light, on an aircraft the luggage is in the hold, and therefore invisible. Worse still, the transport part of the journey, which was once a pleasure and a party in the days of the ocean liners, has become a chore on an ordinary aeroplane, and all that is associated with it, including luggage, has suffered in consequence. The 'cost per hour of use' of a Vuitton trunk or rigid suitcase becomes prohibitive, as the hours of use trend towards zero.

Faced with this situation, and not wishing these luxury objects, the symbols and pride of their house, to become merely museum pieces, Louis Vuitton started with the fact that trunks often served as travel furniture (Savorgnan di Brazza's trunk-camp bed, the suitcase-clothes racks set up for a week's stay in an ocean liner cabin, etc) and that, nowadays, urban mobility was a fact of society for part of their clientele – even if only in their heads! To own a trunk, or several, as a piece of furniture enclosing the products that are dear to us enables us to think that we could leave with it if we so wished, taking them with us.

On this basis, the trunks have found a new lease of life, in the form of either special made-to-measure orders, or on the second-hand market, or rather the antiques market. Each Vuitton trunk has a number, and the Vuitton house has kept all its archives: when you buy an old trunk, you can therefore find out when, by whom and why it was purchased. The 'Vuitton trunk' product is therefore still current and very much alive, but on the urban furnishings market.

Structuring the luxury range: how is the range of a luxury brand organized?

We have already presented the typical architecture of the luxury brand (Chapter 6 on brand equity), which must balance its products according to the four cardinal points: the iconic, trends, status and accessibility.

A narrow range

The principal characteristic of the luxury brand is its narrowness, its concentration on a very small number of products – or even a single product with few variants (like the Hermès square and its designs, or the Vuitton trunk and its internal arrangements). The reason is simple: it is extremely difficult to truly succeed with a luxury product, and the perfect combination of utility–aesthetics–price is often unique; moreover, concentration on one product makes communication and the creation of a symbol of social stratification, which must be widely and easily recognized, much easier.

Each product has its raison d'être

Since the range is narrow, each product must have a precise role to play, fulfil a precise function, in such a way that the whole spread of principal uses is covered.

For example, in a complete range of urban handbags, you need at least:

● one shoulder bag, one one-handled bag, one two-handled bag, one rucksack, one women's handbag;
● one large capacity, one medium capacity, one small capacity;
● one holdall bag, one organizer bag.

The role of the creator and the product chiefs is to ensure that each function is found in at least one product. As we are in luxury, once the functional need has been met, the application of anti-law number 3, 'Don't pander to your customers' wishes', makes it possible to satisfy the customer: 'You want a rucksack? No problem, we have them; here is the one we've designed for you.'

Each product has its own personality

A brand's luxury products are like children of the same family, and moreover each product often has its own first name. This is true in all sectors of luxury, for example the hotel sector: the rooms may have names in smaller hotels, and numbers in larger ones, but suites are always named (for example the Suite Royale at the Plaza Athénée, the Eiffel Suite and so on). In the luxury hotel chain Barrière, each hotel maintains its name and personality (Ermitage at La Baule, Negresco at Cannes, Fouquet's in Paris).

Of course certain details may be modified, provided that they do not change the characteristics of the product itself in any way: you can adapt the dress from the haute couture fashion show to the client's measurements, but you do not change the cut or the materials, and you offer a (highly restricted) choice of specific colours for the chassis of a Ferrari.

Price differences between products are significant

As a consequence of the fact that each product has its own personality, it is counterproductive to cover the price range too specifically: this create confusion in the client's mind.

The price difference between products in the same range should be at least 15 per cent, and if possible 30 per cent, and should be backed up by simple criteria, if possible visible to all (for example, with Cartier, five-strand watch bracelets are all steel, or all gold, or else with either two gold strands and three steel, or vice versa).

The range comprises at least one entry-level product

We have seen in Chapter 6 that brands developed access products for two types of clientele: the 'future faithful' and the 'day trippers'. Here we are interested in the 'future faithful'. The entry-level product(s) should offer the quintessence of the brand's dream, in order to seduce the client, and at the same time be as accessible as possible, without, however, being too accessible (the luxury brand is segregationist). These contradictory aspects make the design of these products very difficult: moreover, and unlike entry-level products for 'day trippers', generally very clearly signed and with high margins, these products have a lower margin and should not be sold in too great a quantity.

Innovating through a new product range

If launching a new product is a complex decision in luxury, deciding to introduce a new range is even more difficult: often a single range carries the essence of the brand, which may in fact be happy to settle for this (Monogram, at Louis Vuitton), and often does settle for this (Oyster, by Rolex).

Launching a new range is a strategic decision, which comprises an aspect specific to luxury: it is above all a demonstration of strength ('What I used to do was and remains perfect, but I can do even better in another field'), and not of weakness ('What I used to do has fallen out of fashion, or has been surpassed technically, and moreover was too expensive; since you no longer want it, let me offer you something else'). The objective of a new range should be to innovate, complement and strengthen existing ranges, not to substitute for them, and to enrich the substance of the brand.

Central ranges (brand core) and peripheral ranges

Before focusing in detail on the manner of launching a new range, we must first of all clarify an important point: the differentiation between central ranges and peripheral ranges. Central ranges are an integral part of the brand, and should be present in every point of sale under the brand's name; peripheral brands are not indispensable to the brand's image, and can be distributed more widely (but still in a controlled manner).

Let us take the example of Cartier, since the strategy of the 'Must' is a model of its kind (Figure 8.1). The central ranges are jewellery and watches, which must be present in any Cartier shop, and the peripheral brands are perfumes, leathers, lighters, glasses, etc, which may be sold outside the specific Cartier universe without damage.

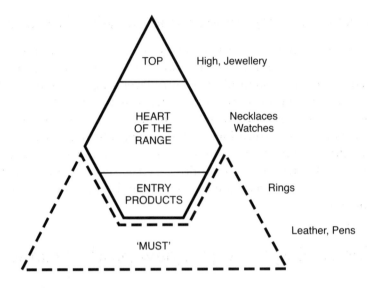

Figure 8.1　Cartier core business and 'Must'

Launching a new range in the brand's core

In what follows, we will concentrate on the brand core, since peripheral brands are dealt with in Chapter 7 on brand stretching and Chapter 13 on business models. The essential point is that the launching of a new range in the brand's core is a demonstration of the innovation and strength of the house.

Right and wrong reasons for launching

The first thing to check is that the new range is being launched for the right reasons, and not for the wrong ones; let us analyse these.

Let us begin with the wrong reasons, which are sadly all too common, and which generally follow the sequence below:

1. The company is tired of its product, having seen too much of it, or thinks that the product's success has caused it to lose its 'luxury' rank. It is high time to 'inject some new blood'.
2. A new team arrives, naturally confirming this analysis, since it was hired to do so, and wishes to demonstrate its talent and usefulness by launching a new range, often with the ulterior motive of dethroning, or even replacing, the old one.
3. Since the existing range is selling itself, there is a desire to use the available cash to launch something new, following an approach known as 'cash cow

milking' (that is, by transferring all the advertising costs of the brand that is selling well to the new product).

4. This strategy leads to failure, and sometimes brings the company to bankruptcy, by gravely weakening the flagship range, the source of profit. The trade where this error is most often committed and the failure is most obvious is in perfume, in which a new perfume is in fact a new range.

The most incredible case experienced by one of the authors in this field is that of Louis Vuitton and his monogrammed line in 1986. At that time, two camps were fighting:

- The majority camp, made up of those who felt that the success of the Monogram range (the LV-signed canvas) was such that it had become a commonplace product, counterfeited everywhere, and that the Louis Vuitton company, in order to remain in luxury, should abandon the Monogram and replace it with another canvas or with leather, and at the same time should step away from the heart of its trade (luggage and fine leather goods) by launching watches, perfumes and scarves.
- The other camp, strangely in the minority, of those who felt that you do not kill a product that sells, and that it is not the visibility of a product that causes it to cease being luxury, but its vulgarization, essentially due to counterfeiting.

To the author it was clear that the majority camp had only wrong reasons for launching new ranges; convinced by the analysis of the minority clan, he immediately worked with the teams to seek for better reasons to launch a new range.

This brings us to the right reasons to launch a new range:

- A new creative idea, enriching the brand universe, but not to the detriment of other ranges: the Pacha range of watches by Cartier did not damage the Tank, Santos or Panthère ranges.
- Strengthening an existing range: a range of soft luggage by Vuitton, accepted as carry-on luggage, completing the traditional range of rigid trunks.
- Reaching a new clientele without rejecting the old one: Hermès silks (square scarves, ties) made it possible to reach a younger, more modern clientele, which was not interested in Hermès' fine leather goods or its saddlery.
- Reaching a price territory where the brand is legitimate, but the existing ranges are not.

To give an example of this last point, let us return to the case of Louis Vuitton in 1986. There was at this time an excellent reason for launching a new range: whereas luggage under the Louis Vuitton range and with the monogrammed canvas sold well at over $5,000, bags in this canvas had not succeeded in crossing the $1,000 threshold in retail prices, as they were perceived as chic, but casual, city bags; the formal handbag market was therefore out of reach. The company had tried to cross this threshold by launching models where the natural cowhide and the metal pieces in brass, highly resistant raw materials used for luggage, which aged well but were unsophisticated, were replaced by calfskin and gold-plated metal pieces. In vain: the client no longer found in these new, more sophisticated materials the dream carried at Louis Vuitton by luggage and transposed, via the canvas and the 'rustic' raw materials, into the handbag.

The situation was clear: Louis Vuitton as a brand was legitimate to ask $2,000 and more for a bag... if it was not a monogrammed one. A totally new line was necessary. Luckily, owing to the 'minority', it has already been developed, under the name of Epi.

The decision was taken to accentuate the aesthetic choices of this line, which were already very strong (bright colours, geometric and ultra-modern lines, rigid leather, discreet LV logo, no canvas), the complete opposite of the Monogram line (dark colour, rounded, classical lines, soft leather, highly visible LV logo, significant use of canvas), in order both to avoid any risk of cannibalization of the Monogram line, and to attract a new clientele in search of aesthetic modernity.

The strategic choice, clearly stated within the company, was to prefer the failure of the new line over the weakening of the old one... and success validated the choice: the Monogram line continued its strong growth, and the Epi line achieved resounding, worldwide success.

Not only that, but the brand universe was considerably enriched: in order to remain coherent with the dream carried by Louis Vuitton, it was necessary to have rigid trunks in Epi leather. These were therefore manufactured and sold, but it was not these that legitimized the handbags, but rather the other way around: Louis Vuitton had become a true fine leather goods dealer, while also remaining the premier luggage maker in the world.

Don't sacrifice the past to the future

A successful launch in the context of a strategy of strength in luxury presupposes that the past is not sacrificed to the future. In order to ensure this, three management rules need to be respected:

- Do not systematically recruit the best individuals or teams to the new line: managing the heritage and the past is not, in luxury, an activity reserved for the incompetent and lazy.
- Give yourself new, ambitious sales targets for the old range, and prudent ones for the new range (in contrast to ordinary consumer goods).
- Launch the new range at a markedly higher price than the old one: this is proof that you are a luxury house.

The aforementioned Epi line was introduced at a price 50 per cent higher than that of the Monogram line, which did not prevent it from enjoying significant commercial success.

Remember that all these rules relate to the brand core, and not to peripheral ranges.

A mode of production as a lever of the imaginary

Since the product (in the wider sense) is at the centre of the client's dream, and since it carries values well beyond pure functionality, its production is a major act. It must contribute to the dream. To achieve this, two conditions are indispensable.

The human hand must have a significant role in production

Originally, every luxury product was made specifically for each client, by an artisan known to the client; it was moreover the said artisan or artist, and not the client, who defined the product. With the development of the brand, the majority of models are made by several people, and moreover standardized, and therefore produced in advance and available in stock.

If the product is no longer manufactured for a specific client, it is nevertheless important that it is not manufactured in an anonymous manner: during production, the end client must be considered as being present. Hence the extreme importance of the manual part of the production process, carried out in a precise location known to the end client, so as to maintain this original connection.

This does not mean that tools, even sophisticated ones, are not used (Ferraris are not 'handmade', and nor are Aston Martins); these tools must be perceived as an extension of the human hand, obeying it as the chisel obeys the sculptor, and not autonomous, like the assembly-line robots of mid-range car factories.

Likewise, there must be parts that are entirely handmade, and this must be well publicized (every client knows it) and justified: a piece for which manual quality is superior to machine quality ('hand sewn': the seating of a luxury car), a piece for which the irregularity of the human hand adds soul (Baccarat glass, blown and engraved by hand).

More generally, in order to maintain the 'handmade' while guaranteeing a sufficient level of technical quality to avoid any major discrepancies, correct reproducibility and the productivity essential to avoiding cost spirals, it must be a rationalized manual production, with productivity through organization (assembly procedures, templates, etc) and not through mechanisation.

This aspect only concerns classic luxury products: think of the key role of the chef and their final touch in a great restaurant; each client knows that the chef did not make the entire meal, much less peel the potatoes, but they know (or believe) that it was the chef personally who went early morning to the market to buy the vegetables or the fish, who participated in the creation of the dishes... and who appears to greet the house at the end of the show!

Production must not be outsourced, much less relocated

This is the second condition for maintaining the dream:

- Outsourcing means losing control and familiarity with the production process. It cuts the connection, which is fundamental to luxury, between the artisan, or group of artisans, who manufactured the product and the client: the company that carries the brand becomes a simple intermediary, and the creative teams lose contact with the terrain where the product will be created.
- Relocation means denying one of the fundamentals of luxury: cultural specificity. This is one of the major points of divergence at the product level between luxury and premium: a luxury product is linked to a history, a territory (physical or cultural) from which it cannot be extracted without losing its aura; a premium product is linked to a strict set of technical specifications, and it must be manufactured where it makes greatest economic sense, always provided that there is strict respect for quality.

A recent illustration of this difference in treatment between luxury and premium was provided by the announcement in September 2006 of the closure of Burberry's British factory in Treorchy (Wales). The brand would from now on be manufactured outside Britain. When questioned, management responded that: 'Britain, unlike Italy and France, is not a country that celebrates manufacturing of fine clothing and in comparison to the aforementioned countries, there is little export in the way of ready-to-wear fashion.' For the directors, Burberry is clearly on the fashion side, and therefore does not need to follow the laws of luxury defined in Italy and France.

The opposition between luxury and relocation

The 'dream aspect' that characterizes the luxury product transcends the product itself, and all the components of this dream aspect must be preserved, since they form a whole (luxury is holistic). The manufacturing of a product by an artisan is an integral part of the dream, and is a major component of it from the very beginning; and this artisan is not just any artisan, but someone who knows the product well, who belongs to the same cultural universe. A French artisan will not work in the same way as an Italian artisan, or a Chinese artisan like a Japanese artisan, since they do not see the shapes, colours, details or balance of a product in the same way. For example, and caricaturing somewhat, the Italian will seek originality at the expense of rigour, and a German will seek rigour at the expense of originality; a Japanese will purify the shapes to the extreme, whereas a Chinese will complicate details to the extreme. Nobody is at ease when not working in a familiar cultural context, and not only will globalization not change anything about these cultural specificities, but it will in fact encourage each one to exaggerate them, if only in rebellion.

The place of production, even more than the shop since it is much less physically accessible and is closed to the public, is a kind of temple where the mythical alchemy of the product takes place, where the brand myth is born, where the cult is celebrated. It is important for the brand substance that this place may be visited, like the Asnières workshop for Vuitton or the Maranello factory for Ferrari; this visit must be accompanied by great ceremony.

To insist further on this point of cultural specificity, not only should production be located strictly within a culture, but most of the time the geographic location of production itself is part of the product. It may be a specific place (Le Puy lace), a defined region (Champagne, or Caspian Sea caviar).

Outsourcing production is the sign that a brand has given up on being luxury, and has accepted, for economic reasons, the inexorable loss of legitimacy due to relocated production; we may note that this does not only concern the top luxury brands, like Chanel, which remains French and thus prevents the disappearance of very refined artisan trades (such as embroidery), adding a supplementary symbolic value to products of a very high quality, but also relates to less prestigious brands, such as Longchamp, which bases all its production in France and is very successful.

The nadir is reached with today's famous slogan: 'Created in France, produced elsewhere'. The reverse is true: creation is a mental process, which unlike production is not located either in time or space. Creation must be as close as possible to production in order to remain strong and original: the great painters mix their own pigments; the biggest cause of the disappearance of haute couture in France is the disappearance of the dress-making trade in the country, whereas its strength in Italy, in contrast, explains the economic and creative power of Italian haute couture.

Licences signal the departure from luxury

The immediate consequence of the above is that the production licence immediately causes the brand to depart from the luxury universe (even if non-connoisseurs take some time to realize this), because it breaks this intimate relationship between creation and manufacturing. This does not mean that a luxury brand should never grant licences, but that when it grants a licence, the licensed products are no longer luxury but 'premium' products (and even then, not always!) bearing the signature of a luxury brand. They can never effectively compete with luxury products on their turf, even if the licensee is a luxury brand. For example, Yves Saint Laurent watches, made under licence by Cartier, were excellent premium products, aesthetically very pleasing, but were not luxury products.

We will deal with this point in greater detail in Chapter 13, dedicated to luxury business models.

Having said this, we are not more royalist than the king on this subject, and our position should not be caricatured: when you depart from the domain of the pure luxury product and confront the domain of luxury services, things are much less clear-cut. At the extreme, for example in luxury hotels, the refusal of the concept of relocation would have no meaning, since service is rendered locally. The licence (or franchise) is in this case a legitimate and effective means of development, provided that there is strict – and friendly – control! In this context, the decision of the great Italian luxury names, such as Bulgari, to diversify into the hotel business is an interesting one to watch.

9 Pricing luxury

When we evoke the word 'luxury', the adjective 'expensive' immediately comes to mind, and yet it is probably in the relationship between luxury and price that things become most complex and surprising. Moreover, many of the 'anti-laws' of marketing analysed in Chapter 3 relate to price.

At the conceptual level, we know that luxury is translated in a product through a high 'symbolic value'. This symbolic value, essential to luxury, is very difficult to quantify, and in any case is highly relative: it cannot be given a precise figure. And yet luxury must be paid for, and therefore must have a price...

It is in the domain of price that the major cause of confusion between 'upper-range' and 'luxury' lies, a confusion that comes from a reading of the 'price factor' that is one-dimensional. Being expensive is not enough to be luxury. Moreover, the question of price must be raised at different levels of the range, and not in a one-size-fits-all manner.

Finally, since luxury products are bought infrequently, the cost is quickly forgotten, and as luxury products are quite specific, it is difficult to compare prices. The price is therefore generally not the major factor in the strategy, contrary to the way things are in the rest of consumer society, where every new product launch is prepared by comparative studies to decide the price difference that will separate it from 'the competitor'.

Contrary to received wisdom, luxury and price are not always inseparable. Many luxuries have no determined price, or are 'priceless' for some (health for the sick, free time for the stressed manager, clean air for the urbanite). Even today, a large part of what may be considered luxury is outside the merchant economy (beauty, art, happiness, nature, ecology); but this is a question of 'luxury for yourself'. These intimate luxuries can never become luxury markets, inasmuch as the sociological dimension of luxury is lacking.

It happens that price is a major factor in the strategy of a luxury brand, and it is then loudly proclaimed: 'Bugatti Veyron, the world's most expensive car', 'Joy, the world's most expensive perfume', while attempting to back it up with impressive figures (10,600 jasmine flowers and 300 roses for 30ml of perfume). Alain Ducasse's arrival in New York was achieved by proclaiming the opening of the most expensive restaurant in the city. Richard Mille, a newcomer to luxury watches, launched the RM 008 at €415,000.

This being said, this type of strategy is rarely attended by financial success, and when there is success it does not last: someone else, more expensive still, will always come along quickly. Moreover, this price strategy sharply reduces the size of the market and gives rise to suspicion. Even in luxury, the underlying 'worth the cost' dimension is always there: what is the symbolic value created by this claim? That of someone who 'can really afford it', or of someone naive enough to be sucked in by such a claim? The slightest disappointment will set off the word of mouth of the opinion leaders in the microcosm, and immediately causes the client to fall into the second category, one of the 'mugs'.

What about price elasticity?

Let us now look at the famous price elasticity, the foundation of all classic economics: when the price rises, demand falls.

In fact, the price–volume relationship is a key factor in a traditional marketing strategy, and it is essential to understand and to measure it, through the classic means of elasticity coefficients, about which there is an abundant literature. This classic concept of elasticity in price, however, does not apply well, if at all, to luxury, for reasons that we will now analyse.

The coefficient may not exist

In order to define an elasticity coefficient, you have to suppose that in the price–volume relationship a small variation in price always corresponds to a small variation in sales volume, and never to a brutal leap in one direction or the other (a crumbling or an explosion of sales).

While this hypothesis may be reasonable for ordinary products, it is rarely applicable to luxury products, even when they have reached a sizeable sales volume (Chanel bags, Cartier watches). This is illustrated by the 'threshold effect': below a certain price, the product is no longer considered by the target clientele as a luxury product. By dipping under this threshold, the product ceases to sell, and by rising above, the product once again sells well... if the quality justifies it!

A well-known example in France (prior to the euro) was that of champagne: at a retail price of fewer than 100 Fr, a bottle was no longer considered 'real' champagne. Dropping the public price from 100 to 99 Fr halted sales, and it was necessary to drop the price much lower in order to find another clientele, that of mere sparkling wines.

Inasmuch as there is a threshold effect, it is the existence of a price zone that is completely ignored by clients, between products considered 'luxury' and those, beneath, that are called 'mass prestige'; the latter are obedient to the laws of classic economics and traditional marketing... and never hesitate to play on the words to create confusion ('Champenois method').

This threshold effect is linked to that of physiological perception, which is applicable both to the price difference between products of the same range, and the price difference between ranges. In luxury, the relationship to price is more qualitative (too expensive/not expensive enough) than quantitative (how much?); the perception of the price is therefore more psychological than rational.

Price differences, in order to be perceptible, must reach a physiological threshold (in the order of 30 per cent, like perceptions of weight difference); a few per cent one way or the other will pass completely unnoticed.

The elasticity coefficient may be negative

It is sometimes the case that luxury products behave like everything else – that is, a lowering of the product price leads to an increase in sales volume – but it is relatively rare: if, for a normal consumption good, even 'premium', when you aim at a public price of 100, you must label it 99, this is not the case for the luxury product!

Other than in exceptional cases, if a luxury product that was selling well is now selling less well, you will not find a larger clientele through dropping the price, but by recapturing the whole concept of the offer.

The coefficient may be null

This case is relatively common in luxury: when a product has found its market, there is often a fairly broad price zone within which the number of clients does not change, whether the price rises or falls (a seat in a box at the opera or at a concert by a famous artiste, a house or a dream apartment).

The coefficient may be positive

Objects or services for which demand increases along with the price are called 'Veblen goods', after the Norwegian Veblen, a theoretician of the 'leisured class' at the beginning of the 19th century. This behaviour of 'Veblen goods' is very frequent in luxury and is somewhat counterintuitive, particularly as it is in flagrant contradiction of what occurs with ordinary products.

Increase the price to increase demand and recreate the distance

In general, a luxury brand must cause its average price to grow continually: its client development dynamic is not the increase in the number of clients through the lowering of the access price, which devalues the brand, but through the increase in the number of clients who are willing to pay to access the brand.

The launching of cheaper lines to capture a less well-off clientele, known as the 'day trippers', practised by many brands, and which is one of the engines driving the development of the 'luxury business', is a sign of the weakness of a brand. It is the advance warning of an exit from the luxury universe, if these lines are not managed with all the codes of luxury. The launching of entry-level products is not fundamentally opposed to a luxury strategy, provided that the products are of a very high quality. The goal is not to sell a lot (or the average price would automatically fall), but to initiate new clients into the brand universe. This is typically what Louis Vuitton does with its smaller leather goods, Tiffany with small, silver jewellery, Pierre Hermé with little macaroons; we will return to this in Chapter 13 on business models.

Independently of this general virtuous circle effect of any powerful brand (concomitant increase in sales volume and average price), it is in fact common for an increase in the price of a given luxury product to lead to an increase in its sales volume – within certain limits, of course; this is to some extent the specificity of luxury.

This Veblen effect is paradoxical for anyone who does not comprehend the profound difference between the luxury product and the classic product, but in practice it is quite difficult to manage. We will therefore expand on the subject in three common cases of professional life.

Increasing the price: the case of an existing product in the range

Increasing the price on principle, thinking that clients will buy more of it because they are 'mugs', will be immediately punished. The luxury client is a connoisseur, and is perfectly well aware of what they are paying (for themself or as a gift) and what it is worth.

In fact, if a product is selling well, in luxury as in elsewhere, it is because it is at its correct price; the 'Veblen effect' does not work in this case, and the price should not be changed except for very good reason, and clients should be notified. This is how Louis Vuitton proceeds in leather goods, with its local prices in Japan or the USA, when currency variations become too large; in the case of Japan, where the affective relationship between the brand and its clientele is very strong, the company goes so far as to publish it in Japanese newspapers, with a detailed explanation of the evolution of the yen–euro exchange rates.

If, nonetheless, you decide to increase the price slightly, and you wish sales to remain steady, you must be careful to increase the perceived value proportionally much more in the client's eyes, and be certain that they are ready to pay for it: you will not increase the sales of a given product just by putting more gold or diamonds on it and charging the customer more. You must clearly understand the client's 'part of the dream', and how the product can satisfy it further.

It is furthermore necessary to play for the duration, and over the long term, making sure that clients are following along, as Krug has done for almost 15 years, supported by the family management of the Remy-Martin house, which has prioritized value created in the long term over short-term growth and was even ready to lose some distributor clients: exchanging bad clients (there for the price) for good ones (there for the increased value).

In addition, the sales force and communication must accompany this increase; it is generally indispensable to explain this 'plus' to the client, since it is rarely something that leaps to the attention. Finally, it is necessary to know the price zone in which you are legitimate, so as not to move 'up' beyond it, in which case the client will abandon you and your sales will crumble.

Another consequence of the systematic growth in sale price is the use of cost savings through productivity. In luxury, as elsewhere, it is necessary to increase productivity and reduce costs; in luxury this should not lead to lower prices, but to an increase in the quality of the offer. To take an example, once again from Louis Vuitton Malletier: the strong, regular growth in sales volume of the great classics of the Monogram lines have led to a considerable economy of scale effect on supplies such as zip fasteners, but also to additional costs on leather) since the economies exceeded the increases, in the end the products as they were became much less expensive.

Rather than reducing the retail price, the decision was taken to maintain it, and to significantly improve the characteristics of the zip fasteners, fine-tuning a new technology with the Japanese supplier YKK, which made the zip considerably easier to slide, and building new machines whose production was reserved for Louis Vuitton.

Increasing the price: the case of launching a new range within the brand's core trade

A preliminary clarification is required here: we are not talking about extending the brand into new product territories, a point that is dealt with elsewhere, and is known as brand stretching, nor about complementary ranges, whose goal is to seduce 'luxury day trippers', but with the introduction of a new range within the core of the trade, which is addressed to loyal clients of the brand, or to those that it wishes to lastingly seduce.

The essential characteristic of a luxury brand, within its core trade, is that a new line should be launched at a higher brand than the old ones. Luxury is distance, and must constantly recreate that distance for its own clients.

A new line is not designed to 'vulgarize' the brand, but conversely to increase its attractiveness, its dream value. This is a classic strategy in luxury, and particularly in the hotel or technical trades (cars, electronics, hi-fi, etc) where it is systematic. Weak brands launch new, cheaper products: a Renault Vel Satis costs €43,000, or 35 per cent more than a Mercedes C-Class with the same characteristics, but Renault is launching the Logan at €5,000, Mercedes the SL 65 AMG at €230,000...

If, nevertheless, a luxury brand decides to launch a cheaper line (as with the BMW 3 Series, then the 1 Series), it must be made clear to all that it is not a strategy of brand weakness (we are not capable of launching more expensive products) but a strategy of strength (we are capable of being innovative); the launching of this new range should be immediately counterbalanced by the introduction of products at the very top of the range: the average price of the core trade must continue to grow.

Increase the price: the case of launching a brand-new product for which nobody knows the real market

Here again, the luxury product shows paradoxical behaviour. Classically, when launching a new product, you position it relatively high, targeting the 'pioneers', then, with the rise in volume and the economies of scale and distribution that it affords, you progressively reduce the price to reach a larger audience... and protect yourself from competitors.

Numerous industrial companies, such as Bic, even anticipate the 'experience curve' to lower their prices even more quickly from the beginning, and thus create a barrier to entry.

With luxury, it works completely differently: it is preferable to begin at the low end of the spread you think is correct, and then to increase it by successive steps (see below, 'Fixing the price in luxury').

What price premium?

In mass consumption marketing, the brand is not necessarily linked to a price premium: easyJet and Ryanair are the two flagship brands of low-cost air travel. Bic is the brand of the cheap ballpoint. For luxury, the price premium is there and is the proof of the 'part of a dream' of the luxury product.

- The price premium proves the brand's value, as in the case of consumption goods, but it is much higher in luxury, since the price of the 'part of a dream' and the recreation of the distance are added to it. This price difference in comparison to a 'comparable' product sold under the same conditions without the brand should be at least 30 per cent if you wish to be a luxury brand. It frequently reaches 100 per cent, or even higher.
- The quality of the distribution is one of the factors that explains and justifies the price. The distribution (or rather the service) forms an integral part of the product.
- The premium is always higher when the brand is within its territory of legitimacy.
- It is important to measure it regularly, since it is one of the best indicators of a brand's strength, and one of the few that are objective.

Two examples reveal the price dynamic in luxury. Compare champagne and sparkling wines (*sekt* in Germany), made using the 'Champenois method': an ordinary champagne clearly sells at a much higher price than a Spanish cava, even if the cava is of a higher quality. The price of the part of a dream is easy to measure in this case.

Luxury watches and the price of a ounce of gold provide a second example. The comparative study of the retail price of watches and bracelets by weight of gold makes it possible to check the status of a luxury brand; Cartier does these studies systematically, and the alarm sounds when the distance from less prestigious brands drops below 30 per cent.

Fixing the price in luxury

The price is the 'exchange value' of a product, but what makes luxury is the 'symbolic value'. This means that the stronger the symbolic value of a luxury brand, the higher a price it can command; in fact, a brand is a genuine luxury brand on its territory if it can ask any price without being ridiculous: the greatest Swiss watchmakers, like Blancpain or Audemars Piguet, can easily offer, in limited quantities of course but nevertheless successfully, watches at €1 million.

For Rémi Krug, who turned the eponymous house into the very prince of champagnes, true luxury is attained when you have the complete freedom to set your price.

Of course, we said at the beginning of this chapter that price is generally not a major factor in the strategy of a brand, inasmuch as it is only the consequence of the strategy pursued; it nevertheless remains true that setting the price remains a crucial operational decision, even if in this field a luxury product enjoys more latitude than a classic product.

The first step is to understand your competitive universe properly, as with any classic product, with the particularity that this universe extends far beyond its direct competitors (see Chapter 8, 'Luxury product and competitive universe'). The immediate consequence is that the price is not defined on the basis of a 'cost-plus'-type method, through addition of the costs, but conversely you begin with the price in order to construct the product (in the broader sense). It is similar to reverse engineering, in which both the functional part and the part of a dream, the basis of the symbolic value, will be properly proportioned.

The second step is to begin to sell the product quickly, and to pay close attention to what happens at the level of the final client (not the distributor).

Given that the price of a luxury product should always increase, the most effective way of setting it is to begin at the bottom of the zone of price legitimacy (defined above), and then progressively increase the price, adding improvements to the offer as necessary, until you find the zone of equilibrium between the volume and the margin that, at a given moment, will be optimal for the brand.

The reason for this tactic is simple: since we cannot know a priori the symbolic value of a product, that is, what the client is ready to pay in addition for the part of a dream, and since luxury products are generally 'Veblen products', only by beginning at a (relatively) low price, and then progressively increasing it and the volume offered for sale until demand ceases to grow, can you discover the figure of this 'symbolic value'.

From that moment on, you can adapt your price strategy to the company's economic constraints and its strategy (profitability, growth, image, etc).

Let us note yet again to what extent this is the opposite strategy to that practiced by classic products, where you begin with a high price, in order to attract innovative clients (pioneers), prices that are then progressively dropped with the increase in sales volume, in order to reach an increasingly broad market (the followers).

The price objective can be expressed as follows: 'what my client is willing to give for my product, for it to be considered a luxury product, but which they can afford to give'.

Managing the price over time

From the moment that the price has been correctly set, that is, the profitability and sales volume are in accord with the company's objectives, and a sufficiently large core of clients exists, the problem arises of managing the brand over time, which means the application of a pricing policy.

Overall there are two major families of possible pricing policies in luxury: those linked to the offer, and those linked to demand.

Price policies linked to the offer

In these policies, the price of the product is set in advance, and the client pays the set price. Since luxury marketing is 'offer marketing' (as opposed to traditional demand marketing), these policies are the practical outworking of our anti-law number 12, 'Luxury sets the price, price does not set luxury'.

To begin with, as we have just noted, the market is small and the clients are few, and therefore easy to get to know individually; the price is the adjustment variable of the strategy.

Once the price has been correctly set, and with the development of sales and the increase in the number of clients, the situation changes altogether, and the price is no longer an adjustment variable, since the brand's price territory is now fixed; you will need to be strict in managing it, both:

- diachronically, since the price adjustments must be carefully measured according to the (hopefully positive) evolution of the brand's 'desirability';
- and synchronically: the problem becomes that of a global price strategy.

Once success arrives, luxury products in fact become global products, for which the transport costs are relatively low and demand almost universal. In these conditions, they travel easily, and as luxury clients also travel a great deal, a strict worldwide coherence between retail prices among the different networks and countries is vital. In order to achieve this, there are two dominant strategies:

Local price modulated according to local distribution costs

This is to some extent a 'cost-plus strategy in distribution': the price difference between two countries is strictly linked to the travel costs (transport + customs, exchange rate fluctuations) and local distribution costs (local retail costs, taxes); this strategy, whose paragon is Louis Vuitton Malletier, has the significant advantage of enabling prices to vary according to real costs incurred, and therefore protecting margins, while being able to clearly explain to the consumer the cause for price differences between countries; the consumer remains free to buy wherever the product is cheaper (Paris or Hong Kong, in the case of Louis Vuitton), while remaining certain of receiving the same quality everywhere.

The key points to manage in this approach are:

- Public, transparent and clearly expressed information on the coefficients applied by country, which will vary according to the currency rates and local taxation, often scalable.
- Management of retail sales in lower price zones, in order to avoid not only a flow (known as the 'grey market') of products towards the higher price zones, which is awkward not for the brand itself (the margins are the same) but for its local distribution operations, and even more for the risk of indirectly financing money-laundering operations.

The well-known example of Louis Vuitton in Paris, which has lasted for decades, perfectly illustrates the problem: the difference in retail price between Paris and Tokyo was around 40 per cent, justified by customs duties and the very high cost of 'retail' in Japan. For an ordinary Japanese tourist, it was therefore advantageous to buy yourself or your family a Vuitton bag in Paris, by way of souvenir, but once the customs duty had been paid (around 30 per cent in 1986), it was not an extraordinary bargain.

But if the bags could be introduced to Japan without paying taxes it became very advantageous; if, moreover, you had Japanese money to be laundered (in which case the criminals are ready to pay around 30 per cent laundering commission), the bargain became extremely profitable: the demand for Vuitton products in Japan was such that a new bag was sure to be resold immediately, at the local market price. Under these conditions, the pressure exerted on the Avenue Marceau shop, the only Vuitton shop in Paris at the time, was terrible. The company therefore decided to limit sales to one product (bag, suitcase) per family and per foreign traveller, in order to halt the traffic, despite French law, which did not permit this limitation. The result: every passer-by was stopped in the street, and offered a cash commission to go in and buy a Vuitton bag. We know of many students of our generation who earned their pocket money this way, but who never understood why normal Japanese people were giving them money to buy products in the shop close by!

The global price

This is the strategy that is required when the product price is very high and its size small, and therefore easily transported (or hidden from customs). The paragon of this is jewellery and watchmaking. In these cases, the price is the same everywhere, accounting for exchange rates. In this case, there is no risk of trafficking or pressure exerted on the company, but conversely, all the monetary fluctuations, taxes and transport costs eat into the margin.

The case of Duty Free

This is a hybrid of the two previous cases, inasmuch as it is not a genuine global price, nor a genuine local price: the status of Duty Free Zones is specific, and Duty Free is cheaper than the local market.

This 'travel market' is best considered as a separate universe, in particular because of its monopoly situation: the manager of the airport has a de facto monopoly, and is therefore the only client; they can therefore impose conditions – often stringent ones. Moreover, it is necessary to master the frontiers with local markets.

In luxury products, it is perfume that is most closely concerned with this market, since the case of alcohols and tobaccos is very specific, due to the heavy taxation that they are subjected to, and the quota system on 'duty-free' imported objects.

Pricing policies linked to demand

These were originally the norm in luxury, in the era of 'case by case', client by client, with orders that were unique every time. Then they became marginal, with the democratization of the latter half of the 20th century. New technologies (the computer, then the internet) gave them a second lease of life. Here again, two major families can be distinguished.

Price variation is linked to time, but is managed by the brand

This is the well-known field of 'yield management', which principally concerns the leisure industry (transport, cruises, the hotel business). It will become increasingly important in the luxury domain, since the sectors involved are developing rapidly, and this technique can be easily adapted to luxury, in particular as a gate of entry to the brand for new consumers. They can access the desired service at a lower cost, the economy being clearly justified (an 'out-of-season' Relais & Châteaux, for example). This is therefore not a marked-down product. However, it should not be used as a method for filling spaces, as is commonly done in classic products.

Take the example of a luxury cruise, where the clientele is often somewhat older. If the company that charters the boat does a 'special newlyweds offer', the clients who have paid the full fare will not feel affronted, because a honeymoon is an exceptional time, and they would not be shocked if on such an occasion a favour was done for newlyweds. On the contrary; it will remind them of the good times of their own youth. If, however, the company makes a 'last-minute' offer, addressed to everyone over the internet, leading to complete filling of the boat and therefore saturation of the services offered during the cruise, those clients who have paid the full fare will not be happy to receive in return a less effective service, to the benefit of ordinary clients who have obtained exceptional financial conditions. Those of us who have already experienced this situation, particularly common in air travel, have certainly not enjoyed it. The luxury brand is exclusive: if it leaves the door ajar, it is only for socially justifiable reasons (special occasions, etc).

This example is a good illustration of the rules to be observed:

- Never penalize existing clients through a lowering of service quality due to new arrivals, and at all costs avoid them feeling insulted, since they have paid 'full price'.
- Have a positive explanation for the special price ('honeymoon', 'low season', etc).
- Do not lower the service quality for those who have profited by the special offer: it must remain a luxury product for all clients.
- Ensure that those who have obtained a favour are worthy of being part of the club of clients (anti-law number 4: 'Keep non-enthusiasts out'): the luxury brand is segregationist.

The price varies freely according to the offer and the demand

This is the world of auctions, originally reserved for exceptional products (namely art) and concentrated in a few, relatively inaccessible places (auction rooms), but which modern technology is revolutionizing and allowing to generalize: since a luxury product gains value as it ages, an important second-hand market will grow up, and computing and the internet will enable it to be monetarized (via eBay for example).

No sales in luxury

The sales, a significant and public reduction in price whose aim is to sell off unsold or poorly-selling products, are the total opposite of luxury. The price, and therefore the value, of a luxury product should increase over time, and not suddenly crumble, showing that ordinary clients have been robbed:

- A luxury product should be timeless, not quickly become obsolete.
- The purchase of luxury is a deliberate, considered act, not an impulse; sales play on the mimesis of appropriation, an acquisitive fever, not on dreams.
- The price should be in the background in luxury, and not in the foreground as it is in sales – a gift from the sales is a depreciated gift: in the sales, you buy the price, not the product.

Consequently, any brand that holds sales cannot be a luxury brand, or, more precisely, the products in the sales cannot be luxury products. This is generally the case for complementary 'fashion' ranges of luxury brands. Sales are vital in fashion: fashion is the collective organization of programmed individual change. Several times a year, it is necessary to bring the client into the shops and cause them to buy. Shops therefore need to make space for the new offer. Unsold items from the previous collection may be subject to sales, or turn up in a brand sales centres (such as McArthur Glenn) where the brand boutiques sell new products from old collections.

Although they are structural to textile and footwear lines in fashion, sales are proscribed in luxury: on this point, there is total divergence between luxury and fashion, and we can even say that this is the concrete aspect that most differentiates a luxury brand from a fashion brand. Strict control over product policy, manufacturing and distribution is indispensable in order to avoid them. For example, a house such as Louis Vuitton, which sometimes sells 'fashion' bags, will destroy the unsold stock at the end of the season rather than sell it at a discount: this apparently anti-economical action is in fact the consequence of the strict application of a luxury strategy in leather goods, and the benefits to its image of this rigour largely make up for the cost of the destruction of a few fancy handbags.

Price reductions?

It may be opportune to give a price advantage in certain cases to particular clients.

In order not to damage the brand and to legitimize a reduction in price, this approach must be personalized and individualized: you do not lower prices because you can't sell off the product; on the contrary, it is the brand that decides to enable such or such customer to benefit from favourable treatment. The key point is to manage this personal aspect well: by lowering the price, you are not devaluing the product, but giving greater value to the client, since you enable them to make a good bargain.

The two most legitimate reasons and ways of doing this, both at an image and an economic level, are:

- Seducing discerning clients who are blasé, or who feel guilty because they already own many of the brand's products: they will buy yet another product, on the pretext (either to themselves, or to their partner!) that it is 'a bargain'. The key point is this: it is a brand that they like, and continue to like; not only does this offer not put them off the brand, but this advantage makes them like the brand even more; in fact, it is a loyalty gift that the brand is giving them. Moreover, rather than being compulsive buyers, they are shrewd buyers. The *sine qua non*: never do this with anyone who is not already a loyal client of the brand.
- Giving a new client the opportunity to discover the brand universe. In order to avoid any misunderstanding, the reason for the advantage should be clear, and moreover be clearly perceived as legitimate. This could be, for example, a special offer for newlyweds, or for a first child, or for obtaining a prestigious degree.

As we have seen above, 'yield management' is a very effective tool for areas such as leisure and tourism, since it makes it possible to manage with extreme precision.

The price and its communication

This point summarizes all the specificities and complexity of price management in luxury: when, how, and to whom should you communicate the price of a luxury product (in the broader sense). This is a game of seduction, of the unsaid; this is the eroticism of luxury: 'Always thinking about it, never talking about it':

- The price should be known, but as an 'understatement'.
- 'If you have to ask the price, you can't afford one' (Charles Rolls, co-founder of Rolls-Royce).

In general, the price level (not the exact price) of the brand's flagship products should be known, not only by potential clients, but also by a broad fringe of the population, as broad as possible (a function of luxury's social restratification, and of the signalling of social distance).

Moreover, it is desirable for the presumed price to always seem higher than the actual price. Here again, we find the opposite of the entry-level price strategy of common consumption goods, where the idea is to lure clients in with very low prices, trying to sell them a more expensive product, for example by means of supplementary options, as with cars, where the basic version has a steering wheel and four wheels and not much else.

There are two virtuous effects of the presumed price seeming higher than the actual price:

- It gives higher value to the gift. A large part of the luxury market is in fact a gift market, with its own rules: in particular, when giving gifts, a high price, or better yet, a reputedly high but unknown price, is a plus.
- The uninitiated client discovers that 'for what you get, it's not all that expensive': the price of the luxury is fully justified (reassurance after the purchase).

The price is not publicly advertised

This is the consequence of the price logic in luxury. Advertising for a luxury product never mentions its price, or indicates it very discreetly, but it is also necessary to avoid mentioning it in the shop, and particularly in the shop window; if legal constraints make it necessary, it should be done as discreetly as possible.

The ideal strategy is summed up in two points:

- the price level is known to all, and if possible overestimated;
- only the person who pays knows the exact price.

The best example is a luxury restaurant: menus without prices for the guests, a menu with prices for the person who pays the bill (discreetly identified: nowadays it is not always the man who pays...), or a prepaid bill, or a bill sent later. In any case, the intimate relation between luxury and gifts should be management's guide to the way in which prices are communicated.

The price must be sold

We will deal with this point in Chapter 10 on distribution, but here is the key aspect: price is often the only thing that there is to sell at the shop level, since a luxury product is not sold – it is bought by the client; in any case, it is the last thing to be sold, and sometimes not sold at all: the blank cheque, the person who signs the bill apparently without even looking. The salesperson's role is key in this process: it is to explain to the client the entire symbolic value of the product, explain in detail the refinement of its raw materials, all the work that the object embodies, which more than justify the price. The client must understand that, for the quality and the prestige that are obtained, the product is in fact quite cheap: this is very important in the rationalization and reassurance after purchase that always takes place.

The price must retain some mystery. Consequently, all communication must make an effort to position the product at the highest possible, still credible, price, all without ever mentioning it directly.

Note that this is one of the trickiest points on the use of the internet in luxury, and is one of the major reasons why luxury has so far avoided the internet as a means of selling: we will deal again with this problem in Chapter 10.

10 Distribution and the internet dilemma

In every major city of the world, luxury shops are flourishing, luxury malls are opening up, and the most beautiful streets are being transformed into luxury streets. This ostentation is proof, if proof were needed, of how distribution plays a key role in luxury management.

Luxury is in the distribution

The watchword of luxury brand management nowadays is 'experience', the multi-sensory total of what is lived and felt at each point of contact with the brand. The shop is where the client can live the brand. This is how Zara built its reputation: although it is a very cheap fashion range, the shops themselves do not look cheap; they are pleasant and add value, from Madrid to Shanghai. If the sales point is a source of value creation for mass brands, we should expect much more from luxury brands. Moreover, the origin of many luxury houses is in distribution:

advice' aspect of the sale is very important in luxury. Hence the importance of stability of the staff in boutiques and the continual training of sales personnel and the greater importance of their feeling of belonging to the house.

As a consequence, distribution must be done in such a way that the client buys in calm (no forced sales, no pressure from the salespeople) and security (the true product at the true price). In fact, you are not selling the product to the client, but it is the client who buys the product – giving rise to the following apparent paradox.

It is the price, not the product, that is sold to the client

When you walk into a supermarket, you are assaulted by a number of signs, hanging from the ceiling or attached to shelves, where enormous figures are spelled out in the largest possible font and in the most visible colours: these are the prices of the product that the shop is recommending to you. Not to mention the profusion of promotional offers of the three-for-two, or BOGOF ('buy one get one free') variety. When you come closer to the products to pick one up, the prices are again advertised in large letters: in contrast, if you want information on a product, you must roam the store until you find a salesperson to inform you... if one is available. In fact, you have the impression that the act of buying in these stores is limited to the choice of a price – which is often the case.

Conversely, when you enter a luxury shop, no price is visible at first glance; if you want to find the price of a product for yourself, it is necessary to under-take complex research; indicating the price of a product is clearly the last thing on the mind of the person in charge of laying out the products ('merchandizing'). You are left with the impression, rather, that you have wandered into an art exhibition, where objects are displayed, and not a 'point of sale'. Even on the watches aisle at the Galeries Lafayette department store, it is significant that the nine Chanel watches presented side by side do not each display their price: all the prices are indicated to one side, separately, in a pres-entation that reproduces the visual arrangement of the nine watches so that you can tell which watch corresponds to which price.

There are salespeople there, of course, available; but if you ask them the price of the product that you are interested in, they will initially respond at a tangent, showing you the refined details of the product; you have to be insis-tent for them to tell you the price. In fact, salespeople in the store are not there to sell, but to make you understand, to share the mystery, the spirit of the place, of the objects, and the time embodied in each object.

When the client discovers the price, in the end they will find it not that high for the quality of product that they are buying.

Our anti-law number 12, 'Luxury sets the price', is applied to the letter here: the role of the store and the sales personnel is indeed to make the potential purchaser understand all the refinements of a product, all those aspects that make it a luxury product. This leads us to a conclusion that is surprising for classic marketing: the true role of the salesperson is not to sell the product – it is to sell the price.

The price is even often the only thing that the store really has to sell: the product the client desires is often on allocation or on a waiting list. If the product, nevertheless, requires selling, since the client is undecided (a common case with gifts), the price still needs to be sold.

Sometimes, there is no need even to sell the price (the blank cheque, the person who signs the bill apparently without even looking). In this case, the role of the store and the sales personnel appears in its purest form: sell the luxury of the product. This has a fundamental consequence: the sales personnel should never earn direct sales commission.

The sales personnel should never earn direct sales commission

This is logical, since their role is not to sell the product! If the salesperson does their work well, but doesn't close the sale, the client will buy later on; often, the client comes back within the hour to make the purchase, having needed the additional time to finalize the decision. If the person who has done the long work of selling has gone to lunch, and another salesperson closes the sale, often in this case in just a few minutes, an individual percentage bonus on the sale would be unfair.

Moreover, sales commission induces aggressive behaviour among salespeople (this is, after all, its purpose!): they rush at the client, or even fight among themselves. In such conditions they are far from showing respect for the client's desire and the creation of the dream!

Distribution shows that the brand dominates the client... but respects them

In every affective relationship, there is a dominator and a dominated; in the case of the affective client–brand relationship, it is the brand that dominates the client. But, as in the affective parent–child relationship for example (very close to the brand–client relationship), the fact that one dominates the other does not mean that they do not respect them; otherwise, it is not an affective attachment, and a brand that does not respect its client is no more a luxury brand than a father who does not respect his children is a true father.

This relationship, intrinsic to luxury, is a logical one: if the client is seeking social elevation in a luxury product, it is clearly with a brand whose social status is higher than theirs; to carry it is to appropriate part of the brand's value to increase your own. Let us also note that in consequence, each product sold carries away part of the brand value and weakens it; it is therefore necessary to continually regenerate it (see the dream equation, page 129).

This specificity of luxury in the client–brand relationship is manifest in the distribution:

- the client often asks the brand, through its sales personnel, for a prescription on what they need, or rather what it would be right to buy;
- in the case of a gift, the client often gives the salesperson free rein.

Here we find another of these contradictions that abound in luxury, and one of the most difficult to manage since it is a doubly subjective universe: from the side of the client (who is king, but expects help), and the side of the salesperson (who manages the game, but must convince the client); this implies a rigorous choice of personnel, and training of sales teams in listening to the client.

Here, again, the role of the sales personnel is key in the application of anti-law number 6: 'Dominate the client', that is, don't look for equality. It is clear that this law applies to the brand, and not to the sales personnel; on the contrary, the warmth and friendliness of the sales personnel should reassure the client and cause them to feel that they are indeed king (or queen): the true 'class' of a salesperson is that of charm, elegance and finesse, not arrogance or pretension.

This is much harder to achieve than one might think: despite the genuine friendliness of almost all the sales personnel in the Louis Vuitton stores, there were constant complaints towards the end of the 1980s about the 'arrogance' of the staff. They were not responsible for this: the stores were too cold and impersonal (architecture as rigid as the suitcases, colours as dark as the Monogram, products under glass cases to protect the leather, sales behind a counter). It was necessary to completely rethink the store concept. With the new, warmer, more open concept, where you could touch the products, the complaints disappeared... although it was still the same staff in attendance!

Distributing is first of all about communicating

A famous management proverb reminds us that when you are not seen in a store, you cannot say that you have distribution there. Distribution is communication. We should add that nowadays, this perception goes beyond sight; it is also tactile, olfactory and auditory. The store is a screen (for the projection of the brand's history) but also a metaphor for the setting that places the object of desire at a distance, in order to increase that desire. Let us examine the facets of this communication.

The window of the luxury store is a privileged place and a major tool of public communication, and the only one in which the brand controls all the parameters. It is a good way of making non-customers aware of the status of the brand, and of the people who carry it: windows play a big role in the 'dream equation', so important in luxury. The store is always located in a highly symbolic place, and every care is taken over the window: a good shop window is the place to present complex and refined messages, in particular through the use of lighting, impossible to transcribe into advertising photography.

The store is the showcase in which products are presented; it must therefore display them to advantage, but also in context. It is also the scene in which the representation of the brand universe is played out, with the sales personnel as its actors – and with audience participation!

The whole universe of the brand must be able to be displayed at a sales point; this does not mean, of course, that all sales points should express all the dimensions of the brand, but that there must be at least one store in which all the dimensions of the brand are expressed together, just as a great symphony orchestra must be able to bring all the instruments together in order to make them play an orchestral score.

The development of the great brands into many luxury universes has led to the concept of the 'megastore', which is both a manifestation of the coherence of all the brand universes for all to see, and a demonstration of power.

The store must make explicit (without words!) the brand's evolution, hence the notion of the 'store concept'; it is imperative that this accompanies the brand evolution.

We have seen above the influence of the new concept at Louis Vuitton in the late 1980s on the clients' perception of the sales and welcoming staff, but the evolution was much deeper: it coincided with the launch of the Epi line, whose bright colours and market core (fine leather goods) marked a departure from the Vuitton past (darker colours of the Monogram, travel market core).

It was therefore necessary to rethink the entire architecture of the store, without, however, giving the impression of a rupture. It was absolutely unthinkable that the 'new concept' should make the Monogram line and the image strategy centred on travel brutally obsolete. On the contrary, the new store concept had to communicate to the client that, while remaining a great luxury brand in luggage, symbolized by the Monogram canvas, Louis Vuitton had also become a great brand in fine leather goods and town bags.

Distribution should not only show off, but enhance the product image

Let us go further: we have seen already to what degree art and luxury are linked, and even more so luxury and modern art; the store must signal that the luxury object is an *objet d'art*. The 'performance' by Vanessa Beecroft, with these bodies intertwined with Vuitton suitcases in the luggage section of the Champs-Elysees store, is an illustration. We should also quote Andy Warhol: 'someday, all department stores will become museums, and all museums will become department stores'. Hence the systematic recourse, for the megastores mentioned above, to prestigious architects: the modernity and prestige of the brand should be evident as soon as you lay eyes on the store.

It is distribution's job to communicate the brand's price level

A luxury brand never communicates directly on price. One of distribution's roles is therefore to communicate the price to the client, in two ways: the store must communicate the price level, and the salesperson must indicate to the client the exact price of the product.

Everything should be done, in the appearance of the store and the management of client relations, to suggest the product's price level, without announcing it in so many words; the sales points should of course be very elegant, but placed at the brand's exact level, through their placement (hence the 'luxury streets') through their architecture and their internal design, and of course through the style of the sales personnel. Take care, however, not to go overboard, or you will be met with financial disaster, with clients refusing to enter a store that is too pretentious in relation to the brand's standing. You need to know in which category you are competing.

A luxury purchase is a lengthy act

The moment of purchase is only one step, although of course a vital one, of the process through which the client enters the brand universe; in fact, the purchase of a luxury product is a long process, where each step is important:

- The pre-purchase, where they dream of the product. The brand must prepare the dream through its communications strategy, and long before the act of purchasing; in luxury, the time lapse between the act of communication and its practical outcome is often counted in years. The marketing director of BMW in the USA, when asked what was the point of his advertising, replied: 'My job is to make sure that all young Americans over 18 dream of a BMW before they fall asleep at night.' This implies that you cannot 'launch' a luxury product, much less a brand, as you would a washing powder.
- The moment of purchase: the pleasure that they should feel at that moment is an integral part of the luxury of the product itself. The aesthetic environment is of course very important, but the human environment is even more so: the client should not feel simply at ease faced with the brand; they should also not feel under pressure to buy.
- The after-purchase: it is necessary to reassure the client that they were indeed right to spend so much, putting in perspective the heart of the brand itself, its values, its heritage, its fundamentals, its demands.

The luxury product gains value over time, either in itself if it is durable (a bottle of a great wine), or in the memory if consumption of the product is immediate (like that of a journey or a cruise). In the latter case, the brand should help in commemoration, through objects, such as the metal ashtray that Air France used to offer each traveller on Concorde, or through the personal contacts afterwards; we continue to receive greetings from the Oriental in Bangkok several years after our stay. We also recall the role of the luggage labels of palaces.

The brand must absolutely foster, and help to create, this feeling, both on principle (remaining a luxury brand), and through commercial effectiveness: clients will come back, and will tell their friends. 'Buzz marketing' is a child of luxury.

This has given rise to the concept of the 'magalogue' (such as 'Le Monde d'Hermès'), a hybrid between the luxury magazine that makes you dream and initiates you into the codes of luxury, and the brand catalogue, designed to make you buy. Hence the little booklets which accompany the product, containing of course the instructions for use, but mostly beautiful images of the brand universe, of which you have purchased a part along with the product.

There is therefore no concept of luxury without:

- monitoring of the product right up to the end client;
- personal knowledge of this client, not only their tastes and preferences, but also lifestyle;
- accompanying of the client, so that the purchase gains value over time.

Strict control over distribution, in all the key aspects of the brand (product policy, price, merchandizing, communication) is vital in luxury; the personalized human relationship is crucial, and the idea of the 'client file' is to be discouraged, in particular in the form of automatic IT management, which is often used in CRM (client relationship management) strategies.

However, a very discerning CRM is necessary to maintain the unique relationship that you can have with a shop manager who knows you so well that they alert you to new products that you in particular will like. It makes it possible to anticipate a client's annual journey from New York to Monaco, and to alert the Monaco store. Luxury's main clients are great travellers: they expect that their brand will recognize them everywhere they go.

Distribution is luxury's weak link

Each of the four aspects of the luxury relationship (affective relationship, dominant position, communication of codes, long-term management) is already difficult to manage; the major difficulty in managing the 'one-to-one' of luxury is that all four must be managed at once, and by the same people; the sales teams are therefore one of a brand's great strengths, and their stability is of the utmost importance.

The principal difficulties to be managed are the cost of distribution, and the maintenance of its quality from day to day.

The cost of personalized distribution is very high

Based on human relations and not on systems, it is very difficult to rationalize, both because you cannot use standardized 'instruction manuals' for salespeople to read (it must be passed on through ongoing and very personalized training), and because you cannot rely on written reports from salespeople on the problems clients have encountered: it is vital to discuss them face to face... and therefore to be continually on the move.

Not only is the cost high, but it increases as the brand develops; you could even call it a 'diseconomy of scale' in this case. In selective distribution, there are of course economies of scale on material aspects (furniture and shop design, software), but for the most expensive aspect (the personnel), the opposite is true: competent salespeople are rare, and it is difficult and costly to move them when you need to open a new sales point, particularly in another country.

Opening a new sales point is to a brand what having another child is to a family: a marvellous and longed-for, but very costly event.

Day-to-day management is a delicate matter

The most difficult problem is that raised by the multicultural aspect of sales nowadays.

If conflicts of culture are to be found at all levels of a multinational organization, it is at the retail sales level that they are most obvious, not as a result of language problems, but of cultural and behavioural problems. By working hard at a language that is not your mother tongue, you can relatively easily become bilingual or trilingual; becoming bicultural is extremely difficult. If the client is to perceive the brand universe clearly, it is necessary that the salesperson should be from the same culture as the client: Japanese in Japan, Chinese in China, French in France, but also from the same universe as the brand (Italian for an Italian brand). Bicultural people are rare and expensive.

This is why it is so important to find a good local partner who will manage all the 'retail' aspects of operations, even when you have integrated distribution; in fact, if you cannot find a local partner in a particular country or city, it is better not to open a store there, since there must be a problem there that has escaped the central management. This is also why it is important that managers travel regularly, so that they can truly understand what is happening on the ground and immediately rectify any aberrations.

The choice of a new sales point is not delegable

The decision to open a new sales point should never be made without a prior in-depth visit by the CEO or managing director. This is the main weakness of distribution licences at the brand's core: you are de facto delegating location decisions that have a long-term structuring effect on the perceived level of the luxury brand in question – which is often far from the level desired by the brand, and which, moreover, risks blocking its development. There is no other way at this moment but to buy back these licences, but the cost is often very high, and above what these licences have brought in: in the spring of 2007 Ralph Lauren had to buy back its principal Japanese *prêt-à-porter* licence for $155 million.

As for licences linked to complementary ranges, they involve taking major risks due to an absence of control prior to the opening of any new sales points specific to the accessories in question, all the more so when located in a distant country. This is how to destroy value while increasing sales: when the Richemont group bought Lancel, it found itself confronting a serious problem in Japan, since the brand had lost all value due to licences on all sorts of articles, sold in locations without any kind of prestige. These licences, which had previously brought in a great deal of income, were no longer bringing anything in at the time of the buyback, and had in addition destroyed the status of the core range products, bags and suitcases.

Distribution must manage rarity

By its own construction, from the beginning, luxury, being reserved for an elite, is rare; rarity and luxury are thus consubstantial.

From the moment that luxury democratizes, if it loses the attribute of rarity, it loses its essence and becomes common; if the only differentiating factor is the price, it becomes snobbish. In order to maintain its status, a luxury product must deserve it, whether through financial (price) or cultural (initiation) effort, by dedicating time (going to a given city and into a specific shop) and patience (waiting list) to it, etc.

Part of the rarity follows automatically from the conception of the luxury product: precious raw materials, manual work by qualified artisans, hence the inertia, both upwards and downwards, of the production system. On the 'non-automatic' aspects, there should be an organized penury; management of rarity is an integral part of the luxury strategy, and selectivity is the consequence of this where distribution is concerned. This rarity should be perceptible at all levels:

- few sales points;
- precise locations;
- quality sales personnel;
- the shop as a showcase;
- merchandizing as staging for the product.

Distribution protects you from competition

At the retail sales level, there is no competition, but rather two brands complementing each other.

A specificity of luxury is that, since each brand is its own universe, it is difficult to compare two luxury brands, except in vague terms such as 'level'; in fact, a client does not desire a product from house X or a product from house Y, but a product from one and the other.

Consequently, the proximity of two stores for two brands of 'equivalent level' is not a problem, quite the reverse: each strengthens the other from the image and social codes point of view. It is perfectly natural to walk into a Cartier store with a Hermès product wrapped in one of the brand's paper bags; you will not be asked to leave it at the door, but rather, they will try to find out what you bought at Hermès, in order to sell you a complementary Cartier product!

Hence the 'luxury streets' that we have already discussed, where you are among the right kind of people, and where less noble brands seek to implant themselves to increase their value, in the same way that we seek to frequent the society of people 'superior' to ourselves in order to elevate ourselves.

Luxury and mode of distribution

Almost any system of distribution can work for luxury, always provided that all the rules we listed above are respected. Having said this, according to the products and the markets, some are more suitable than others.

The own brand store

This is of course the first distribution system that we think of, since it is the most natural and the most coherent with the origin of luxury and the notion of personal relationship.

Admittedly there are considerable advantages: perfect control over the brand from all points of view (products, price, image) and high economic efficiency. Intermediaries are expensive in terms of margin points, but also in spoiled products, mismanaged stock, and are also a distorted screen placed between the client and the brand, which is very damaging in the management of product ranges.

An own brand store makes it possible, in particular, to know exactly and in real time which products are selling, leading to a very precise steering of the logistical chain.

On this point, the system is very effective: we calculated at the time that a competitor, not having integrated their production and not selling through their own network, would have had to sell a bag at twice the price that Louis Vuitton sold it in order to make ends meet. In fact, the exceptional (sometimes criticized) margins at Louis Vuitton did not arise from excessively high prices,

- Only distribution (Fauchon).
- Essentially distribution (Hermès).
- Workshop/shops in tandem (Louis Vuitton).

Distribution is also the most awkward part to manage on a daily basis, once the brand has a global reach: ensuring coherence and strategic rigour, while remaining profitable, when you are embedded in countries that are totally different culturally and economically, requires considerable engagement and energy from management. Furthermore, the distribution is often entrusted to local partners, which in fact comes down to entrusting client service and client experience to them.

Distribution is generally the weak link of luxury strategy, and this is where many brands die or lose their status. Note also that in the world of fashion and luxury there seems to have developed a kind of first division: the brands capable of financing 'cathedrals' on the most desirable main streets of the world. The costs of the ever-increasing rents on Ginza or 5th Avenue lead the large luxury groups to think in terms of real estate and to build genuine real estate strategies in order to be able to compete in this first division.

You sell to someone before you sell something

During the sale, a personal, quasi-affective relationship must be created between the brand and the client. This relationship is vital in luxury: at its roots, a luxury product is remitted (rather than sold) by a given person to a given person. This 'one-to-one' relationship is an integral part of the DNA and universe of luxury. You sell to someone before you sell something: this relationship has an affective side that is very important from the beginning (even a king places himself in the hands of his suppliers), and persists in today's world (you put your trust in 'your' salesperson).

Both in its 'social stratification' aspect and its 'for yourself' aspect, luxury has a strong human, purely relational dimension. Its role is also to offer human warmth in an aggressive and impersonal world. Contrary to too-popular belief, the salesperson in luxury should certainly not be distant, but on the contrary warm and friendly. They do not know who tomorrow's good clients are: these future clients will walk in like anyone else into one of the brand's boutiques, and will also judge the brand on how it welcomes an anonymous shopper.

The client often enters the boutique without any idea of what they will buy, particularly when looking for a gift; they often trust entirely in the salesperson's opinion, and will prefer someone they already know: the 'personal but from the removal of all costs and damages due to intermediaries. Louis Vuitton's competitiveness was therefore structural.

The other major advantage, and perhaps the most important, of the own brand store is the human aspect: the sales personnel are really part of the brand, and are the brand for all clients; the quality of the link with the client is therefore very strong: at Louis Vuitton, the store managers have always had priority access to the company management.

One final point: it is the only distribution system that completely protects the client from counterfeiting and enables the company to counter this scourge effectively; since the brand only sells in its own stores, any product bought elsewhere is of dubious origin, to say the least: a fake, or a product that has been used for money laundering.

Having said this, this system has the major failing of any vertically integrated system: it is very rigid, both at the top and at the bottom. It therefore presupposes a very reactive and anticipatory management, but also a stable product range. It also presupposes that the product can be sold in sufficient quantities and at a sufficient pace to make a store profitable (which excludes a trade such as jewellery, but is appropriate for fine leather goods), but conversely the quantities sold and the sales pace should not be too much for a store network (which excludes perfume, or strongly diffused products such as Cartier's 'Must').

Exclusive distribution

This is also very suitable for luxury, since it preserves the personal relationship to the brand, provided that the distribution agreement specifies that sales can only take place in the specified location, and by the specified personnel, and that there should be total transparency regarding the clientele and the conditions granted them. This system is particularly suitable when there already exists a vast, quality sales network, and the product has strong after-sales constraints that require a vast network; the best-known examples are watchmaking and cars.

Rolex, for example, has succeeded in becoming the global number one luxury watchmaking brand, and the most profitable, without developing any stores under its own name, but by relying on a network of very high-quality exclusive distributors.

The biggest advantage in comparison to the exclusive own-brand store network is that this system is much more flexible and the break-even point of a store here is much lower (overheads are shared with other brands). Moreover, it is very easy to have a mixed network (own brand stores and exclusive distributors) without damaging the brand: the success of Cartier is ample proof.

Selective distribution

The major difference relative to exclusive distribution is that the brand no longer chooses its distribution network. In the European legal context, any sales point that respects the brand's specifications can distribute its products.

This admittedly protects the product environment by respecting the brand's codes, and therefore makes it possible to preserve a minimum of the universe, but it is the first step towards departure from the luxury universe, since the direct link between clients and brand has been broken: they are clients of the sales point, no longer of the brand.

The advantage of this system is that it enables wide diffusion of the product, without, however, making it common. This distribution will therefore be used for luxury products with wide distribution and frequent purchase, such as perfume.

The major disadvantage, on the other hand, is that you very quickly cross the barrier that separates 'luxury' from 'premium', and we may legitimately ask how often products sold in selective distribution, such as perfume, remain in the luxury universe. It is also enough to see how far the 'gift with purchase' has invaded the perfume market over the past 10 years, illustrating the fall in the product's status.

The other disadvantage of this distribution system is the 'grey market': since the prices are no longer controlled, products arriving from zones with lower prices, and particularly Duty Free zones, have the troublesome tendency to invade the zones with higher prices, exerting a strong downward pressure on prices, and therefore on margins. The vicious circle of brand impoverishment is set in motion.

One final disadvantage: since it is very difficult to check that all sales points respect the brand's 'code', qualitative degradation is inexorable (bad money drives out good). Despite the armies of controllers and constant court cases against 'discounters' who sell perfumes, the outcome of the battle is inescapable: you must spend more and more money on communication and advertising to recharge the product image, while margins continue to fall.

The example of perfume in selective distribution is a good example of what we said at the beginning of the chapter: 'distribution is generally the weak link of luxury strategy, and this is where many brands die'; the risk is very high for perfume, despite being one of luxury's flagship products, that in a short space of time it will no longer be a luxury product but a 'mass luxury' product, a modern neologism that speaks volumes.

At-home sales

For the sake of completeness, we should not neglect this final mode of distribution, which in fact was luxury's original mode of sale (the artisan travelled to the client to take their order, then to deliver the product) and whose legitimacy remains total, in particular for very prestigious products such as *haute joaillierie*; you could not dream of better service, and in addition everything is carried out with the greatest discretion and security; the risk of the client being attacked by criminals is removed.

Luxury and internet distribution (the internet dilemma)

This is one of the problems for luxury today: an internet strategy is indispensable for a luxury brand. If the use of the internet as a means of communication, or an advertising and experiential tool, is unproblematic, the same cannot be said for distribution.

A luxury product can communicate via the internet, but should not be sold there

This position will no doubt come as something of a surprise to those readers who have visited the Gucci online store or Armani Collezione online. It is true that, one by one, some luxury brands are arming themselves with internet sales. Our point of view is not concerned with fashion or upper-premium brands, but with those that wish to follow a luxury strategy. Are Gucci and Armani correct?

Why are we opposed to the sale of luxury products on today's internet? Our opinion is governed by the dynamic of luxury itself.

On today's web, the personal relationship disappears quickly: the internet is an anonymous universe

You do not know who is talking to you, or rather who is really behind the computer; of course, this is not the case when you already know your interlocutor and the links are secure, but when this is not the case, the very concept of the internet makes it a universe on the opposite extreme from luxury as a sales tool (remember the importance of the personal human relationship in luxury). However, as far as existing clients go, the development of Web 2.0 is a significant opportunity for the brand to maintain an effective and legitimate exchange with them on everything to do with after-sales, presentation or even reservation of new products, with the objective remaining that of making the client come to the sales point regularly so that they maintain a physical link to the brand.

Today's internet world is a sensually reductive world: it is not experiential enough.

If the eyes and ears are well served, which is useful for presenting a hotel room or a concert, the senses of smell, taste and touch are ignored, or served in such a reduced, summary manner that the refinement and the multisensory component of luxury are excluded.

The internet world is a transparent and explicit one

Luxury, highly nuanced and difficult to quantify, is an intruder; in particular, the delicate price management of a luxury product is impossible to carry out correctly on the web, where everything is public. Moreover, for many, the internet is above all a good way to buy more cheaply – the opposite of the luxury approach.

The internet world is a virtual universe

Luxury is part of the real world, where its role is to bring the dream; the internet is a world of illusion, of the artificial, and in which the false can easily be introduced. We can see this clearly in the serious consequences that its use can lead to in terms of human relationships and the affective manipulation of adolescents (internet predators), but it is also visible in terms of counterfeit product sales: a recent study estimated the percentage of 'spam' linked to the sale of counterfeit products at 23 per cent.

The internet is a world of the instantaneous, the immediate, much closer to fashion than to luxury

In consequence, a product freely placed on sale on the internet by a brand is no longer a luxury product. If a luxury brand wishes nevertheless to sell products on the internet, whether to broaden its clientele or to sell off products, it will do so for articles that it has decided to exclude from its luxury universe. For example, a Chanel perfume might be sold over the internet, but Chanel would never sell its Chronographe watch online.

What luxury brands expect from Web 3.0

For luxury products to flourish on the internet, two conditions must be fulfilled: correct, personalized identification and multisensory experience. We will call this new 'luxury compatible', personalized, secure internet phase Web 3.0.

The absence of certainty of identification is prohibitive to internet sales; to be 'one to one', it is necessary to be sure that it is you I am talking to on the web, as I am sure that it is you who is coming into my shop. The current developments on internet security suggest that there will be a successful solution to this in the next decade.

On the other hand, what we have called 'negation of the senses', is obstructive but not prohibitive for luxury products. In this field, the evolution of the internet shows great contrast. It is gripping and fast for sound and vision – hence the interest of luxury sectors where these two senses are dominant, for example an online visit to a cruise ship and the showing of its ports of call. It is almost impossible for smell and taste, which will always be excluded – the scent of the atmosphere obtained by a device linked to the internet will never have the subtlety of a real perfume. The revolution is inexorable in terms of touch – we are beings for whom tactile communication is important (the caress of a loved one, the feel of a fabric) as is, more generally, 'increased reality'; they will have to be part of Web 3.0.

In conclusion, luxury brands wait impatiently for Web 3.0 in order to be able to consider the internet as a real channel of distribution. Therefore, our recommendation, as of today, is clear for luxury goods: always communicate via the internet, never sell on the internet. It is a significant difference between luxury on the one hand, and fashion and 'exclusivity' on the other: the latter two can sell on the internet without difficulty... and, moreover, they take full advantage of it.

11 Communicating luxury

Luxury and communication are consubstantial, since one of luxury's two fundamental roles, that of recreating social stratification, is pure communication. Moreover, luxury is a transmitter of taste. It must therefore be active at a cultural level.

Given that this aspect of luxury is strongly original and differentiates it from the universe of classic consumption goods, it results in a completely different use of communication from the habitual function of 'making sales'. In luxury, you communicate in order to create the dream and to recharge the brand's value, not in order to sell.

Luxury brand communication is situated far upstream of the purchase; the product and the brand universe are spoken of in a dreamlike way. It must also be sufficiently vague that many people can identify with it and find their personal share of the dream.

This implies refined and artistic communication, highly coded (luxury creates social codes) without being too dated, never direct, highly allusive. The practical consequences of this approach are that you can never judge the effectiveness of luxury communication by measuring its impact on a sales campaign.

Its qualitative impact is measured using classic tests, but also, most importantly, by asking existing clients, who are always delighted and flattered to be consulted, whether during a visit to the boutique, through a mailing to their home, or via the internet. This point is very important: a communication campaign aims at least as much to comfort existing clients, who will make another purchase or convince others to do so through 'word of mouth', as to conquer new clients:

- The value of a luxury brand depends on the quality of its image, much more than on its recognition.
- It is better not to communicate at all than to communicate in a mediocre way.
- A good campaign should be pursued for a long time, despite the often contrary opinion of the creative directors within advertising agencies.

The 'weariness' of advertisers, who live in a world of immediacy and fashion, is not that of clients, and the tempo of luxury is not that of fashion.

You don't talk about money

We concluded, in our discussion of the sociology of luxury in Chapter 1, that money was a raw material that luxury transformed in order to obtain a much more refined social stratification than that produced by money alone. When the transformation has been done well, the raw material should no longer be seen in its raw state, and it is pointless to communicate about it. To talk about money for a luxury product is to admit publicly that you have nothing better to say about it, and therefore to devalue it in the eyes of those 'in the know', precisely the people who support the dream.

In practical terms, the closeness between luxury and gifts offers a simple guide: you would no more communicate on price in luxury than you would leave the price sticker on a gift.

Not talking about money means:

- Not talking about the price of a product in communication, and if you are legally obliged to do so, it should be in small, hard-to-read characters.
- Talking about discounts or savings even less: we recognize an ordinary car from its advertising, which states the price in large type, and then in much smaller writing that this price relates to the basic, bare-bones model.
- Never talking about financial results, which are the acme of materiality.

One of the great advantages of Chanel is that, since it is not listed on the stock exchange, it is in no way obliged to give out its figures. In contrast, a serious problem for Louis Vuitton Malletier was the publishing of its results and its management secrets when Louis Vuitton merged with Moët-Hennessy to found LVMH, and then during the struggle for control of the group that followed the merger.

About its results

For clients, buying a Vuitton bag no longer meant participating in the brand's dream, but contributing at a rate of 80 per cent of the purchase price to increasing the net profit of a financial group, since emphasis had publicly been placed on the company's 'gross margin rate': this figure has little meaning in luxury, and even less for a vertically integrated company such as Louis Vuitton.

About its methods and secrets

Many began to copy its strategy, in particular at the distribution level, which was at the time completely original for a 'single product' luxury brand: creating an exclusive sales network in own brand shops.

You communicate because you sell

Let us pick up again on one of luxury's fundamental characteristics: each product sold carries with it a portion of the dream, and therefore weakens the brand. It is therefore necessary to recharge it constantly, as you recharge the battery of a torch that you are using: this is the second role of communication, with the first being to create the dream.

Remember that in the dream equation (p. 129), the dream is the function of the difference between brand recognition and brand diffusion. It is therefore necessary to compensate continually for this structural effect of image dilution, created by commercial success. This is unique to luxury: for a classic consumption good, or for a fashion product, diffusion in fact strengthens the image.

You communicate, you don't advertise

Since the role of communication in luxury is different from its role in classic markets, it is therefore hardly surprising that luxury's communication methods should be fundamentally different from the usual methods. As Figure 11.1 shows, the importance of the means of communication varies according to the level you are at on the pyramid. At the mass market level, media advertising plays a key role, with the stores being promoted. The closer you get to the summit, the less of a key role advertising plays; in luxury, it is secondary.

Of course you buy pages in glossy magazines, the media streets of luxury. What matters, however, are press relations and public relations. From this point of view, everything the brand does should be 'PR-able'. A brand that is not spoken about, that is not quoted, mentioned, whether in films or on television, or carried by a celebrity who is then caught on camera during her arrival at the Oscars ceremony – is that really a brand that counts? The brand is a transmitter of taste: as such it should be a sign of 'good taste'. In order to be recognized as such, it should display the visible signs of its adoption by those who make the front covers. It should be present in the high places of taste, living culture, and fashion, a little, as well.

Let us examine this luxury communication in detail.

No, or little, passive advertising (television)

With the well-known exception of perfume, luxury does not use the great media of television. Nowadays perfume is ruled more by the codes of premium and mass prestige than by the codes of luxury: it is found in integrated perfumery chains (Douglas, Marionnaud) or in the shops of the global Duty Free operators (DFS, etc). This is why it is delegated to traditional marketing institutions, who have mastered the techniques of large-scale

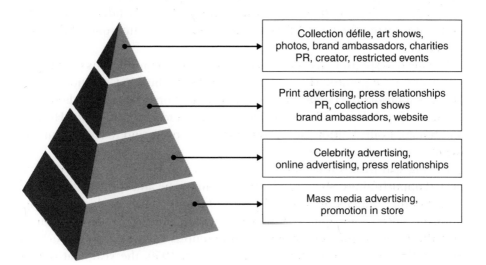

Figure 11.1   Layers of luxury communication

marketing. Delegating perfumes to traditional marketing experts leads to a profusion of new perfume launches, but also to a watering down of the identify of each one, and thus of the brand itself: traditional marketing begins with the client, not the brand. There are many clients, but only one brand.

Luxury seeks participation and active membership from the client; the use of a mass medium such as television does not meet this requirement. Moreover, television is a very expensive medium, and not at all selective: its strength is precisely that the cost per contact is very low... if you assume that all television viewers are potential clients. This is the case for perfume, but certainly not the case for luxury products.

Finally, a minimum time span is required to create a dreamlike universe, as luxury requests it; on television, every second counts.

A great deal of event PR and corporate patronage

At an event, you invite a physical person and can therefore take care of them: you can initiate a new client into the brand universe in a very personalized manner, or treat a very good client in the appropriate manner. Moreover, it is very easy to direct every detail of an event, and therefore ensure its coherence with the brand. The quality of the invitees reinforces the stratification.

Sponsorship and patronage are both equally legitimate for a luxury brand, always provided that they are coherent with the brand – which is not always easy, nor as obvious as in the case of the Lalique trophy for figure skating: everyone immediately makes the link between ice, elegance and a luxury crystal glass brand; on the other hand, apart from Hermès, very few luxury houses have their roots in the world of horses. Under these conditions, sponsoring the Grand Prix de Paris, as Louis Vuitton once did makes no sense.

You need to sponsor an event – since you can then control all its parameters – but not a competitor (Louis Vuitton sponsors the LV Cup, not a boat; Hermès sponsors the Grand Prix de Diane, not a horse); you must choose, an event that is coherent with the universe of the brand's core, its roots (Hermès and horses; Louis Vuitton and travel, therefore boats), and to concentrate on the most prestigious events.

Having said this, you need to be pragmatic, and know how to seize unexpected opportunities. Shaking a bottle of champagne and spraying the crowd is part of the winner's ritual at a Formula One race. This ritual is surprising, however, since champagne is a luxury beverage and not a shower product, and the Champagne region has no indigenous racing-car constructors. Where, then, does this custom spring from? In 1950, the year that the F1 World Championship was formed, the French Grand Prix took place at Reims, in the heart of the Champagne region. Paul Chandon Moët and Frédéric

Chandon de Brailles, who were great fans of motor racing, offered a Jeroboam (the equivalent of four bottles) of Moët et Chandon to the winner, Juan-Manuel Fangio. This gesture was appreciated, and was subsequently generalized to other prestigious motoring events. In 1966 the champagne offered to the winner of the Le Mans 24 Hour Race, Jo Siffert, was warm; the cork flew out and the wine sprayed out, showering the crowd around the foot of the podium. In 1967, the winner, Dan Gurney, voluntarily shook the bottle and sprayed the crowd. A tradition was born.

One last point: the luxury brand should not disperse itself across multiple events in multiple sectors but concentrate fully on a single universe, in which you can develop a very strong image by devoting all your available means to it.

The creation of a universe, and not simply pack shots

Every image should nurture all of the brand's imaginary, and not concentrate on a single product, which is only one element of the universe. This is why you must take care to define, make known and respect the brand's semantic constants and their system of codes.

Stability of the aesthetics over time

Given the hysteresis of communication in luxury (often many years elapse between the client's first contact with the brand and the first purchase), the strategic and aesthetic coherence of the communication is crucial, since it alone makes the cumulative effect possible.

No personalities in the advertising

We come now to one of our most surprising anti-laws, number 16: 'Keep stars out of your advertising'. In fact, we will even go further: don't put anyone in your advertising; if one or more human beings appear, they should be in the background, as part of the scenery.

This might seem provocative at first glance, but it is in fact both logical and coherent. Recall our conceptual analysis in Chapter 1: one of the specificities of a luxury brand is the personal relationship that the client maintains with it; it is necessary to allow the client's imaginary for the brand free rein, allowing the affective relation between the client and the brand to establish itself without interference, respecting the fluidity of this relationship and not coagulating it by interposing a third person, however well known. It is the relationship with the brand that is sought after in luxury, not the imitation of a third person.

This very important point has been repeated many times, in particular in the context of the analysis of René Girard's thinking: it is precisely because a luxury brand is desired for itself, and not only because you desire the desire of someone else for it, that luxury escapes the trap of 'triangular desire', the register of mass consumption goods and in particular of fashion.

The best way to avoid any ambiguity on this point is not to have any 'significant' personality appear in your advertising. If this is easy to do in markets other than personal apparel (cars, cruises, hotels), or for very technical products, such as watches or jewellery, it is much more difficult for the market of so-called 'fashion accessories'. Yet it is here, due to the risk of trivialization of the product and confusion with fashion products, that it is most important to take care on this point.

Using a 'star' is not helpful to the success of a beautiful advertising campaign; indeed, it is often harmful, since it screens off the direct affective client–brand relationship, or even destroys it by replacing it with the affective client–star relationship, while reducing the richness of the imaginary. In luxury, only the domination of the brand, as abstract as a god, is legitimate in the client's eyes, and not that of such-and-such an individual, especially not that of such-and-such a film star, who will fall out of fashion.

Often, the conspicuous use of a star is a way to hide the absence of creative ideas, replaced by the use of the cheque book to buy the celebrity of the moment. Luxury, however, owes it to itself to be particularly creative in communication so that the brand is not aged by the continual sale of 'eternal' products such as Hermès' Kelly bag.

The role of 'brand ambassadors'

After what we have just said, it might seem surprising to see famous personalities frequently appearing in luxury brand advertising. Does this mean that we are contradicted by the facts? Not at all! It means that you must underline the difference between paying a star to appear in an advertisement and using a personality as a 'brand ambassador'. In the latter case, you are placing yourself within the concept of 'ordinary product for extraordinary people'; you show the extraordinary personality using the product in everyday life. This is the case with Louis Vuitton's current campaign, showing Gorbachev, in his car in front of the Berlin Wall, using a common Vuitton product, in this case the Speedy bag that hundreds of thousands of people own, in their normal professional life.

The nuance between 'star', 'ambassador' and 'testimonial' is important. In luxury codes, you do not use a 'star' who exhibits the product, but a great personality using the product, or testifying that they use it. Or the brand ambassador might be taking an active role in the cultural or artistic projects of the brand. The luxury brand dominates the client (anti-law number 6). You should therefore not use a star whose recognition benefits the brand, through photos that implicitly suggest that the star's status is higher than that of the brand, which is an admission of weakness. You must have a 'testimonial' – that is, show that highly respected people normally use this brand's products, thus confirming their status as common products for exceptional people, and in so doing recognizing the power of the brand. A great luxury brand that applies this policy with continuity is Rolex, with great sportspeople respected by all, such as Meissner in the past or Justine Hénin recently.

The brand ambassador strategy (a single person who is paid to serve as an emblem of the brand, exclusively, and for a given period) is very different from the testimonial (various different personalities testifying at the same time that they use the product normally and not exclusively). This strategy is a source of difference between premium and luxury.

In order to illustrate this difference, let us take the case of perfume, a product for which the separation between 'luxury' and 'premium' is less clear. In this sector, the majority of luxury houses use different muses in turn: even Chanel, who have no brand ambassador, now use this strategy for 'No 5' perfume.

Some decades ago, with the famous example of Marilyn Monroe, who said that she wore nothing but a few drops of No 5 to bed, they were within the scope of the testimonial, and therefore within the codes of luxury. In 1968, associating No 5 with a star (Catherine Deneuve) in classic mass market advertising, Chanel toppled into a brand ambassador strategy, which it pursues to this day (currently with Nicole Kidman). This strategy is identical to that pursued by 'premium' brands such as Lancôme.

In fact, as we saw in Chapter 10 on distribution, the status of perfume as a 'luxury product' is increasingly debatable... and debated. Moreover, most great perfumes are in the universe of fashion brands, a universe in which the use of a muse is almost a generalized practice; in the case of No 5, the age of the perfume and its quality from all points of view make it a true luxury product in itself; adding a 'muse' makes it possible to keep its image up to date while keeping the perfume unchanged.

Tightening the social driver of desire

The social function of luxury is the permanent recreation of distance. This is why luxury is a club, which must appear all the more exclusive as the stores open up to an increasingly broad clientele. Being sold to more people should never mean that you are everybody's brand; quite the opposite.

How do you translate this club? In advertising, for example, it appears that all the luxury brands appear in the same glossy magazines: this is a typical manifestation of the club. The essential, however, is elsewhere: advertising is not the essential vector of luxury. The essential vectors are events that are simultaneously exclusive and incomparable, intensely translating the brand's values, to which only a minority are invited.

Little by little, over the years, in each global capital, the luxury brand thus builds itself a reputation as a creator of events that become 'musts', like the royal parties of yesterday.

What is the function of these events? First, to legitimize the brand's status as a creator of taste, a cultural transmitter. But also to create this social distance through the game of inclusion and exclusion: who is 'in'? who is 'out'? This is the management of buzz.

The black and white ball organized by Truman Capote on 28 November 1966 at the Plaza Hotel in New York remains a model of the genre. The dress code was dinner jackets and long dresses, with a mask: even the journalists and bodyguards had to wear masks. Truman Capote invited 540 friends, only the rich, powerful or famous. But he made 15,000 enemies that evening: in fact, he organized a leak and the *New York Times* published the list of invitees. All those who had not been invited therefore knew that they were not members of the club, and would do anything to be invited next time.

This is how the brand recreates distance. This brings us back to anti-law number 8 ('Protect... the big from the small'). Paul Ricard is the creator and promoter of a very popular aniseed brand. His success stemmed from this essential phrase that he would repeat to his salespeople: make a friend every day! After 50 years, that makes for a lot of friends. In luxury, to caricaturize the situation, it is sometimes the opposite: 'make enemies, by excluding them'.

Once the brand has been marked out as a transmitter of taste and events, this creates expectations each year. When winter arrives, rich Russians can talk only of the coming Martell evening at Courchevel. Two of luxury's essential constituents are present: time (the wait) and desire. Of course, as art demands, the brand must be very creative at these events.

In addition, if the luxury object leads to what Thorstein Veblen called conspicuous consumption, the event organized by the brand, if it has an artistic or cultural dimension, leads to what we must call 'conspicuous cultivation'. It must stimulate the connoisseur in everyone. Thus Royal Salute, a luxury whisky brand if ever there was one, brought John Major, the former British Prime Minister, to Shanghai for a meeting organized privately for over 100 Chinese company managers. Martell cognac would not hesitate to bring its cellarmaster from France for an exceptional occasion, such as a Hollywood party hosted by Steven Spielberg.

Permanently encourage word of mouth

One of the key consequences of these events is the fact that the media will relay it. It must be talked about. Rumour, as we know, is fed on marvels (Kapferer, 1990). Such events assume an attention to detail that will give rise to word of mouth. Thus, people still talk about the party organized by one of the world's richest men, Lakshmi Mittal, for his daughter's marriage in 2006: 1,000 people around the world were invited to a party that lasted for five days at the famous Chateau of Vaux le Vicomte in France. The buzz talked particularly about the invitation, 20 silk pages, in a silver casket, delivered in person to each invitee, wherever they were.

Everything the brand does should be made use of in press relations. A brand that the press does not talk about does not exist in this world. It is therefore necessary to feed the media constantly with news, stories, events, facts, etc, which weave the tale of the adventure of its products from conception to use. For example, two months before its launch, the Karl Lagerfeld advertising campaign for Dom Pérignon was presented to all *Condé Nast*'s editors. The brand must be 'mediactive', constantly generating content, whether through a press trip, press releases, leaks, etc. To borrow Danziger's expression (2005), the luxury brand should not be only expensive but expansive, that is, ever-present in selective media and locales.

What balance should there be between local and global communication?

One question is raised: who is negotiating with whom? Is it the brand's headquarters, in a centralized manner, or the countries? More generally, how is the local–global division managed in luxury? This is a central question for all brands: each is trying to find the right balance. In fact there are eight modalities for managing the global brand (Kapferer, 2008, p. 459). The luxury brand is one all to itself: it centralizes not only decisions, but also the execution of communication.

Headquarters defines and carries out all strategic communications, unifies the country-specific internet sites, comes up with and designs worldwide events, sponsorships, fashion shows, etc. The local management should take responsibility for perfect implementation of these, and for maintaining the cult of the brand. This is why it has a vital role in press relations, local public relations, relationships with VIPs and major clients. One final point: one of the sources of the brand's dream is its international character. Anything that 'localizes' the brand too much in the country of sale causes it to fall from its pedestal.

The internet and communication in luxury

We said in Chapter 10 on distribution that you should never sell a luxury product on the internet, and should limit internet use to CRM, and even then, with some care. In contrast, the internet offers remarkable and completely new opportunities for communication: doing without this new medium in a communication strategy would be an error. The basic rule of luxury is: 'Always communicate via the internet, but never sell on the internet.'

The codes of luxury communication

The luxury brand is a universe, not a promise. The luxury brand is experiential first and foremost. Its language is mostly non-verbal: it is primarily visual, and sensory. It is more its way of doing things, its referents, its aesthetic, its modes of expression that will weave the emotional relationship with its audiences than the words themselves.

Making the brand's visual language denser: the nine signatures of the brand

Of course the notion of brand codes is hardly new: any brand must have its codes, otherwise it would not be recognized. But the specificity of the luxury brand hangs on the number of codes and their extreme coherence over time. The luxury brand is continually using more codes at once than any other brand, and varying them in greater depth.

What are the nine systematic and necessary elements of the signature of a luxury brand?:

- The figure of the brand's creator, he or she who made the brand a work and not a production: the effigy of this person will be found in its shops and communications.
- The logotypes, generally short and very visual, such as Chanel's double C, Dolce & Gabbana's DG, etc. Originally this was a way of protecting themselves against counterfeiting: it has become an aesthetic form of signature, capable of being repeated ad infinitum, as Louis Vuitton was the first to do with LV in its famous monogram canvas.
- A visual symbol that accompanies the logotyped signature: Aston Martin's wings, Mercedes' circle.

- A repeated visual motif: this is typical of all brands, from *prêt-à-porter* to luxury. The latter use the repetitive motif as a visual signature on their textiles.
- A brand colour: Tiffany's blue, Veuve Clicquot's orange.
- A favourite material, such as silk for Hermès or python skin and ostrich leather for Prada.
- The cult of detail, to the point of obsession, which is expressed visually for example through close-ups on the seams and the lock details at Louis Vuitton.
- The constant hymns to the manual work, to the excellence of the artisans who have contributed to each object, to the know-how.
- A way of doing things that is typical of the brand: whether it is the 'Chanel style' so visible in the woman's suit – an icon of the brand – or the quilting of the Chanel bag, or the typical driving experience at the wheel of a BMW.

These codes are found in the communication, of course, but also in the store, on the products and on the packaging, a veritable antechamber of the product, the theatre of the brand, a signature and factor of surprise and the tension of desire, all at the same time.

It is interesting to note that even the most recent brands reproduce these nine codes: Ralph Lauren, Paul Smith are recognizable on sight, even without the names, so successfully have they developed their eight types of visual signature. They have defined their semiotic constants and use them all, systematically, all the time. Veuve Clicquot has been doing so since 1772.

Making the brand denser through tales, stories and rumours

The traditional brand wants to be a landmark: it has therefore developed tools that reduce it to a promise (the famous 'positioning'). This is the consequence of the economy of hyperchoice: each brand is summed up in a simple proposition ('I am the best for...'). Here you can recognize the famous USP (unique selling proposition), born of the fact that in a televised or poster advertisement you can say only one thing, since clients' attention is fleeting and their involvement low.

The luxury brand does not obey these pressures: on the contrary. Far from being reduced to a promise, it offers its universe. It is not subject to a comparative logic and its communication is first and foremost about word of mouth. Its distinction is based not on its advertising budget but on what clients say about it among themselves.

This is why the luxury brand should be thought of like a story: there is no luxury brand without storytelling. As all studies on the diffusion of rumours and urban legends show (Kapferer, 1990), we like to tell stories that are perceived as authentic, somewhat secret, and capable of transmitting an implicit message, loaded with collective values. This is why the luxury brand should reveal its story, both in the historic and the mythical dimension: they give it status and at the same time feed the word of mouth. This is an ongoing task: everything is suitable for becoming the object of word of mouth, from the search for the rarest raw materials, to the number of silkworm cocoons necessary to create a single Hermès scarf, the manufacturing methods at Ferrari's Maranello home, the creator's life... Everything is useful for feeding the myth, the cult through the communication of a luxury brand.

Note that recent brands have invented their myths from scratch: countless books have been published by the Ralph Lauren House about Ralph Lauren himself (in reality Ralph Lifschitz), a man become a legendary personality in his lifetime, and presented throughout these books or magazine reports among his collection of old Jaguars, or at his timeless ranch.

Adapting the communication register to the type of luxury

The communication of a luxury brand forms an intrinsic part of the brand: it is the visible lever of its creative deployment in the media. But intuition and creativity are not enough: the brand is strengthened through the coherence and relevance of its communication, boosted by surprise. How then should it talk to its clientele? What elements of value should it promote? What registers of communication should be used? The ones that will resonate with the target clientele.

At this point, we need to return to the four types of clientele revealed by our study of luxury attitudes (see Chapter 5). In order to become a market, luxury cannot be only an intimate personal luxury, but must return to its essential sociological dimension: being a marker of social restratification. Luxury is both personal pleasure and a way of distinguishing yourself. This aspiration to distinction is not uniform in degree and can take several modalities, each of which determines a certain relationship to luxury. What are these four types of relationship with luxury in the world?:

- internalized luxury, comprising the search for an authentic experience, almost an art of living, exclusive – and therefore distinguishing you from others through a discreet elitism;

- luxury of self-expression through strong creativity and singularity;
- luxury of certain values, prestigious institutions, for those who seek status;
- luxury of self-affirmation relative to others, through the display of wealth, the visibility of consumption famously reserved for a minority.

These four types of relationship to luxury do not expect the same communications:

- To the first client type you will talk of the brand's patrimony and heritage, timelessness, and exclusive know-how.
- To the second type, you will talk of creativity, and references to contemporary art will be important.
- To the third, you need to reassure them through the myth, the proof of prestige, celebrity and social success.
- The fourth type wishes to stand out from the rest: they are sensitive to the transgressive discourse, the values of wealth and glory, excess and power reserved for a small minority.

As they grow, luxury brands will of course number all four types among their clientele, but to varying degrees according to the brand, its novelty, its status and its style. They must therefore communicate in several registers at once. How then can they avoid incoherence?:

- partly through controlling the register of the most visible part: the advertising;
- partly by remembering that luxury communication goes well beyond advertising (events, foundations, charities, public relations, art).

A great luxury brand such as Louis Vuitton communicates in reality with all four types, as Figure 11.2 shows, but using varying tools.

The dialectic of the local and the universal

Globalization causes new problems for brands, especially luxury ones, which were the first to go global, ambassadors of a culture and a vision of the world. They are by nature very centralized in terms of their management; their identity is non-negotiable. Chanel has been Chanel ever since Mlle Chasnel created it. However, in reality the same brand is different according to the country, depending on whether it is a newly emerging or seasoned brand. Take the case of Louis Vuitton: this brand in Asia is currently the ultimate symbol of social ascension, of conformism and of success. In Europe, in the

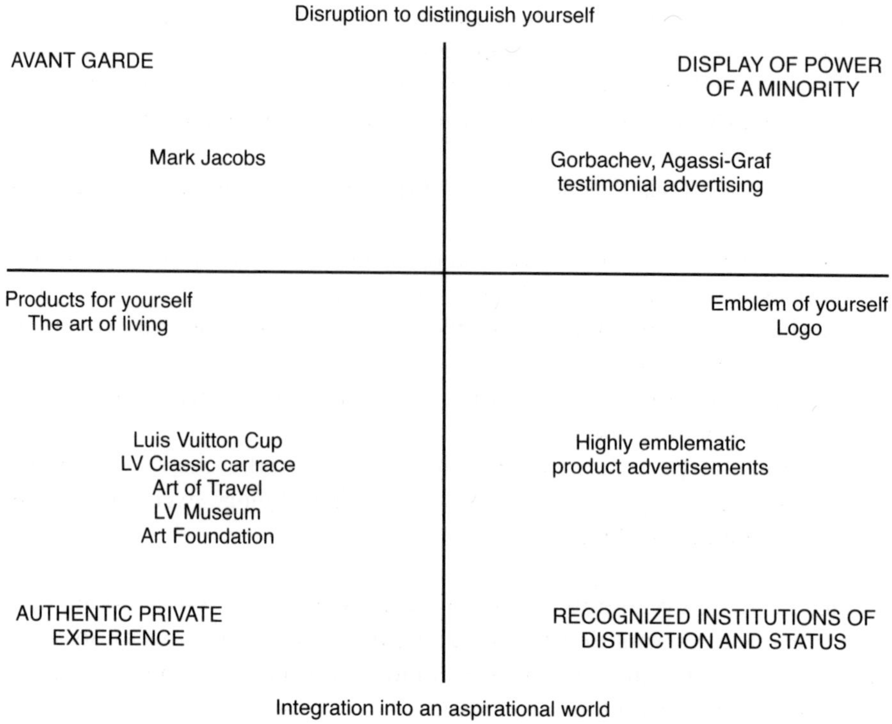

Disruption to distinguish yourself

AVANT GARDE	DISPLAY OF POWER OF A MINORITY
Mark Jacobs	Gorbachev, Agassi-Graf testimonial advertising
Products for yourself The art of living	Emblem of yourself Logo
Luis Vuitton Cup LV Classic car race Art of Travel LV Museum Art Foundation	Highly emblematic product advertisements
AUTHENTIC PRIVATE EXPERIENCE	RECOGNIZED INSTITUTIONS OF DISTINCTION AND STATUS

Integration into an aspirational world

Figure 11.2   How Louis Vuitton balances its communications for different targets

countries where it is successful, it is a symbol of creative genius that is the influence of Mark Jacobs. Where it is not very successful it is associated with 'bling' or is regarded as passé.

As Abeles (2008) reminds us, globalization maximizes space and time; it makes everything contemporary (even time), and the geographical spaces are all interconnected. What happens to a brand in Asia impacts on the Western market and vice versa; everyone in the USA and in Europe knows that Louis Vuitton is a demi-god in Asia. Brands are therefore transformed by being international, where they have to adapt like any living species (Becker, 2002).

The mistake would be to look for a position of compromise, a middle way using a combination of the emotional levers of the brand in Asia and the levers of globalization that cause an emotional response in Europe. From this would come a position which would satisfy everyone and upset no one, of the all too often seen 'traditional and modern together' type.

12 Financial and HR management of a luxury company

It is through marketing, in the broader (strategic and operational) sense, that luxury companies distinguish themselves strongly from others, but this brings with it various specificities in terms of the financial and human relationship aspects.

Financial specificities of luxury companies

The first is the importance of the brand's value, by far the most important of its 'assets', which is due, as we have seen in Chapter 6, to the extreme concentration of intangibles that it embodies.

The value of a luxury company is above all the financial value of its brand

In 2008 the value of the Louis Vuitton name made it the 19th brand in the world (Table 12.1), according to Millward Brown, with a valuation of $25.7 billion, just behind BMW ($28 billion) and far ahead of Mercedes ($18 billion), L'Oréal ($16.5 billion), or Nike ($12.5 billion). This shows how luxury brands, even if small in size, can be profitable. Those estimations of brand equity illustrate the fact that a luxury strategy leads to a better financial valuation of the brands than a fashion strategy. It is also interesting to mention that the Apple brand, whose value was down to zero in 1997, is valued 10 years later at $55.2 billion, at the same level as IBM; we will analyse later the strategy of Apple (Chapter 15, 'Learning from luxury').

In consequence, the financial strategy of a luxury brand will be to maximize not the net profit, but the brand's value: this is very different from traditional strategies.

Another consequence: since brands have never figured on the balance sheet at their true worth, particularly as long as the company remains controlled by the family, luxury companies generally have a very high 'return on equity', a phenomenon accentuated by often very high profitability.

The keys to financial profitability

The benefit for luxury derives of course from its productions, but also from its financial results. It is a small business in size, compared to Toyota or PSA Peugeot Citroen, but very high in terms of net profit when it is profitable. However, it should not be forgotten that the overheads are high, taking into account the degree of rigour expected from the start in all facets of the brand experience (distribution, products, services, communication), and at an international level: the brand must be handled perfectly everywhere it is sold, therefore there are no 'marginal countries'. Likewise, the classic strategy of covering overheads through marginal volume is not applicable to luxury.

Table 12.1   Luxury brand valuations in perspective

Brand	Ranking	Valuation	Growth
Google	n° 1	value 86 MM $	+30% vs 2007
Microsoft	3	71	+30%
IBM	6	55	+65%
Apple	7	55	+123%
Toyota	12	35	+5%
BMW	17	28	+9%
Louis Vuitton	19	26	+13%
Mercedes	36	18	+1%
L'Oréal	38	16	+34%
Cartier	80	9	+32%
Chanel	85	9	+15%

Data from Millward Brown 2008

It should also be remembered that it takes lots of time and money to build a luxury brand: high net profit now is the reward of several years of loss in the past.

Luxury and profitability

Luxury can be extremely, and lastingly profitable. But under what conditions?

One precaution is required from the start: avoiding the classic error of the uninitiated, who relish (or are outraged by) the high gross margin levels: given the importance of the investments to be made in creation, communication and distribution, a very high gross margin (in the order of 80 per cent) is crucial to the brand's survival.

When we talk about profit, we are therefore talking about the net profit (after tax). Let us note in passing that this very high gross margin rate, applied to products of low complexity (T-shirts, sunglasses) onto which a simple logo is affixed, is a windfall for counterfeiters. A 'downwards' extension, for an easy profit, is therefore very dangerous and weakens the brand by facilitating, or even provoking, counterfeiting: the loss of brand value due to this strategy is often greater than the profit generated. This substantial net loss is often not perceived: the financial profit is always posted annually, but the loss of brand value only rarely.

In practice:

- Above a net profit rate of 35 per cent on sales, constantly obtained for more than 20 years, we find the biggest stars, the brands highly concentrated on a product niche, like Louis Vuitton Malletier, or Rolex.
- Above 25 per cent, we find more diversified brands, but with coherent universes, like Cartier or Chanel.
- Fashion brands that flirt with luxury, like Dior, Gucci, or Yves Saint Laurent, undergo highly contrastive highs and lows, according to their standing at the time.
- Brands at the upper end of the range, but too expensive to find a significant client base: Rolls-Royce (the cars, not the reactors) or *haute joaillerie*, are not profitable.

You might even say that luxury should be extremely profitable, since:

- Profit is the proof of the brand's success: it has matched the dream of a significant clientele, ready to pay the price, knowingly (as we saw in the 'Luxury and art' section of Chapter 1).

- Very high profitability is crucial in maintaining the brand: investments in distribution and communication are very heavy, since they are strongly qualitative, and are only profitable over the long term; it is therefore necessary to be able to make them without worrying about the short term.
- Falling profitability can force a reduction in structural expenditure for maintaining the brand, particularly if the brand is undergoing short-term shareholder pressure. The problem is that at first, these cuts in 'useless' expenditure have an immediate positive effect on the operating account, but the harm done to the image is invisible, due to the hysteresis mentioned above – hence there is plenty of encouragement to pursue this strategy right to the bitter end, which generally arrives quite quickly.
- Only a high profitability can protect the brand from these mistakes… but not from the avidity of financial predators.

This very high profitability must be maintained over the long term. In order to do this, some basic rules must be followed:

- Remain concentrated on the core trade (Rolex), and extend it only progressively and in a controlled manner (Chanel, Hermès).
- Ensure human stability and coherence of teams: in particular, you should be mindful of troop morale when you launch into diversification. It is often taken as a rejection of existing lines and their teams (management is generally in love with the new business), and as an impoverishment. With diversification consuming a great deal of cash (since you want desperately for it to succeed) to the detriment of the principal business, whose teams would need to invest that money, and with a better return.
- Remain above the daily pressure of the stock market, and avoid publishing your financial results, either by not being listed (Chanel), or by hiding your results within a larger group, which is much less profitable, but provides a screen (LVMH for Louis Vuitton).
- Resist the drift towards fashion, unless it is core to the image (Chanel).
- Continue to invest strongly in the brand and in distribution: a strong brand is a great protection, provided that it is properly maintained; the same is true for the network of stores.
- Avoid ostentatious, or structurally useless, expenditure (when you have very high margins, there is a strong temptation to 'let yourself go'). Luxury is for the client, not for the managers. Here again, a beautiful brand and a high profitability can mask any drifts for a while, but not always.
- Manage regular growth, systematically checking that you remain within luxury.

Be profitable in the core trade first of all

Before creating new ranges, or diversifying into different trades, a luxury brand should first and foremost make its core trade profitable. We have seen how a luxury brand is deep in deficit at the beginning, since it cannot waver on the product quality it offers, and its low recognition makes it impossible to sell at high prices: this deficit should be considered as an investment on the brand's content.

You must then set the virtuous spiral in motion:

● an increase in sales volume, and thus in production;
● a lowering of costs, enabled by the experience effect, which leads to a rise in the margin, since retail prices are maintained;
● the release of a level of finance making it possible to invest in communication;
● increasing sales prices, made possible by recognition.

Diversifying into other products before achieving profitability would be a calamitous error.

Globalizing

It is rare that a local clientele is large enough to set this spiral in motion, once again for reasons specific to luxury:

● maintaining the price level does not help to increase the volume;
● economies of scale cannot be taken too far, since it would require a sales volume such that the brand would lose all the status linked to its exclusivity.

Under these conditions, you must seek the minimum volume beyond your own borders: internationalization, and then globalization, is the law of luxury. All the great French luxury houses have a percentage of foreign clients above 90 per cent. However, relocating production in order to reduce costs destroys the brand, as we have repeatedly seen. It is therefore a question of globalizing the image and the distribution, but under no circumstances the production.

Luxury, volume and profitability

Another reason for not following the logic of economy of scale too far is due to the fact that the luxury product comprises one part functionality and one part dream, and these two elements do not obey the same economic laws:

- Through volume increase, the functional part obeys the classic industrial laws of cost reduction owing to experience effect (put forward by the Boston Consulting Group – BCG), but also of diminishing returns on investment (ROI). For this reason, in all good industrial as well as distribution management, it is normal to invest in improving productivity and reducing cost through volume increase, as long as the ROI is acceptable. However, according to the BCG, you need to double production to reduce costs by 30 per cent. Even through globalization, following this volume strategy leads sooner or later to a departure from luxury.

- The sociological part (awareness, reputation), a key component of the dream part, initially obeys the laws of word-of-mouth diffusion and rumour (Kapferer, 1990). This leads to an effect that starts very slowly, but then grows exponentially (networking behaviour) up to a certain awareness threshold. Investing a great deal in advertising, before this threshold is reached, is extremely expensive and gives poor results. We know that the impact of an advertisement in a magazine (the fact of noticing and remembering it) depends on prior awareness of the brand: when it is not known, it is unlikely to be memorized. Beyond this awareness threshold, created by buzz, on the other hand, advertising investment rapidly becomes more profitable; the marginal profitability rate on invested capital in communication and distribution grows.

Consequently, we note the presence of two volume thresholds (Figure 12.1):

- A first swing threshold, after which it is more profitable to invest in communication than in cost reduction: the marginal profitability is higher.
- A saturation threshold, after which it is better not to invest to increase sales volume of the product, since the loss of exclusivity would asphyxiate the brand, leading to a loss of its dream value and therefore the price it can ask, and generally to a crumbling of the margin. This is the moment to invest in new products or new ranges.

In summary, in the financial management of the luxury company, you must therefore:

- Initially, concentrate the bulk of your small capital on the development of your production volume in order to be profitable at the desired sales price: avoid the 'Rolls-Royce' effect of a brand that is very well known, but does not sell enough to be industrially efficient and therefore profitable. This volume logic has a limit, however: causing a departure from luxury (as in the case of Mercedes).

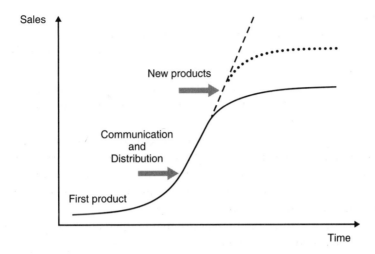

Figure 12.1 The two thresholds of luxury business development

- Know how to spot the moment where you have reached a reasonable cost price: at this point, you should swing the majority of your investment into communication, including the distribution network. It is important at this stage not to 'invest' the economies of scale obtained by the development of sales into a lowering of prices, but into communications and the construction of a quality distribution network.

Luxury and price–earnings ratio

In addition to an exceptional profitability on turnover, luxury has also historically enjoyed a price–earnings ratio clearly above the market rate (25 to 15). There are four causes for this situation:

- The brand is a valuable asset, since it is easy (in theory!) to 'leverage' it on other products or markets (see Chapter 7 on brand stretching), while relatively sheltered from direct competition (and thus protected in price terms), and practically immortal: this asset is very difficult to account for, and therefore is rarely valued at its correct price, except in the case of an acquisition. This is taken into account in the share price valuation, but only partially: hence the rapid rise in price of a good luxury brand at the time of an acquisition.
- Communication expenditure is considered as operating expenditure and not as investment. This is of course the case for all brands, luxury or

otherwise. What differentiates luxury, and explains this higher 'price–earnings ratio', is that expenditure on communication is in fact investment: carried out in one year, it is not intended to increase the sales or the margin for that same year, but to recreate the dream to prepare the future; it therefore reduces the immediate profit (the denominator), but increases the value of shares, and therefore the share price (the numerator).

- The phenomenon of the 'boss's dancing girl', or an investment that serves no commercial objective. Few CEOs of major groups can resist the temptation to add a luxury brand to their portfolio; the public justifications fool no one, but the automatic effect is to create stronger demand, and therefore a higher valuation, of luxury brands.
- The fact that analysts themselves are major clients of luxury brands; they are secretly in love with them.

Luxury and financial volatility

Possessed of such advantages, luxury certainly inspires enthusiasm among financiers. The problem is that this profitability is volatile if the laws of luxury management are not scrupulously respected, which is not that easy. These rules are:

- the opposite of classic marketing laws, and therefore often completely unfamiliar to non-specialists;
- highly subjective and qualitative, and therefore far from the quantitative that is dear to financiers; in particular, their business plans have no great value, owing to the non-linearity of the growth of sales volume and margins, and their high volatility (see the history of Gucci during the last 15 years).

Luxury has therefore left many financiers with a bitter taste in the mouth, as we saw in Chapter 2, 'The end of a confusion'.

The most common error is the brutal reduction of 'image expenditure' and in particular communication expenditure, in order to improve the before-tax profit: the resultant weakening of the brand does not appear in the accounts until the following year at the earliest. The effect on results is therefore very positive the first year; since the punishment is not immediate, the temptation to reduce these expenses still further the second year is too strong for a financier to resist... and this is when everything falls apart, because the loss of volume and the fall in the margin rate at the end of the second year are immeasurably greater than the savings made over the first two years.

Managing the human capital in luxury

Luxury companies' major specificity is their people. We talked about this in Chapter 1, and then again in Chapter 8 on product and Chapter 10 on distribution, so important is this point. In luxury, the human hand, its presence, is everywhere. It is always people who make a brand. In luxury they need, in addition to great professionalism, talent, creativity, and sensitivity to detail. To these traits are added those aspects specific to luxury, often ignored or underestimated.

Luxury is 'left-brain and right-brain'

Succeeding in luxury requires you to be both highly creative and imaginative (right cerebral hemisphere) and highly rigorous (left cerebral hemisphere). Of course, each of us has two hemispheres, but one is always dominant. Unlike classic industry (left-brain), where it is often initially one person who creates an empire alone, or art (right-brain), where it is always an individual, success in luxury is achieved at a minimum through a tandem of right-brain and left-brain with neither dominating the other; each has its own territory.

The partnership formed by Pierre Bergé and Yves Saint Laurent is a famous one, like the association of Tom Ford with Domenico di Sole. In fact, all luxury brands originate with a couple, and the brand can be considered their child: The creator–manager tandem is a characteristic of luxury.

In contrast, Pierre Cardin's solitude was the cause for his decline, despite his immense talent.

A luxury company is a team

Not only can success in luxury not be the work of a single person, but it cannot be the work of a single pair, either: it is critical to seek to form complementary teams.

In luxury, there is room for artists, artisans, and managers.

Artists

Luxury is extremely creative and refined, particularly at the product and communication levels. The team should comprise at least one artist, who should simply know how to bow to both the brand (whose universe they must respect) and economic and practical reality: a luxury product must of course be beautiful, but it must also sell; a luxury watch must be beautiful, but it must also tell the time.

Artisans

The importance of the manufactured side of the product is such that, in fact, all those who contribute to the production should be genuine, experienced artisans. This is a rare resource, and you should defend them and make them loyal. Each time that Louis Vuitton Malletier wished to open a new production workshop, it sought a place where there was a strong shoemaking competence: the near-disappearance of this trade in France left a number of worker-artisans out of work, who were specialized in leatherwork and could be easily retrained to fine leather goods; all of their competence was preserved and valorized.

Managers

Here, again, you need both 'right-brain' and 'left-brain'. The ideal is to employ people who have proved their worth in the classic world (sales or marketing at L'Oréal, P&G, Carrefour, or production in classic industry), and who are therefore familiar with 'real life', but who have that little 'something extra' that means they know how to work with artists and handle fluid concepts, since they have an artistic side – and know their limits in this field. If they have spent too much time in traditional marketing companies, adapting managers to the specificities of luxury proves difficult.

In general, in order to succeed in luxury, you need to know yourself (all aspects of your personality are used in this trade) and know your limits, and in particular remain humble in the case of success (it is not yours, but the brand's), and always remember that luxury is for the client, not for the internal teams. In particular, vast expenses are reserved for the external universe, not the internal one; the client's money is not theirs, and daily intercourse with 'extraordinary people' can turn the head of weaker people.

The great luxury houses have splendid stores and beautiful production workshops, since these are places that transmit the brand's image to the public, but modest offices, since clients do not visit the offices; it is a very important sign that the high price of a luxury product is not due to vast, wasted expenditure, but to extreme quality in production and distribution.

Humans are part of the brand

Stability of teams is key, and we have seen above that 'human capital' was an important part of giving value to a luxury brand.

Traditionally, 'employees' spent their entire career in a single luxury company, which was often, in fact, a family (hence the term 'house'). The faithfulness of these teams led to a certain cultural originality, apparent in the product and the stores. Without demanding total stability, which is also a factor of immobility that is particularly dangerous in a universe as fluid as ours today, you should not move to the other extreme of many companies, where employees change company constantly: this instability leads to permanent hybridization, which, added to the incessant benchmarking, causes all originality to disappear.

This is one of the problems of 'luxury' perfumery, which must absolutely remain original. If there is no longer a 'house nose', the scents no longer carry the house's 'mark'. This is more and more the case in many 'luxury' brands, where creation is steered by 'product chiefs' – talented, but entirely interchangeable. The result is that 'premium' perfumery brands, such as Lancôme, succeed better economically today than 'luxury' perfumery brands, like Guerlain.

Finally, not only are the true luxury houses characterized by high team stability, but they also have a role in the preservation of certain artisanal trades, which would not be economically viable without their help: hence Chanel recently (2007) bought six dying French artisan companies.

The 'inverted pyramid' of human resources management

In luxury, other than the creator, the most important people for the brand are the workers, those who make the product, and the salespeople, those who are in direct contact with the client. All the others are really at their service.

The luxury house therefore functions according to the famous principle of the 'inverted pyramid', except that in this case it is a real and daily practice, and not a vague slogan contradicted by the facts (who honestly believes that a worker at Lever or Renault, or a salesperson at L'Oréal or Toyota is more important than the CEO?)

In a house such as Louis Vuitton, a store director has priority over all other departments, always has direct access to the CEO; any new employee in a managerial position of any kind must compulsorily begin by working in the store, in order to understand fully what goes on there and how their job can serve the sales network and thus the client. This period in sales is not only a matter of personal training, as in the case of major successful brands, but really a structural question: the whole organization serves the store, in order to serve the client.

The choice and the ongoing training of the sales teams is the consequence of this, but it is not enough, management should always be travelling to sites in order to create, and above all maintain, personal links between everyone.

This is one of the reasons why luxury management is so difficult: genuinely assuming the concept of the 'inverted pyramid' is often difficult for managers accustomed to giving orders from their desk; travelling endlessly to the four corners of the globe is tiring; knowing how to stay in the background is unnatural to the ego of the Western 'chief'.

This is also one of the reasons why this management is so exciting: the human relations are so rich and real within the company.

Finally, this is one of the reasons why wanting to introduce fashion, with its 'star system', within a luxury house is so difficult: the rejection is immediate, if the teams dealing with fashion do not have the right human behaviours... and God knows that it is difficult for them and contrary to their nature.

Luxury groups and management of brand portfolios

We will not dwell on this subject, since it is not core to this book. However, two points differentiate luxury from other trades.

The importance of family companies

One characteristic of luxury is that, in general, it is built by several successive family generations, a fact that they freely mention (Rothschild, Mellerio, Krug). Moreover, family companies are often more profitable than anonymous groups, and survive well, at least while the family has the ability and will to manage the house... and is not too numerous!

One of the biggest differences between family companies and listed companies is that the former think first and foremost of the maintenance of value and the image of the name, which is often their own name, whereas the latter seek growth at any price.

This is also true when the name is not that of the family: from this point of view, it is perhaps useful to remember that one of the factors in Chanel's lasting, continual success is the fact that it was a family company from the beginning (the Wertheimer family); this is also the case with BMW (the Quandt family).

Brand portfolios and luxury groups

Unlike traditional metiers:

- The notion of brand portfolios does not work in luxury. Since each 'house' has its own specificity, and luxury does not work in direct competition within a single market, there is little sense in constructing a portfolio of brands in order to cover this market with complementary brands, as the major food or household products groups do.
- There are few real synergies within a group. In fact, groups that work well, like LVMH, are associations of companies each with its own brand,

teams, CEO, and considerable freedom of management, with just a small central holding activity, limited to the management of only part of the finances and human resources, and not rigid, heavy structures managing subsidiaries dependent on an all-powerful headquarters.

- In consequence, the logic of poles (brands of the same trade grouping together within a group) has proved disappointing: the best managers do not want to be brand managers, due to the lack of autonomy at this level. As we know, a luxury brand needs dedicated and talented management; therefore the contradiction is total between poles and luxury.

PART 3

Strategic perspectives

13 Luxury business models

In the previous chapters we have examined the management rules to be applied in order to succeed with a luxury strategy. It is now necessary to explain how to apply them in order to succeed financially. Although these rules are clear, comprehensible, coherent and effective, they do not guarantee economic success.

The management of companies highlights the importance of the brand as competitive advantage, but above all the importance of the business model on which it rests. Our analysis therefore cannot be limited to the exegesis of brands known as luxury without:

- On the one hand, examining whether they are truly luxury brands, other than in their own statements or in the perception of the mass audience: for many Japanese, Burberry is luxury, and for many French, Cardin is also.
- On the other hand, deciphering the models of working of the companies that manage them, integrating the creation, production, distribution, human resources and finance aspects.

One of the contributions of this book is to relocate luxury within the business models that underlie it: there are several of these. We will examine them all in turn.

In luxury, a product is always accompanied by a service, and we can distinguish four major families of luxury business models, according to whether the product or the service is dominant:

- Two for the 'luxury products', according to whether the brand has a core range with a sufficiently large and profitable market, or whether this market, being too narrow, forces the brand to sell other articles outside the core trade, benefiting from its aura (brand stretching) in order to be profitable.
  - To these two families we can add another very specific one: the perfume model.
- One for 'luxury services'.
- One for 'luxury in high-tech'.

Luxury products with a profitable core trade

The core trade is sufficiently powerful to ensure by itself the company's long-term survival. The prototypes are the personal accessories market (watches, jewellery, fine leather goods) and the car market. Their daily use and their visibility make them ideal products for luxury. In effect, their 'cost per hour of visible use' is low, even if the purchase price is high, since they are used often and the product is seen. Let us take two examples.

Louis Vuitton Malletier, the historical core of the Louis Vuitton brand

LVM is concentrated on the leather goods and luggage market. Admittedly, over the past 10 years a few products outside the core range have been sold under the Louis Vuitton brand, such as shoes, watches, textiles, etc, but these activities are marginal, even if the noise that the media make about them enables them to animate the brand (which is their role); they will be left out of the analysis of the business model.

The ordinary object for extraordinary people is the trunk, the 'special order'; the extraordinary object for ordinary people is the flexible bag (the Keepall), and the city handbags.

The link between the two objects is made through the materials used: the same raw materials (natural cow leather for the Monogram line, patent leather for the

Epi line), the same visual appearance (LV monogram for the Monogram line, graining for Epi).

The worldwide success and recognition of Louis Vuitton rests on this balance and this complementarity, which must be maintained: the Louis Vuitton bags and luggage will remain luxury products just as long as elites the world over continue to buy Vuitton trunks and 'special orders' with the LV name, even if the middle classes the world over queue up in Vuitton stores to buy bags made of the same materials. It will also be necessary, of course, for these products to remain of impeccable quality, manufactured by the company, and sold exclusively in Vuitton stores.

Audemars Piguet

In 1875, in the Swiss village of Brassus, two young admirers of *haute horlogerie*, Jules-Louis Audemars and Edward-Auguste Piguet, pooled their know-how in order to design and produce intricate watches. The history of the brand is a succession of creations. We will mention two of them. In 1892, Audemars Piguet designed and achieved the first minute repetition wristwatch: it was a world first. In 1972, breaking with the codes of *haute horlogerie*, Audemars Piguet created Royal Oak (2121 calibre), the first upper-range steel sports watch.

Today, Audemars Piguet remains the oldest manufacturer of *haute horlogerie* to have remained in the hands of its founding families. It has more than 700 employees worldwide, 550 of whom work on the three production sites in Switzerland. It produces 24,000 watches per year. The Royal Oak watch is priced from €600,000 (ordinary product for extraordinary people) to €8,000 (extraordinary product for ordinary people); as with Rolex, another highly representative example with its Oyster model, unchanged for decades and always current, a single design is used for the entire Royal Oak range.

Of course, €8,000 is a steep price for 'ordinary people', but if the watch is worn every other day for 10 years, the classic situation for a watch designed to resist aggression (shocks, water), that gives 20,000 hours of use, or less than 50 euro cents per hour, which makes it reasonable for an 'ordinary' person.

The specificities of the business model illustrated here relate to the product, production and distribution levels, as detailed below.

At the product level

- Focus on a core trade: luggage, including handbags (urban luggage), and small leather goods for Louis Vuitton, watches for Audemars Piguet.
- The products are permanent (a product is never officially retired from sale).

- A strictly controlled offer of highly differentiated products, whose aesthetic and technical territories overlap very little, so as to cover the maximum of client needs (handbag with handle, with shoulder strap, backpack) with the minimum of SKUs (store keeping units). Parsimonious launches of new products (a new product is managed like a new child in a family).
- All products sell and are profitable.
- The most profitable products are those of the middle of the range: the entry-level products are not there to make a profit, or even for volume, but to facilitate the first step into the universe of the range, and engender loyalty through the intrinsic value of the product. Those entry-level products, therefore, are highly qualitative.
- Parsimonious introduction of new ranges, which are not there to supplant existing ranges, but to round out the offer; these new ranges are sold at a higher price than existing ranges. You can see the difference from the approach – in our view, a mistaken one – used by Porsche with the Boxster, or the weakening of Mercedes' status through the commercial success of the A-Class, or the risks linked to the 1 Series for BMW.
- If, nevertheless, the introduction of a cheaper range is necessary, it must be compensated for by the parallel introduction of markedly more expensive products, in order to express clearly the message that, if the brand has introduced a cheaper product, it is not because it is incapable of renewing itself 'upwards' (see Chapter 9 on price), but from a desire to open an entrance door for a new clientele.

At the production level

- Totally controlled vertical integration, from the production workshop to the customer.
- No structural subcontracting of production, since the manufacturing of the product by the artisan is an integral part of the dream. Rapid growth can lead to a search for production subcontractors, but the objective will be to integrate them as soon as possible, as Hermès did with its Lyonnais silk manufacturers, through the acquisition of Perrin.
- Small, artisan production workshops, but highly organized, and not a huge mechanized factory. The place of production, even more than the store, since it is much less physically accessible and is closed to the public, is a sort of temple where the cult has its rituals. It is important that the substance of the brand can be visited, like Vuitton's Asnières workshop or Ferrari's Maranello factory. This visit should be carried out with due ceremony.

At the distribution level

Distribution will be completely controlled. Given the extreme importance of the moment of sale, it is totally unthinkable that these products should be sold in places, or by people, who are not part of the brand universe.

The indispensable rigour in managing this business model is compensated for through exceptional profitability, and leads to a considerable increase in value: the Louis Vuitton brand, whose value was almost nil in 1977 (the company had been offered for sale at 70 million Fr, or around €10 million, and nobody was persuaded to buy it at that price), was in 2008, according to Millward Brown, worth $26 billion.

Under this business model, we find many of the great names of 'personal accessories', such as Cartier, but also of cars, such as Ferrari. There is also the very interesting case of Hermès, which applies this business model across two very different trades: fine leather goods and silk (since it acquired its Lyonnais suppliers).

These exceptional performances are obtained thanks to a very strict management, and require an all-round competence (creation, production, distribution, communication) since these companies are highly integrated, as well as a permanent focus on the product and how it matches the client dream.

An essential characteristic of this model springs from the fact that a genuine core range exists, and the profitability is achieved on the mid-range.

We saw above that very expensive products are very rarely profitable; it is therefore pointless to sell too many, and even more pointless to multiply the references.

Symmetrically, the entry-level products are not very profitable either: since they serve as first access to the brand universe (they target the 'future faithful', and not the 'day trippers'), they absolutely must not disappoint the client on the excuse that they are not too expensive, and must also carry all of the brand's important signs. They cannot therefore be 'economy' products. As a result, they have low margins, and there should be few references (ideally, just the one), so that the client will subsequently make purchases of more profitable products, once they have taken a liking to the brand.

This is a major specificity of this business model: you need entry-level products, that is, 'budget' products, but you need as few of these as possible, since they are not there to 'meet a quota' or 'make money'. This margin structure is the opposite of the pyramid model (see the business model below), where the margin is made on the entry-level products, aimed at 'day tripper' clients.

The working schema is therefore as follows:

- a very short range;
- a few image products, expensive, but not sold in large numbers;

- a very limited number of access products;
- a core range that is carefully wrought, with highly differentiated products, a reduced number of references, but covering a maximum of client needs.

To help make more explicit this concept of entry product and its specificity, let us see how references are managed in fashion, in Figure 13.2.

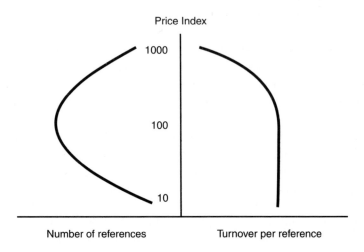

Figure 13.1   Luxury SKU management

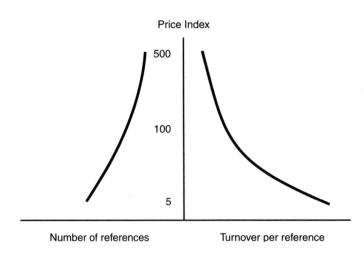

Figure 13.2   Fashion SKU management

What are the pitfalls to avoid in this working model of a luxury product with a profitable core trade?

Diversifications that are not wholly legitimate and are less profitable

The brand is generally only fully legitimate within its core range, a very specific and reduced territory (watchmaking, jewellery and not leather for Cartier; leather goods and luggage and not textiles, and still less fashion, for Louis Vuitton; cars and not computers or watches for Ferrari).

Outside this territory of legitimacy, the brand becomes a 'premium' brand, and profitability falls. Genuine diversification is therefore very difficult, all the more so since the success of a luxury brand cannot be separated from a very strong cohesion of the personnel around a specific universe, leading to a high degree of idiosyncrasy, which cannot be transferred wholesale to another trade. The rigour and seriousness of leather goods has nothing in common with the 'show-off' side of fashion, and the professionalism of leather has nothing in common with that of watchmaking.

The truly successful conquests of new territory, such as that of Hermès, which moved from leather goods into silk while maintaining its original trade and remaining within luxury, are therefore extremely rare; there is, however, a very interesting case of a successful change of trade, that of ST Dupont: with its original trade, cigarette lighters, dying out, the company completed a brilliant transformation into pens. Having said this, there were close proximities between the two trades, both at the technical and the distribution level, and the threat of extinction that hung over the company must have helped enormously in executing the crucial transformation as well and as quickly as possible. Unhappily for the company, the following diversification, without any legitimacy, into leather products and textiles for men, too far from its core competence, was a failure and dragged the ST Dupont brand into a downward spiral from which it has not yet emerged.

The ease of the everyday

Since the 'success machine' appears to be functioning of its own accord, it is better not to meddle with it; there is then a great temptation towards the 'easy life', succumbing to vast expenses and pointless hirings. Luxury is for the client: any huge expense that is not directed towards increasing the dream value weakens the brand.

Internal lassitude

As we saw in the case of Louis Vuitton regarding the Monogram canvas in 1986, this is one of the biggest risks that come with success in this case. The greatest restaurateur can end up tiring of their great dishes, which is understandable; deducing from this that the clients are also tired of them, forgetting that they do not dine on them daily, would be a grave mistake.

The late Claude Terrail showed great wisdom in continuing to cook (and number) his 'Pressed Duck' daily at La Tour d'Argent for decades.

Rejection of the past

Another major risk is a new team assuming power within the company; there is a strong temptation to prove their talent, to reject the past or, simply, to cease to invest in the maintenance of existing products and dedicating most of the cash to new products.

The trade where this is most frequent is perfumery; it is also where we see the most turnarounds following this type of mistake, with the 'great classics' finding favour again in a cyclical manner, following the failure of new launches. Deci-Delà, by Nina Ricci, launched deliberately in order to move out of the brand's traditional universe, was a total failure. The success of Nina is due to a return to its roots: Nina, in its execution (bottle, contents and above all advertising) revitalizes the brand's core identity almost trait for trait, a core identity that had been totally forgotten after the death of Robert Ricci and several changes of management. A luxury brand is a bridge between the past and the future. Its future and its identity cannot be ignored or rejected. The analysis of the historical symbol of the Nina Ricci brand (the Three Graces) had moreover revealed in 1990 what the foundation of the brand was (Kapferer, 2008, p. 280): all that was required was to find the deeper meaning of the fairy in the collective Western unconscious. The essence of Nina Ricci is accession to femininity. Nina's success is due essentially to this return to the brand's essence: its white-clad heroine holds out her hand for an apple.

The specificity of the product life cycle within luxury brands follows from this possibility of always finding a strong and still vibrant core identity, even after years of mistakes: the phoenix can be reborn from its ashes.

Rigidity due to vertical integration

This risk is common to all vertical integration, but with a side that is specific to luxury: the 'artistic fog' that envelops relationships between the different stages of production. The majority of the aesthetic aspects are not quantifiable and good functioning rests more on the intuitive comprehension between individuals about the brand's shared dream than on the establishment of specific technical dossiers. Although crucial, these latter are not enough, since they are too reductive.

Under these conditions, the classic strategy of vertically integrated companies for remaining efficient (installing a genuine 'client–supplier' relationship between the divisions in charge of the different successive stages of product manufacturing and distribution) is impossible to implement in luxury. This leads to risks of cost drift, rigidifying of the production methods, and closed-mindedness to innovation.

Staleness of the product image through saturation and vulgarization

This risk is the reflection of that in the point about internal lassitude; this time, the lassitude is not in the heads of the teams running the company, but in those of the clients... and this is much more serious.

This is even the most serious risk of all for a luxury brand that has met with global success (Louis Vuitton and its LV monogram), where the line between democratization (positive) and vulgarization (catastrophic) becomes increasingly blurred, and all the more so as the brand addresses very diverse cultures using the same discourse, and these diverse cultures have a completely different perception of the accessible–vulgar dialectic (an ultra-democratic society such as Japan versus a democratic, but caste-based, society such as England or India).

The problem is that, in luxury, purchases are infrequent, and therefore this staleness of the brand and this lassitude among clients is very difficult to detect amidst all the false information coming from non-clients, and in particular from the 'people', the 'trendsetters', who in any case quickly tire of everything. It is therefore necessary to listen intently to clients, so as to have an unbiased opinion; having your own network of stores is a major advantage, provided that you maintain a very close relationship with the people on the ground.

Only a wholly controlled distribution in which each client is known, and personally recognized, makes it possible to remain a luxury brand. Own-brand distribution makes client familiarity possible, which in the luxury world means client recognition.

Luxury products with a too-restricted core range

This is the case for those houses for whom the typical product of their original trade is admittedly prestigious, but not profitable or difficult to sell in sufficient quantities to ensure the company's economic development (the market is too small, and you cannot rationalize a quality product), or impossible to extend (restaurant, chateau). In this case, the brand's dream is carried by the original trade, but the profits are made through other trades.

Two typical business models enable the profitability challenge to be met; we have encountered them earlier (see Chapter 7). They are the pyramid model and the galaxy model. In both cases, and unlike the previous business model, the margin (by percentage and by volume) is made on the cheapest products.

The 'pyramid' business model

The most classic example is that of haute couture in France. Nowadays, in France, the haute couture market has vanished and Chanel is probably the only one to balance its books. Its natural extension market, *prêt-à-porter*, is no longer produced in France (once again, except for Chanel), causing the brands concerned to lose all legitimacy – in contrast to what is happening in Italy, where the existence of a local industry enables the success of Giorgio Armani and others.

Faced with this economic failure, while the high street fashion of H&M and others, Zara or Mango, is a success, French haute couture has been obliged to justify this deficit economically as an investment in the brand, which is recouped through other, derivative products which then become, as with Dior, the true 'stars' of the catwalk, with the dresses as mere elements of the show, and often finish by pulling the brand out of the luxury world.

It is therefore necessary to find other products; the haute couture houses conceive their offer according to a succession of strata ranging from the highest exclusivity (the *griffe* at the summit) to the lines that, being cheap in their segment, have become very accessible. This way of functioning is called the 'pyramid' since it begins with a narrow summit made of rare, even unique works – made by hand, priceless, works of art – and is progressively enlarged in both clientele and diffusion (Figure 13.3). The dream is continually recreated at the summit, and it cascades onto the different products: the *prêt-à-porter* lines, fashion accessories, watches, down to glasses, perfumes, cosmetics, etc.

In the pyramid model, the issue is to maintain a strict coherence between the different products that carry the brand, which therefore form a genuine 'brand universe' (the test is whether they can be displayed and sold all within the same store). A common logo is not enough: the entire troupe must be able to provide a coherent show, just as a symphony orchestra brings all its instruments together under the authority of the conductor's baton. It is also necessary for the conductor to be present: nowadays, video technique is immensely helpful for a haute couture brand, since it makes it possible to create an infinite loop of catwalk shows, ensuring the living presence of the myth.

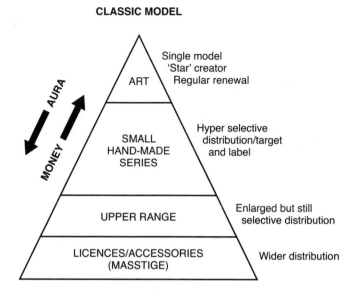

Figure 13.3   The pyramid business model

The two risks of the pyramid model are creative dilution as you move away from the summit, and also contamination from below:

- The loss of the creative power and therefore of its influence on clients and its authority over the other strata may be genuine: leather goods, perfume or watchmaking, being legitimate luxury trades for the brand, may be tempted to run themselves.
- Contamination from below: 'easy money' from small products with high margins leads to the facile solution of highly profitable mass marketing as long as the brand maintains its prestige. The risk of contamination from below is all the stronger if the brand is managed by financiers wishing for rapid results. In this business model, the small products have the highest margin and are sold in larger quantities; their financial contribution is therefore significant, sometimes even indispensable to the company's economic stability – in which case, the brand is extremely fragile. The natural temptation of a fragile brand, under pressure to make money quickly, is to *griffe* everything within its reach, to multiply its licences while providing itself with a 'creative office' supposed to offer its creative talent to licensees chosen principally for their ability to contribute financially, and to relocate to the area of lowest costs.

Using Figure 13.4, we can also see how different is the management of Louis Vuitton-like brands.

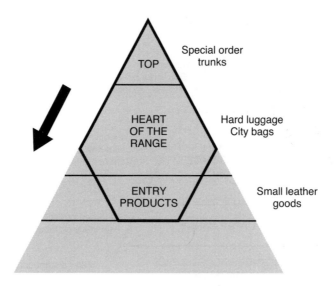

Figure 13.4 Louis Vuitton and the pyramid model

We will now analyse several famous brands according to this pyramid frame: Chanel, Armani, Dior and Cardin (Figure 13.5). We include also Louis Vuitton and Rolex although it is clear from our analyses that their business model is not that of the pyramid.

The case of Chanel is a very interesting one, due to its lasting success and high profitability. Its pyramid is unique since not only the top of the pyramid, haute couture, is luxury, but in addition each product-universe of the brand is also a luxury universe: the leather goods are produced in France, as with Hermès, the perfumes are created by a house 'nose' (Chanel even has its own jasmine plantations at Grasse), the watches are real watches and not *griffe* products, etc.

Chanel has another specificity, which explains its success in haute couture now that Gabrielle Chasnel, alias Coco Chanel, is long dead: the constitution of a tandem of brand (which guarantees luxury) and creator (which guarantees fashion), with the creator in question (Karl Lagerfeld) fully respecting the 'Chanel spirit' and its semiotic grammar in his creations for the couture house. In parallel, Karl Lagerfeld is expressing himself personally through his own brand, and working for other companies (such as Fendi or H&M), thus avoiding any confusion between himself as an individual and the Chanel brand. The Chanel pyramid is therefore made up not of descending strata, but of mini-pyramids placed side by side, hardly descending at all in quality and price level. The only exceptions: glasses, distributed by multi-brand optician chains, or T-shirts.

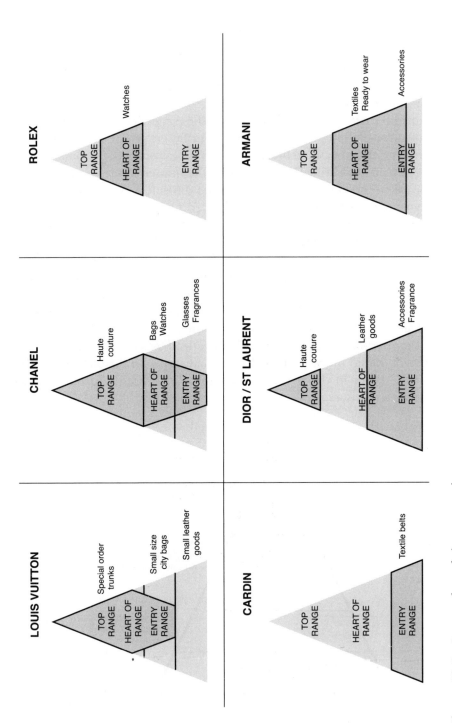

Figure 13.5 Luxury brands in perspective

Up to 2005, Armani had been defined by a pyramid with a truncated summit: its impressive international success did not need the aura of an haute couture *griffe*. Its many complete lines were clearly organized in a descending order from Armani Collezione, Emporio Armani, and then complementary lines and at the bottom Armani eXchange, down to the highly informal Armani jeans aimed at young people. These lines correspond to the strata of price, target and degree of exclusivity of the boutiques. Under these brands we find the complete range of corresponding accessories and, even lower, products that are even more widely diffused in multi-brand stores (glasses, cosmetics, perfume).

Giorgio Armani identified that the void at the summit was leading to a long-term threat to the entire edifice: despite the difficulties (technical, financial and regulatory) of haute couture, he decided to launch his haute couture house in Paris, Armani Privè, since his talent and his financial solidity enabled him to take this risk (see Figure 13.6).

Fendi, since its integration into the LVMH group, does likewise in leaning on Karl Lagerfeld's talent, supported by a management team of the highest quality. The recent fashion show on the Great Wall of China illustrates its success: since the summit of the pyramid, furs had become too weak a trade for ecological reasons: it needed to build another.

The Dior pyramid (Figure 13.7) is characterized by a creative spring at the top of the pyramid in the person of John Galliano, with the bulk of its sales being made lower in the pyramid through accessories, the production of which is often outsourced.

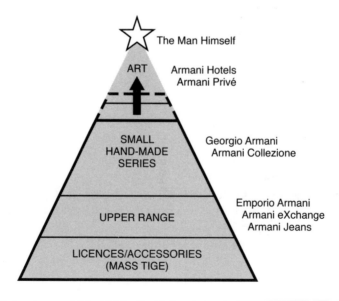

Figure 13.6   Armani pyramid

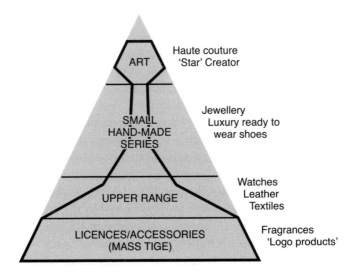

Figure 13.7   Dior pyramid

As for Pierre Cardin, only the base of the pyramid remains, but it is an extremely broad base. The aura is the memory of the now-gone era in which Cardin was a creator and a *griffe*, with the remaining recognition at a truly global level among the mass audience.

The 'galaxy' business model

The other model is called the 'galaxy': it begins at the same economic starting-point (a creator who wishes to develop), but functions differently. Unlike the pyramid, which establishes a clear hierarchy between the summit, small series from the workshop, and the larger series at the base of the pyramid, the galaxy treats all it products equally. Each expresses the brand's dream in identical fashion. They are all doors of entry into the brand (see also page 141).

Just as a galaxy comprises different, separate star systems, which are held together only by the gravitational attraction of the black hole lurking at the centre, this system rests on the talent or attractive power of a single person. One of the best current examples is Ralph Lauren. Here we find not only numerous *prêt-à-porter* lines (organized into daughter brands through their occasion of use: formal, Friday wear, casual, sport, clubhouse, etc), including their accessories, but also RL household linen, RL furniture, RL paint.

In fact, Ralph Lauren is not only a talented man, it is also a film in which each of us are actors, at once a true story, an incarnation of the American dream (Ralph Lifschitz, the immigrant Jew from the Bronx who started from nothing and became rich and famous), and a true invented story, that of the aristocracy of the north-eastern coast of the USA.

In these conditions, we are no longer looking at the myth of creation, but the true field of luxury, that of the dream; moreover, RL himself has said: 'other designers have taste; I have dreams'. RL's talent is to enable many to share his dream.

Let us note here a point that is very important strategically: whereas, in the pyramid model, we are dealing with a luxury brand that sells products that might not be luxury products, when a brand functions on the galaxy model, as long as the creator is alive, it might not be a luxury brand ('Ralph Lauren' is not a luxury brand), but all its products may be luxury products for those who dream of the brand, if all its products are legitimized by the creator as forming part of his universe. This quickly borders on fetishism: RL even sells the furniture he has used, which become luxury products for his fans.

Unlike the pyramid model, therefore, the galaxy model does not a priori exclude any product, and does not require all products to be sold in the same place to demonstrate the brand's coherence, under the influence of the product generating the dream; coherence is ensured by the personality of the creator.

The risk with this model is that it rests on a single person, and that person must remain constantly vigilant, even with increasing age, or everything falls apart: even a man of exceptional talent such as Pierre Cardin was not able to maintain his name at a high enough level to keep his galaxy within luxury: nowadays, nobody, or almost nobody, identifies with the dream of Pierre Cardin – which, moreover, he no longer seeks to communicate.

In any case, can the galaxy model survive the death of the creator? It is imperative that the creator be alive, in order to ensure the cohesion of the whole.

This galaxy model does not only concern fashion: a luxury restaurateur such as Alain Ducasse functions in this way. Nor is the centre of the galaxy necessarily a human being: this model can be applied to famous monuments, carriers of an eternal dream, such as the Chateau de Versailles, the Chateau de Chambord, or the Taj Mahal.

The perfume business model

Perfume is such an important product, and so singular within the luxury universe, that it is not surprising that it has ended up creating its own business model. For various reasons, one being the specific, non-quantifiable relationship we each have with perfume (see *The Perfume* by Patrick Süskind, 2001), and another being the possibility of selling very high-quality perfumes at prices accessible to many, perfume is in fact the first species of the luxury island to have successfully colonized the continent of consumption goods, and has interbred in a viable manner with the local species.

The specificities of the perfume market

This market has three strong, original and structuring characteristics.

You do not communicate about the scent

Even when a perfume is 'single scent', this scent is not mentioned in its name, nor in its communication: Pour un Homme by Caron is not about lavender, nor is Opium pour Homme by Yves Saint-Laurent about Bourbon vanilla, although there is no olfactory ambiguity there.

When you talk concretely and precisely about a specific smell, with very few exceptions you are immediately relegated to the world of deodorants, or worse, of air fresheners, which officially 'smell' of pine or lavender.

There are simple technical reasons for this: contrary to images or sounds, no one has yet found a way to reproduce a scent on a large scale, with great faithfulness, and at low cost. Moreover, describing a smell in words is impossible, without naming smells that everyone knows (mimosa) – but then, where is the originality of the creation, so indispensable to luxury?

Mass communication should therefore be based essentially on the image: the perfume bottle assumes its full importance here, since it provides the visual (it 'embodies' the perfume in advertising) and tactile (it is the first physical contact with the perfume) aspects to the crucial multisensory perception: smell alone is not enough to make 'luxury'.

It is a product with a long lifespan, and frequently purchased

This characteristic is practically unique in luxury: a perfume is simultaneously a timeless and immutable product (No 5 by Chanel dates from 1921, Shalimar by Guerlain from 1925), and a product that is purchased regularly. The bottle itself lasts a long time, but it is rapidly emptied. The intimate mixture of these aspects makes it a unique product within the luxury universe, but also one of its biggest markets: its extreme proximity in distribution terms with common consumption goods (frequent purchase, low unit price) have enabled rapid development.

Very high gross margins, no more than respectable profitability

The price of success is that, despite a very high gross margin, its final profitability is only average.

The cost of launching is very high (for a luxury perfume, on average one year's anticipated turnover), since it subscribes to the logic of the mass product and not of the elitist product, and the cost of maintaining the brand is also very high, since it requires investment in communication both to maintain the dream, and also to push sales. At P&G's prestige and beauty division, which manages perfumes under licence, the media advertising investment is 20 per cent of turnover.

While there was still hope that the perfume would easily become a great classic, these launch and brand maintenance costs were justified.

Nowadays, the life expectancy of a new perfume is getting shorter all the time, due both to the direct competition between luxury and premium in this market, leading to a logic of constant launches, and to the introduction of lots of star perfumes (Delon, Dali, Spice Girls, etc), of which companies such as Coty have become specialists.

Under these conditions, the luxury perfume market is today not very profitable.

Segmentation of the perfume market

We have already seen that perfume is a product for which a great part of the market is luxury. In fact, around half of the market is 'premium', held by the major actors in consumer goods, such as L'Oréal with Lancôme, or Procter & Gamble, and the other half is a luxury market held by the great names of the trade, such as Chanel.

Even more interesting: these two strategies coexist in the same market, in the same distribution networks, and in the same price zone.

The business models of luxury and premium perfume

The haute couture–luxury perfume coupling

The first specificity is that, whereas perfume has always been a luxury trade (it can be traced at least as far back as Ancient Egypt), and it requires great and very specific technical prowess, there are very few great luxury perfume houses that are not linked to haute couture.

Among big names, only Guerlain, and to a lesser extent Caron, are 'pure perfumers'. All the other great and lasting successes come from couture: No 5 by Chanel, L'Air du Temps by Nina Ricci, Opium and Paris by Yves Saint-Laurent, Angel by Mugler...

The luxury part of a product is its dream part; the specificity of perfume here is that its dream is located outside its 'natural' market: scent. This is not to say that luxury perfumes do not have wonderful, complex, captivating scents – quite the reverse; but it is to say that the dream that they carry is not, in our modern society, supported by the smell, but by something entirely other, issuing from another, 'smell-less' universe: the universe created by a great couturier.

The true business model of the luxury perfume is therefore of the introduction of a single fragrance, made to last forever and immortalize the couturier's universe. Chanel No 5, or L'Air du Temps by Nina Ricci are the paragons of this genre, and it is in this same way that the most recent of the great successes in luxury perfume was introduced (not launched!): Angel, by Thierry Mugler.

You do not 'launch' a perfume in this case 'because you need to', but you 'introduce' a new perfume because you have found a new olfactory composition, coherent with the couturier's universe. Opium was a part of the Yves Saint-Laurent universe, Paris another one.

This strategy is the only one that leads to lastingly high financial results, coherent with other luxury activities.

The premium and 'mass premium' strategy

The other profitable business model in perfume is that of premium and 'mass premium', with high and regular frequency of launches, followed by an abandonment of the product. These accelerated launches make it possible to create a true corner or shelf relatively quickly and to gain from the sales of the first the resources to advertise the second, the third, etc.

The justification for these repeated product launches typically arises from increasingly detailed segmentation analyses, where three types of parameters interact:

- The nature of the basic motivations for purchasing a perfume: for me, or for seduction?
- Gender: is this a perfume for men or women?
- The psychological profile of the target, arising from a segmentation of the brand's potential market into client types: each type then sustains a different perfume project.

In this business model, value is not placed on the product, the scent itself, the packaging, or the bottle, but in the advertising and merchandizing. This is typically 'demand marketing' and not offer or supply marketing, based on a strong brand identity. The advertisements for this type of perfume are interchangeable since the link with the creator, or a creative root that provides coherence, is lost in favour of target analysis and the use of advertising skits based on the stereotypes of each target. These are not very numerous.

Another approach to justifying these repeated launches consists of following the vagaries of fashion. Thus Calvin Klein has been able to spot emerging trends and capitalize on them to sell to the masses thanks to his reputation as a designer. In 1980, Obsession surfed the wave of moral liberation, and later Eternity, its opposite, signalled the return of cocooning.

The business model of luxury trades with very high overheads

The previous three business models concerned what are known as 'light industry' trades.

The opposite is the heavy industry trades, characterized by very high fixed costs, requiring high volume of sales to balance them. They are found mainly in the services (hotels, restaurants, air transport, cruises). The need to cover the overheads leads to the integration of yield management-type price logic, making it possible to constantly adjust the price of luxury services according to demand.

However, owing to the specificity of price management in luxury (see Chapter 9), and namely the fact that the price must not be advertised and that 'no sales' is a law, implementing yield management requires tact.

When the price reduction is for everybody at the same time (low-season fares), there is no specific problem. When this not the case, it needs to be managed in such a way that neither the people who pay a higher price nor the ones who pay a lower price for the same service are harmed.

The people paying a higher price

Luxury is segregationist. People paying full price want to belong to a club, with access limited to a 'happy few', the cost of the service being one of the barriers. If they know somebody has joined them without paying the toll, they need to find a good reason why not to discard this person. For instance, the special fare can be linked to a specific and gratifying event (honeymoon, graduation from a prestigious school)

The people paying a lower price

Luxury implies scarcity. Unless specially explained, a lower price, like sales, means that there is no scarcity and that the product is no longer a luxury product. The lower price has to be justified as an exceptional and personal gift reserved to the specific person, either as a good customer (*soldes privées* or 'private sales'), or as somebody chosen to join the club ('entry product' strategy in the service business).

In these trades, we find two types of establishments and methods of management.

Those that offer shared enjoyment: first class on common transport (train, underground, aeroplane, certain large cruise ships)

In this case, already dealt with in Chapter 4, the differentiation is achieved through the luxury in the service, in discretion... but also in ostentation (the first-class traveller who is ushered past the rest during boarding). Here we find both aspects of luxury.

One example of this business model is Singapore Airlines. This company, created in May 1947, is regularly named by *Fortune Magazine* as one of the world's most admired companies. It is also the world's most valuable carrier. Its first class is a true luxury product, but what is striking is the ability of the brand as a whole to surpass all other airlines. It has four key values: permanent innovation, the best technology, authentic quality, and excellence in customer service.

While these values come as no surprise to anyone, it is nevertheless their lasting implementation at the highest level that represents a genuine feat:

- Singapore Airlines has always, systematically, been the first to launch most innovations concerning client experience on board and on the ground, as well as their entertainment. The most recent was the installation of a PC at every seat!
- Singapore Airlines also has the most up-to-date fleet of any airline: it was the first to buy the new A380.
- Every luxury brand has an icon. The icon of Singapore Airlines is the Singapore Girl, created in 1968 and the focal point of all its advertising since then. Pierre Balmain was asked to create her uniform, a special version of the Malay *sarong kebaya*. This icon symbolizes the hospitality and warmth of the company's welcome and service. In order to maintain it, ongoing training is given to the hostesses, stewards and personnel in contact with the client, in order to increase their competence: for example, they take courses to better recognize wines and cheeses and be able to talk about them, recommending them to passengers who themselves are so competent and demanding. Singapore Airlines' advertising has systematically promoted this icon of service for 40 years.

Those that offer a clearly separate enjoyment, such as luxury hotels (Relais et Chateaux, Burj Dubai and its seven stars), special trains (the Orient Express) or private jets

What is the economic balance of a Parisian palace? Sixty-five per cent of turnover and 75 per cent of profitability come from accommodation (with an average room occupancy rate of 51 per cent). Restaurants provide 35 per cent of turnover but 20 per cent of profitability: in a 'palace', half of the personnel work in catering. Hence the importance of the marginal filling rate and the restaurant's fame in capturing local clientele (tourists like to dine elsewhere).

Table 13.1 details the delicate balance for restaurateurs and explains the systematic rise in prices.

Faced with these costs, the only solution is to raise the level of luxury in order to raise prices.

In order to develop further, luxury restaurateurs adopt the galaxy business model: the great chefs such as J Robuchon, Pierre Gagnaire and Alain Ducasse have become the couturiers of haute cuisine. They multiply their restaurants internationally, often in conjunction with other luxury brands in their flagship stores (such as Ducasse in the Chanel building on Ginza in Tokyo). Even when they are absent – they do not have the gift of omnipresence – they inspire the creation in each of their restaurants and multiply their media visibility during each of their fleeting trips to these capital cities.

Ferran Adria of elBulli is world famous for his *tecnológica gastronómica*, developed in his creativity workshop elBullitaller. This workshop and the elBulli restaurant, considered as the best in the world, create a powerful centre for the galaxy, which includes lots of sub-brands (elBullicarmen, elBullihotel, elBullicatering, elBullibooks, and so forth) allowing Ferran Adria to expand his business far away from Roses, the Catalan city where his restaurant is located, without harming the dream.

Innovation is a key factor in the success of today's luxury hotels: it is a source of buzz among the world's great travellers. The case of the Plaza Athénée in Paris is enlightening (Phan, 2007). Innovation is one of the key values of this 'palace', which requires highly motivated employees, the

Table 13.1   Cost structure of a restaurant in a luxury hotel

Food revenue	43.2 M	66.7%
Beverage revenue	18.9 M	29.3%
Other F&B revenues	2.6 M	4%
Total revenues	64. 7 M	100%
Food costs	10.6 M	
Beverage costs	3.1 M	
Total food, bev costs	13.7 M	21.2%
Payroll	42.6 M	65.8%
Other expenses	8.1 M	12.6%
Profit	0.3 M	0.5%

encouragement of free expression, systematic innovation workshops, the listening ear of a charismatic managing team, and an egalitarian distribution of profits to employees.

In this hotel you find a desire to progress systematically in the four main types of service innovation:

- The adaptation of existing service, such as the replacement of normal television channels with an exceptional array of digital, multilingual channels, or check-in in the limousine that carries the client from the airport to the hotel.
- The introduction of a service that already exists in the market but not yet in the hotel, such as for example the systematic taking of the number of the taxi that drops off a client, just in case the client should leave an object in the taxi, or placing a Maserati at the disposal of all clients of the Royal or Eiffel suites. This was the innovation of the Raffles hotel in Singapore, offering a BMW 7 Series or a chauffeur-driven Bentley.
- The adaptation of an existing service by focusing on a particular target. This is typically the case of a complete makeover of the bar to make it more attractive to the clients' children and also attract a Parisian clientele.
- Finally, disruptive innovation, new for the market, such as the transformation of the court garden into a skating rink in winter.

The 'high-tech' business model (highly innovative industry)

Despite its importance in today's world, which means that we should mention it here, we will not discuss it at any length.

The basic constraint of 'high-tech', constant technological advances, is in contradiction with luxury, which targets stability and timelessness; this constant change is also totally different from that of fashion, inasmuch as it is not purely artificial, but rests on objective bases. A fashion product will one day become fashionable again, just as a stopped watch is right twice a day, but you never know when; you just have to wait. A computer from a few years ago is completely useless, and there is no point in waiting.

The more recent the technology, the stronger this constraint: evolution in the internal combustion engine develops in a manner that is normally manageable for luxury (hence the whole market of luxury cars based on motorization, like Ferrari or Porsche); evolution in electronics does not.

Clients have two, wholly conflicting expectations: the luxury of being at the cutting edge of progress, and that of fully enjoying progress while not having to worry about it; hence there are two conflicting choices for leading a luxury strategy in this sector:

- maximal technical complexity (omnipresent technical product): this is what characterizes cars with a strong sporting component in their make-up;
- ease of use (invisible technical product): this is what characterizes chauffeur-driven 'saloon' cars, direct descendants of the old carriages.

When in the electronic field, the technological rhythm of evolution is such that you need to split your product between the physical object and the service. The service can be easily and permanently improved, allowing the object to be durable, and as a consequence, luxury. But both service and object need to be real luxury. Nokia's Vertu telephone is a perfect illustration of the case: service (the concierge) is the quintessence of luxury, as is the object (the mobile), which everyone can admire, and which is made by jewellers.

The most difficult to manage are the electronic products where object and technology cannot be split. It is feasible, as shown by Bang & Olufsen, but success is very volatile, as design and technology must be both at the top. Founded in 1925 by Peter Bang and Sven Olufsen, B&O has been very successful, and some of its products are part of the permanent collection of New York's Museum of Modern Art. But in the 1980s the company departed from the strict requirements of a luxury strategy. As a consequence, at the beginning of the 1990s the brand suffered big losses, its design being outdated and its technology behind top competitors like Bose: both aspects of luxury were severely harmed. However, B&O being a luxury brand again, it didn't die, and Anders Knutsen made a remarkable turnaround by again implementing a luxury strategy.

The big difficulty in this case is to be both very modern in design but, unlike fashion, staying modern for years and not for months, and staying at the edge of technology – which is requesting the mastering of two very different areas of expertise often contradictory. When you are able to do it, then you can implement a luxury strategy, as described in this book, with huge success. But this is fragile as shown by B&O's poor results in 2007–2008.

14 Entering luxury and leaving it

Everyone has examples of luxury brands in their head, those that exist today. The list, however, is not closed: some brands will die, but tomorrow new brands will be born, and in great numbers, whether in Europe or the USA, or in China, Korea, Japan, India or Russia, since we saw, in Chapter 1, the degree to which the luxury market is growing structurally in these countries and how it is progressively conquering all trades.

Here we will address the three key questions that the founders of new luxury brands should ask themselves:

- Why choose a luxury strategy?
- How do you manage development while maintaining a luxury strategy?
- And, finally, when, how and why should you exit luxury?

Wanting to be luxury is not enough: the conditions of luxury

We have analysed in detail in this work what a 'luxury strategy' is. This analysis was based on practical, concrete experiences, with their successes and failures, each as instructive as the other, of companies operating in the classic luxury markets (clothing, jewellery, personal accessories, cars, hotels, cruises, etc.).

From these we deduced the rules of management, and in particular the 'anti-laws' of marketing, which form a highly coherent corpus, often completely opposed to the strategies and tactics applied successfully in classic marketing. It was necessary to pursue this lengthy analysis to its end in order to convince our readers that success in luxury was not only the recompense of creative talent and luck, but that it was equally the result of marketing practices that were original, but just as structured and professional as those of classic marketing.

If the overall analysis of what luxury is in Chapter 1 ('In the beginning there was luxury') is valid for any company in any era, the practical tools, in particular the '4Ps' (product, price, place, promotion), correspond to a specific environment. It is therefore necessary to adapt them to the trade and culture in which the luxury strategy is envisaged. Pragmatism should be the watchword, and we will return to it frequently throughout this chapter; what we feel important is that you should be clear on why you are not rigorously respecting this law or that one, and that you have weighed up the consequences of this choice. Another point: the '4Ps in luxury' are as consistent together as are the '4Ps' in traditional marketing. It is therefore very dangerous to implement a strategy with one or two 'Ps in luxury' and the other 'Ps' remaining managed the traditional way: all the '4Ps' have to be readjusted. Consistency is of course extremely important in traditional marketing, but it is an absolute necessity in luxury, owing to the importance of all the qualitative aspects.

This is true even for existing products and markets: we have seen several times that luxury marketing must adapt to the client's level of familiarity with the brand. It is necessary to be highly rigorous with the client who does not know the brand, in order to reassure and convince them of the quality and coherence of the brand universe. However, with a client already familiar with the brand, the approach can and should be less ceremonious. This is particularly true in terms of the price, where, even though it is clear that you should never lower the price of a product, you can do a 'favour' for a familiar client, such as reserved offers, or 'private sales'. If this is done well, it will not be seen as a brand weakness, but on the contrary as a privilege reserved for the connoisseur, the friend – in fact as a gift from the brand to someone who deserves it: the affective link is thus reinforced.

Likewise, the role of the internet in a luxury strategy will evolve along with the tool and the sociocultural environment: rightfully completely excluded from luxury some 10 years ago, we now strongly recommend including it in the communications mix, thanks to its considerable qualitative evolution (images, sounds) and technological evolution (high speed); we exclude it from sales today (while still strongly recommending its use in pre- and after-sales, or CRM – customer relationship management), until it becomes more secure and personalized... but perhaps we will recommend it tomorrow. Here again, pragmatism is king!

Conversely, this does not mean that a luxury strategy is always possible, and less still that it is economically realistic: the cemeteries are full of people who believed they were indispensable, but also of companies that thought they were 'luxury'.

The fact that your grandmother was able to stitch together a few garments for the notables of the village, or that your great-grandfather sold a few hand-made articles at the market in the neighbouring town, is not, de facto, enough to justify the historic roots of a luxury brand. Artisanship is not luxury as long as it is not socially coded and a bearer of taste, or even simply art.

Likewise, you should not confuse a product that is not sold with a rare product, by blaming the incomprehension of potential clients and not blaming your own obstinacy and the failings of the offer.

Why envisage a luxury strategy?

Luxury attracts and fascinates. Even the most rational managers and financial analysts are susceptible to it. It is true the luxury brands have recognition out of all proportion to the normal size of their turnover. Moreover, these managers are good clients of luxury: high, immediately disposable income, ready to be invested in objects that signify the beautiful and the taste of the acquirer, not to mention their wealth – but above all their social status!

There are three fundamental reasons why you might be tempted by a 'luxury strategy', as we define it in this book:

The first is profitability.

The figures are exceptional... when there are any. Luxury is a 'jackpot business': you can earn a great deal, with an uncommonly high return on invested capital. In 1994, the net profitability on invested capital by Louis Vuitton Malletier was higher than 120 per cent, whereas the minimum threshold of 15 per cent, demanded by the financial world, seems unattainable for many. Often, however, you can lose everything: Bernard Arnault himself pulled out of Christian Lacroix after almost 20 years without profitability, and this despite the genius of Christian Lacroix and the genuine competence of the succession of managers at the head of the company.

The second reason is the unimportance of the company's size

In traditional markets, whether it is a matter of consumer goods or industrial goods, we know through PIMS (the Profit Impact of Market Share) or BCG (Boston Consulting Group) studies that the 'leader's bonus' is very high: in a homogeneous market (PIMS figures), whatever the product, on average:

- the profitability on turnover of the leader is over 12 per cent;
- that of the second is around 8 per cent;
- that of the third around 3.5 per cent;
- the rest are losing out.

Consequently, if you are not in the top three in any market, it is worth thinking of adopting a luxury strategy, as explained throughout this book, if there is a base for it in your product or service. Small initial size is not a handicap in that case, and it can even be an asset, as we will see later on.

The third reason is desire

Creators are born every day with the ambition of installing new codes of taste and excellence, creating a new luxury house, their own. All of them should remember the three basic conditions that make a luxury strategy conceivable at the beginning:

- the product must have the power to be a valorizing social signifier;
- the product must comprise a significant dream part for enough people;
- the company must be small enough.

If the first two conditions are hardly surprising to the reader, since we have already developed them in full, the third, which can be rewritten as 'start small', is different. We have already seen how closely luxury and time are linked, and how much time luxury needs. A famous Asian proverb says: 'What time has not made, time destroys' – it is now time to apply it!

Start small and become profitable

This recommendation does not mean that you must be minuscule; rather that not only is large size not an advantage, but it can even prove an obstacle, in particular at the client relationship level. We have already seen that the golden rule of luxury distribution is to maintain the direct link with your client, which supposes:

- either that the link already exists with all clients (the ideal case, but a rare one if the company has reached a significant size);
- or that it must be built. If there are already many clients, this is difficult. A process of recentring on part of the clientele, and closing part (perhaps a large part) of distribution and accepting the risk of a significant drop in turnover, will be necessary: this is a financially costly operation and requires the shareholders to hold their nerve.

This latter situation is fairly common in luxury, where the repurchase of licences, given out to 'make money quickly', becomes indispensable in order to regain a luxury image and strategy.

The case of Ralph Lauren is a good, and very recent, illustration: in 2002, it decided to abandon its licences strategy to pursue a luxury strategy, which involved a progressive retaking of control over its distribution network. This strategy worked well (net profit rose from $172.5 million for the 2002 financial year to $401 million for the 2007 financial year, with licences falling from 64 per cent to 17 per cent of the operating profit, and boutiques increasing from 4 per cent to 26 per cent over this period), but at the cost of heavy investment: Polo repurchased its *prêt-à-porter* licence in Japan for $155 million in the spring of 2007, and significant sums were invested in its boutiques (*Fortune*, 17 September 2007). YSL, which launched into a similar strategy following the brand's acquisition by PPR, still cannot see the light at the end of the tunnel, even 10 years on.

Once profitable, grow quickly

Once this 'launch base' has been built, it then conversely becomes necessary to grow quickly, or in some senses to make up for lost time.

The reason for this abrupt change of pace is simple: just as it was necessary to take time at the beginning to be certain that the dream you were offering was indeed a dream for enough people, once you have this certainty, it is equally necessary to make haste to conquer the maximum number of clients, before the dream can fade away with a change of socioeconomic circumstances, or a competitor who fulfils it better than you do. In some sense you need to 'occupy the terrain'.

Here we find the practical consequence of what we called the 'swing threshold' in Chapter 12 on finances: this is the moment when the resource allocation policy must be fundamentally changed. There is no rule of thumb for determining this threshold: it depends on the trade and the brand's situation versus the competing offer. One thing only is clear: as long as the company is not, even slightly, profitable, this threshold has not been reached. Very few of those who have sunk large sums of money into a brand in order to develop it before it reached financial equilibrium by itself have ever recovered their stake.

- Below this threshold it is much more profitable to concentrate your limited resources on the construction of the product offer ('usage part' and 'personal dream part'), in order to seduce a small core of clients from the start, leading to slow growth during this constitution period.
- Beyond this threshold, you should throw most of your resources into the conquest of new clients in order to develop the product's 'social dream part', the only thing capable of ensuring the brand's global expansion.

This is the beginning of the heavy investment phase, partly in distribution, sometimes all the heavier if a licensing strategy has been used from the beginning to 'make money quickly' (see the case of Ralph Lauren), and partly in communication, particularly media advertising (word of mouth is now no longer enough; see Chapter 11 on communication). In this rapid growth phase, the bulk of resources should be invested in communication and distribution, in addition to the development of the production tool (which should follow demand, even with some delay, and not precede it, hence the de facto product scarcity, the price of success).

If you continue to invest too heavily in the product beyond this threshold, in addition to the investments in conquering new clients, the company will generally find itself in severe financial difficulties – for example, the Swedish car company Koenigsegg. Founded in 1994 by Christian von Koenigsegg, the company broke even in 2003 and became really profitable in 2004 with the CCR model. This beautiful car sold at around $500,000, already a very high price, even for a luxury car. Instead of switching his efforts and money to consolidate the success of the CCR, Koenigsegg kept on developing new models, like the CCXR, launched in 2007, and priced over $2 million. The profit of 2004 turned into big losses in 2005 and 2006.

In order to succeed in this development without ruining yourself or draining the brand of its substance, there are certain rules to be respected, as detailed below.

In geographic development: creating your roots

You need to begin local and specific (one place, one product) in order to ensure coherence and the personal link to the clients from the start, and then become regional, and finally national: we have seen that the luxury product always carries the marks of its birthplace, which forms part of the client dream. Wine is French, silk is Chinese, caviar is Russian, Rolls-Royce is British.

The next step is to move beyond your borders, and become global, as explained in Chapter 12 on finances; the trick here is to be recognized as a luxury product by cultures other than the one in which the brand was born, and this is often a stiff challenge.

This step is crucial, and requires skilful steering. In particular, you should not launch 'in all directions', nor choose markets according to their size. You must begin with those whose clients are most receptive to the brand, and who will accept the product as it stands, without modifications, as a luxury product. Remember anti-law number 3, 'Don't pander to your customers' wishes'. This is a way of working that is the total opposite of classic marketing: a luxury product adapted to local requirements is no longer a luxury product... with the obvious technical exceptions, such as left-hand drive for cars in continental Europe and the USA, and right-hand drive for cars in Japan and Great Britain.

We have said that the choice of a new location is never delegated; this is even more true for the decision to open in a new country.

Finally, a brand often finds that the socioeconomic position of its clients is very different from one country to the next: in the 1980s, Louis Vuitton's clients in France were mainly adult women aged 40 and over, and in Japan young 'office ladies' under 30. This was not a serious problem, but it had to be taken into consideration at the distribution and communication level. In contrast, seeking to attract Japanese women over 40 on the pretext that the typical French client was over 40 would have been a complete cultural mistranslation, obvious to anyone familiar with Japan!

It is therefore necessary to choose the country with care, identify the local target clientele, and choose carefully the location of the first sales point; in particular, a smaller store but in a prestigious location for the brand, although not too prestigious since it will suffer by comparison if you aim too high, is preferable to a larger, but less well-placed store. The first opening is effectively a 'statement' on the brand's status, and you don't get a second chance to make a first impression.

In product development: creating your reference

You need to begin with a single product, or, if this is impossible, with a single range of products, at a global level. This is the condition for achieving a minimum of 'scale effect' in production and communication, and therefore being able to finance worldwide expansion: you must stick to this unique product as long as possible (see above, Koenigsegg's financial problems).

It is only later, once worldwide expansion has been achieved, that you can introduce (and not 'launch') a second range, and then possibly a third, within the same product universe, and only after this that can you envisage new product territories.

Acquiring an existing brand

If you do not have the time to build a brand from scratch, taking over a brand belonging to the luxury universe is an apparently elegant and financially satisfactory solution, when you are rich and in a hurry. There are two ways of doing this.

Using a brand that is already within the company but previously not exploited, or whose use has been abandoned

This is what Mercedes, or rather the Daimler-Benz group, did by reactivating the Maybach brand, already part of their portfolio. Willhelm Maybach was the chief engineer at Daimler Motoren Gesellschaft (DMG) on its foundation in 1882, and in this role had launched the Mercedes in 1900, and then launched luxury cars in his own name: the first model, the Maybach W1, dates from 1919. It is a nice story, one on which Mercedes can build. In 1929, Maybach's son Karl placed the company's know-how at the service of the Third Reich in order to produce V12s for Panzer tanks, while continuing production of cars until 1940; the company disappeared at the end of the Second World War.

The Daimler group, familiar with the history of the Maybach brand, was therefore in a position to revive its glorious past, while glossing over the troubled period; it could therefore revive it, particularly since other German luxury brands (BMW, Hugo Boss) were in the same situation between 1930 and 1945. It was a collective problem, and therefore less directly imputable to the brand.

Acquiring a brand

This second strategy is increasingly employed, since (in theory!) it saves a great deal of time that would otherwise have to be spent building the brand universe. It has led to a considerable increase in value of luxury brands over the past 20 years, as we saw in Chapter 12 on finances.

However, it is more complex to manage than might be thought, as the example of Volkswagen's acquisition of the Bugatti brand shows: there was no historical legitimacy in the link between Volkswagen and Bugatti, and the cultures were very different (as their names indicate). Not only must you be certain that the 'dream' of the brand can be reactivated, but there must also be teams in place who know how to run it, which is generally not the case when a company producing mass consumer goods buys a luxury brand, or when the cultural universes are too different (see Chapter 2, 'The end of a confusion').

In all cases where this new brand strategy is chosen, it is imperative that you ensure the coherence of the entire marketing mix in the first stage, before thinking of going further. As we have said, a luxury brand is not launched, any more than a luxury product is launched. If an otherwise effective group has not succeeded in luxury, it is not only because the chosen brand did not carry a dream, but often because the classic marketing strategies, and therefore the competent teams who have successfully applied them, are unsuitable for this new market. There is a serious risk that the graft will not take. It is therefore often necessary to 'begin again from zero', which is very difficult when you have been successful elsewhere.

Departing from luxury

Being a luxury brand is not an end in itself. Remaining one implies a respect for norms and constraints that you may no longer wish to follow, or even that you are no longer able to follow. It is therefore necessary to know how to depart from luxury, which is in no way shameful. There are other profitable business models, such as, for example, that of premium brands, or that of fashion brands. Mercedes exited luxury in order to move towards the status of upper-range generalist. For its management the alternative was simple: either remain luxury and disappear like Rolls-Royce (bought by BMW), or grow, but no longer as luxury. We will therefore examine the reasons that may lead to a departure from luxury and the ways of achieving it.

The end of a luxury brand

We have already seen that the transition from the status of a small, confidential luxury brand to that of a global brand is difficult, but that many different, effective business models make it possible to achieve this.

We also know that luxury is eternal, or at least will survive as long as humans exist, and the luxury market is heading for robust development for the coming years. From these elements we might conclude that, once 'in orbit', a luxury brand remains an eternal success, like a work of art.

However, this is not the case: even if luxury as such will never die, a luxury brand is fragile, and even an entire trade; we are thinking here not only of the furrier business, but also of perfumery, which is imperceptibly evolving from an art to a mass prestige trade under the influence of the repetitive launches of new products under a single brand. Once you cannot or no longer wish to apply our 'anti-laws', the end is nigh: a 'premium' strategy then dominates. As we have already seen, even if a luxury brand never disappears completely and can always be resuscitated (as were Gucci, Balmain and Bugatti), it can rapidly wither away through refusing a change in status to become a premium brand. In the eyes of some (but not in the eyes of the authors!), moving from 'luxury' to 'premium' represents a diminution of the brand. This is a capital mistake: a luxury brand is neither better nor worse than a premium brand; it is simply managed differently. A parallel can be drawn here with the fairly classic behaviour of the heir of a prestigious and wealthy family finding themselves in a difficult financial situation. Refusing to admit that their social situation has changed, they refuse to re-evaluate and to work hard to begin again on a new basis. Thus begins the downward spiral of decline, of selling the family jewels in order to keep up appearances.

The principal causes of the withering away of a brand are:

- uncontrolled extension of distribution (as with the case of perfume);
- contamination of the 'pyramid' from below, through all the non-luxury products bearing the signs of the luxury brand;
- lack of creativity in the core range (death of the creator);
- voracious shareholders (to borrow a familiar expression from the Boston Consulting Group, they 'milk the cash cow');
- but, above all, the short-term pressure (such as that which makes fashion necessary), of a universe that no longer gives time its place – and as we have said, luxury needs time!

According to the chosen business model, the causes of this withering are different.

The Louis Vuitton Malletier-type business model

We have already examined its six intrinsic risks in Chapter 13 on business models:

1. Diversifications that are not wholly legitimate and are less profitable.
2. The ease of the everyday.
3. Internal lassitude.
4. Rejection of the past.

5. Rigidity due to vertical integration.
6. Staleness of the product image through saturation and vulgarization.

However, the most serious risk is the extrinsic risk: that of shareholder greed, attempting to 'milk the brand' to the maximum by pushing it to move away from its domain of legitimacy, and to move towards the pyramid or galaxy models, which are not suitable in this case.

This is death by dilution, dispersion or evaporation of the brand content. A famous example is that of the Gucci family, which succeeded in causing the Gucci brand to almost completely wither away, before it was saved through acquisition by Investcorp and taken firmly in hand by the Domenico De Sole–Tom Ford duo, and then by the French PPR group.

The pyramid business model

The principal risk linked to this way of working, as already examined, is that of upwards contamination, through easy money. At its most extreme, as we see with many couture brands, there is still a summit, made concrete by the fashion show, but there is no longer an intermediate stage of the offer: everyone is concentrating on the base, on the high-margin, easy to sell products, products where they are cheapest. Only the name is luxury: the rest is only a badge.

The products at the base of the pyramid are not sufficiently charged with quality and creativity, but enjoy very high margins, above 80 per cent, since the dream value, which endures for a little while longer, is far higher than the usage value, which becomes almost nil following the drop in product quality: the door is wide open for counterfeiting.

The galaxy business model

The principal risk is that the force of attraction that holds the whole together is no longer enough, either because the centre weakens, or even disappears (such as on the death of the creator who incarnated the myth, the dream), or because too many different universes have been created and the centrifugal force is too great. When the two are combined, as in the case of Pierre Cardin, the writing is on the wall.

There are two possible fallback options in this case: departing from luxury (see below), or moving to the pyramid strategy, by concentrating and restructuring the offer around certain product families only.

This is an advantageous strategy in particular when the creator dies, or retires (as with Yves Saint-Laurent in 2002), while their image is still strong; it is possible to try to continue to feed the dream that descends from the summit of the pyramid, for example by naming a talented designer as head of the house, who will respect the founder's image and be artistically compatible with their achievements (as Saint-Laurent is currently attempting with the appointment of Stefano Pilati).

The perfume business model

Is the perfume business model doomed in the long term? Nowadays perfume has been dethroned by the iPod as the gift product that pleases women most. Its dream potential has been dented.

We have seen above that the financial situation of the perfume trade is being degraded, a logical consequence of the fact that perfume, the first attempt at interbreeding between 'luxury' and 'premium', began progressively to abandon the codes of luxury, and to break our anti-laws, in particular at the distribution level. The causes of this slide are multiple, but the principal one is the pressure of fashion.

We have seen that, in fact, the greats of luxury perfume are no longer perfumers, but couturiers. This, clearly, is the first step in the downgrading of perfume as a luxury product, since the luxury is no longer in the product itself but in its belonging to another universe. The 'dream part' and the 'usage part' of the product (see Chapter 8) are no longer complementary, as they are in any luxury product, but are completely uncoupled from one another – the beginning of schizophrenia, an illness that is fatal to the integrity of the personality, a key point for luxury.

Since the universe of the great couturiers is fashion, perfume finds itself swallowed up by it: perfume is no longer created for the long term, like all luxury products, but is 'launched' like a new collection or a new shampoo. There is therefore no time to construct the dream and nurture it: you must launch massively, and quickly. The launch of a perfume, however, is very expensive: as we have noted, you spend the estimated turnover of the first year on advertising for the launch.

In order to make this enormous investment profitable, there is no longer any question of a creative, sophisticated and refined perfume, which would create too small a segment or take too long to 'understand', but a simple, immediately identifiable scent. Nor is there any question of controlled distribution where the link with the client is maintained: you need a mass distribution, which is catastrophic for the product's luxury image, even if you try to make it selective (see Chapter 10 on distribution). As for its communication, it will exploit the current stereotypes of the targeted client segment: since perfumes target the same segments, it leads to interchangeable advertisements. Beginning with the consumers necessarily creates trivialization: beginning with the brand's values and codes would have preserved the differentiation and the dream.

The consequence of this evolution is that people are no longer seeking a perfume that will last – a 'great classic' – and the economic logic of luxury (continual investment in the long term, made profitable by a product that lasts for a long time) gets lost here: 300 perfumes or variants on existing perfumes are launched every year. Knowing that new perfumes take 15 per cent of the market and that the market grows by 5 per cent each year, it is clear that these new, industrially launched perfumes threaten the others. Coty has become famous for launching star perfumes before buying Unilever's upper-range perfumes (Calvin Klein, Lagerfeld). Its slogan is 'Faster, further, freer'. It is clear that through the emphasis on speed, the relationship to time is that of the mass consumption market. Eighty-five per cent of perfumes launched have a lifespan of less than a year, and less than 1 per cent will become classics, whereas, in the luxury perfume schema and up until the 1990s, a new perfume had a one in two chance of being successful.

Procter and Gamble is typical of a commercial success based on this model of repeatedly launching new products under the same brand, rather than seeking to create sales in the long term: its methods are directly inspired by mass consumption marketing, image marketing, whereas in luxury it is the brand identity that takes precedence.

Likewise, our anti-law number 9, 'The role of advertising is not to sell', and number 16, 'Keep stars out of your advertising', are increasingly neglected in perfume; the systematic use of regularly changing stars in advertising, and the massive investment in television, are completely opposed to a luxury strategy. As for the use of a 'brand ambassador', a strategy that can respect the 'codes of luxury' if it is correctly undertaken, it is practised both by the greats of luxury such as Chanel, and the greats of premium such as Lancôme; it is therefore no longer a factor of differentiation between luxury and premium.

Less controlled distribution, loss of contact with the client, advertising to sell... we are beginning seriously to move away from a luxury strategy. Result: the economic balance has been lost. For almost 20 years now, launching a luxury perfume has been statistically loss-making (the mathematical expectation of profitability is negative); the great perfume houses remain profitable thanks to their great classic(s), which make up the entirety of their profit, while additionally bearing the costs of launching the 'novelties', which are in fact only a waste of money and energy. In fact, these houses find themselves on a terrain that is no longer that of luxury, but that of premium; and on this terrain the big marketers (L'Oréal or P&G) are much better equipped to succeed than they are. Hence the recent handover of YSL Perfumes from PPR to L'Oréal: with the departure of Yves Saint-Laurent, the brand lost the capacity of pursuing a luxury strategy, at least in the perfume business.

One of the extreme strategies is that undertaken for Poison, by Dior: the expensive components of the perfume, essentially the name (hence Tendre,

Hypnotique, Pure Poison, etc) and the bottle (varied in every possible colour), are recycled, with one or two cosmetic modifications (a particularly apt term in this case), while changing those things that are not too expensive to change (the 'juice', the advertising creation). These are last-ditch strategies, which risk voiding the brand of its contents for limited financial profit.

However, all is not lost for luxury perfumes:

- True perfumers can take the opportunity of this 'mass-premiumization' of couture perfumes, accelerated by the influence of marketer like l'Oréal on those perfumes, and the decline of haute couture and the dream it was conveying, to recreate a market for luxury perfumes. Penhaligon's, Serge Lutens, Annick Goutal have a great opportunity if they implement fully a luxury marketing strategy, as described in this book. It is also a great opportunity for Guerlain, which suffered in the last 10 years of 'premiumization' drift and decreasing financial results, to revive its glorious past.
- Some still succeed in launching luxury perfumes within the universe of the couturiers; two of the major successes of recent years (Le Mâle by Jean-Paul Gaultier and Angel by Thierry Mugler) were the work of great professionals (in both cases women) who were perfectly conversant with the codes of luxury (they had started out at Yves Saint-Laurent, back in the 'glory days'), and applied them with rigour and talent. But this is the exception rather than the rule, whereas not too long ago, it was the reference model for success.

Taking a brand out of the luxury universe

When a brand cannot or no longer wishes to respect the constraints of the chosen business model, whether for reasons external to the company or internal reasons, it is time to consider leaving luxury before it is too late.

The external reasons:

- The market where the highest level of the brand is recognized and expressed is disappearing. It was the case for the silversmiths' trade at Christofle, where the heavy, solid silver products were linked to a way of life that has almost disappeared (ceremonial dinners of the haute bourgeoisie of the 19th century). In the same way, as analysed in the previous chapter, ST Dupont (like Dunhill) suffered badly from legislation against smoking in public and tobacco advertising, and therefore the cigarette lighter as a prestigious gift no longer had cachet; the brand succeeded in a first evolution towards pens (thanks to the product coherence between the cigarette lighter and the pen), and then with much less success into leather goods and *prêt-à-porter* in the classic British style. The absence of (technical and image) legitimacy, and therefore of the 'dream part', of ST Dupont in these latter trades explains the failure of this brand stretching. It is interesting to note that the same is true for Dunhill: despite its different roots (one brand is French, the other English), different shareholders and different management, the recent history of these two brands has been almost identical. The laws that we have revealed for management of luxury are indeed structural laws.

- Without disappearing, the market may be considerably reduced: this was the case for *haute joaillerie*, which is much less frequently worn in public, hence the evolution of these brands into watchmaking, a legitimate evolution, and then perfume (again!), a much less legitimate one.
- The creator changes strategy. This is how Pierre Cardin became a brand managing a global business of pure licences, which profitably exploits the afterglow of his prestige among a mass clientele: the stand of shirts, belts and ties at Galeries Lafayette is one of the most profitable of the entire men's department at the Parisian department store.
- The death of the creator, when he alone embodies the dream and therefore cannot be replaced, often leads to a departure from luxury (the Chanel house is one of the rare exceptions). Thus Thierry Mugler has ceased to create: all that remains under its name are the Angel and Alien perfumes, and a few accessories, all managed by Clarins. The same is true for Loris Azzaro, Nina Ricci now owned by Puig in Spain, or Guy Laroche, bought from Bic by a Chinese group.

As for internal reasons, there are two:

- loss of creativity;
- impatient or greedy shareholders.

In all these cases, it is better to get out of luxury before it is too late, that is, before the brand becomes worthless.

For whichever reason the decision to leave luxury is taken, implementing this strategy is not easy: as we saw in Chapter 1, you can be lastingly profitable either in classical brand marketing (L'Oréal, Procter & Gamble) or in luxury (Louis Vuitton, Cartier, Chanel); very rarely can you achieve profitability in-between the two. Managing the transition is a difficult and perilous art of its own.

However, success of the strategy is possible, as shown by a case of clever management of departure from luxury: that of Dior. In fact, the man Christian Dior was never really replaced after his death in 1957, despite the talent of the great couturiers who succeeded him as head of design over almost half a century, from Yves Saint-Laurent to Gianfranco Ferré.

The arrival of John Galliano in 1997, exactly 50 years after the launch of the 'New Look', was a key element in the complete change of strategy: the transition from that of a luxury brand (Christian Dior) to that of a prestige fashion brand (Dior).

Without of course admitting it publicly, so as to avoid damaging its superb image, the Maison Dior passed in a few years from being a haute couture house, in the name of Christian Dior, with a talented designer (Gianfranco Ferré) and superb collections made to be worn, to a brand, simply named 'Dior' (and a set of initials, 'CD'), with an 'artistic director' who is admittedly a great couturier, but also and above all a very talented showman (John Galliano), and whose fashion shows are designed to provoke and to highlight the accessories, not to sell dresses.

This strategy proved economically rewarding (after many difficult years, Dior is now profitable), but at the price of a great separation: the Dior name is always mentioned among the first when people are asked to name French luxury brands, but the Dior products are practically never mentioned when people are asked to name French luxury products spontaneously. It will be interesting to see how long this unstable situation will last, and whether the decision will be taken to return to luxury, or to depart totally from the luxury universe. Today, both strategies are possible; the decision to pursue outsourcing of the manufacture of products sold under the Dior brand will be one of the key factors in this choice: relocation is an anathema to luxury.

Dior is not the only couture house in this situation: Yves Saint Laurent is in a very similar state to Christian Dior's before it became Dior; it could become the prestige fashion brand Saint Laurent, and a set of initials, YSL. As seen above, the sale of Yves Saint-Laurent Parfums to L'Oréal is a big step in this direction

We have already analysed this subject several times: luxury and fashion are both economically significant universes, but completely different (the 'luxury streets' are not in the 'fashion quarters') and have only marginal overlap; while the creator is alive, a fashion brand, even if it is not a luxury house (Ralph Lauren for example), can sell luxury products, if they are given legitimacy by the creator.

Once the creator is gone, in order to remain a profitable luxury brand, it must succeed in forming a 'tandem': of the brand (which guarantees luxury) and the designer (who guarantees fashion), as Chanel succeeded in doing with Karl Lagerfeld; but success rarely follows, since it is markedly similar to a mixture of water and fire, so strong is the deep opposition between a luxury brand and a fashion designer.

We have taken our last examples in the universe of fashion, because it is there that the question is the more frequently aroused, but we have previously seen another example: the Daimler group and the Mercedes brand.

The decision of the Daimler group to have Mercedes leave luxury was moti-vated by the too small size, according to the shareholders, of the luxury market; so, the acquisition of Chrysler, the launch of the Mercedes A-class and of Smart, and the revival of the Maybach brand. As of now, the decision to leave luxury has shown less financial success than the one of BMW, which decided to stay in luxury, but this was the shareholders' decision!

In order to be successful, the departure from luxury must be achieved in time (the brand must have retained its prestige, and must not be under too great a financial burden), and carried out with a great deal of marketing rigour. One of the key points, however, is the transformation of teams: we have seen how much, in luxury, the quality of the teams and their loyalty to the brand were crucial. When you move from a 'luxury' strategy to a 'premium' strategy, the human and technical competencies required are different, leading to a considerable task of recentring, training and conviction to be carried out by management... all without saying so officially, since the key to success here is to maintain the luxury image for the client: the client should not become aware of this departure from the luxury universe if you want the 'dream part' to remain intact as far as possible, since this is what will protect the company during its transformation.

15 Learning from luxury

We have just explained how to develop in a luxury market. At this point, we should broaden our discussion and suggest that, contrary to received wisdom, all sectors can draw elements of strategy from luxury. It could even be suggested that this will be necessary if brands wish to pursue an original and effective strategy, and aim high in the segments where they operate, thereby offering a counterweight to the tendency for trivialization encouraged by mass distribution, discount and so-called 'low-cost' companies. The luxury marketing strategies analysed and defined in this book are not limited to the traditional luxury markets; in fact, you can always find, in every trade or market, a luxury niche, or more precisely a niche in which a luxury strategy could be successful, even in those trades where it is not immediately apparent.

Luxury concerns all trades

First, it is a question of knowing for whom you wish to be luxury, and acting accordingly. And this question is not limited to classical luxury trades.

Let us take the example of surgery: at first glance, this is the opposite of luxury, both because the superfluous is prohibited (you must save the sick or injured person), because it is frightening (being operated on is never a pleasure), because it is not a social stratifier (we do not generally show off the operation scars, or boast publicly of having been operated on). Moreover, its economic model is specific (reimbursement biases the entire system of price fixing and strongly limits the freedom of both the 'producer' and the 'consumer') and is under strong financial constraints (pressure from health insurance funds and Social Security). Finally, it is the subject of ongoing public debate, hardly a propitious environment for drawing up a strategy that takes time to implement. And yet, there is indeed at least one luxury niche here: cosmetic surgery, in which the strategy we have revealed in this book works very well, as the success of the upper range clinics clearly demonstrates. Brazil, and particularly Rio de Janeiro, are carriers of the dream of youth and physical beauty: this is one of the most desirable places to set up a clinic where, in a luxury environment, the 'surgical act' loses all aggressive connotations and is sublimated into an artistic act, which procures for you not deliverance from suffering, but access to greater happiness.

At another level, it is not only at the top of a market that a luxury strategy can prove relevant: in the food market, caviar is admittedly a luxury product, but organic is just as much relevant for a luxury strategy, since it has all the necessary characteristics, and yet without being 'unaffordable', in accordance with our anti-law number 12: 'Luxury sets the price, price does not set luxury'.

In fact, all the elements of the luxury marketing mix are applicable in this case: the dream part of the product is health, its 'social signifier' is respect for the environment, the price is not the primary question (and is moreover higher than for an identical, non-organic product), distribution is controlled, and communication is there to recharge the dream, rather than to sell. In addition, there is a certain rarity due to non-intensive production.

Understand the rules in order to adapt them

When you are not in a traditional luxury trade, it is all the more important to respect the specific rules of luxury, or at least to understand them well enough to adapt them to the trade in question.

Clients do not necessarily decode the rules of luxury when they are applied in a trade that does not traditionally form part of the luxury universe, particularly when at first glance it seems unfavourable to luxury. In this case, the smallest mistake is immediately punished.

Having said this, a trade is particularly favourable to a luxury strategy if its average price is rising, or at least stable. If the average market price is falling sharply and continuously, then anti-law number 13, 'Raise your prices as time goes on in order to increase demand', must be adapted; in particular, it is the relative price to the market that must be taken into consideration, and not the absolute price of the product. The price of the product might be decreased, but it must decrease significantly less than the market price, so as to conserve a high price premium, and in addition it is necessary to plan a 'compensation' strategy for existing clients.

A typical example of this type of market is that of electronic goods, where 'Moore's law' dictates that prices decrease even as the functional quality of the products increases. However, one of the main brands is successfully following a strategy inspired by luxury: Apple.

How Apple follows a luxury strategy

As everybody knows, Apple was founded in 1976 by Steve Wosniak and Steve Jobs in California, around a vision: that of the computer with a human face, the computer as the servant of man and not the other way around. Those who recall this era and used to work on computers equipped with IBM's Disk Operating System will remember the shock created by the introduction in 1977 of the Apple II, its user-friendliness and ease of use, and then the revolution that was the Macintosh. The little smiling man who appeared when you switched on your Mac offered spontaneously to be your guide in this new universe, while the screens of other computers, which displayed reams of figures and terms that were incomprehensible to the ordinary mortal, confirmed from the start that you were an unwelcome intruder into said universe.

Despite the success of this strategy, Steve Jobs was considered too young and too unpredictable to manage a listed company, and in 1983 the shareholders of the Apple company hired John Sculley, the number two at Pepsi-Cola and one of the best marketers in the business, as CEO, thinking that with the launch of the Macintosh (put on the market in 1984), it was necessary to implement a 'true' marketing strategy in order to move to the next stage, and make Apple a challenger to IBM.

The clash of cultures between Sculley and Jobs quickly escalated to the point of Jobs's departure in 1985, due to the personal and strategic conflict between the two men, leaving Sculley with complete freedom to act. Profits began to go rapidly downhill, and in 1996–97 the situation at Apple was dire (Michael Dell declared in *Fortune* in 1997: 'the best solution is to shut down Apple and give the shareholders their money back'). Apple thought it better to acquire NeXT, the company founded by Steve Jobs some years after his departure, in order to regain Steve Jobs and hand the reins to him once more.

Steve Jobs returned to the original strategy, while adapting the management style to the new situation. Everyone knows the rest: the iMac, then the iPod and iTunes, finally the iPhone, an entire series of global successes, both in technical terms and at the level of financial profits... and the queue on 5th Avenue in the spring of 2007 for the launch of the iPhone, on an already saturated and ultra-competitive market, was spectacular proof of the wisdom of the 'Jobs' strategy. In 2007, Apple's stock market value was equal to that of IBM – it has come a long way in 10 years!

The case of Apple is a prime example of the difficulty, even the impossibility, for a brand or a company, to cross this border between 'luxury' and 'premium', in either direction, even within the same market niche, and even if the market is not a traditional luxury market. In fact, Apple's strategy has all the characteristics of a luxury strategy applied to a classic market: let us review them:

- A strong vision at the beginning, a creative Utopia.
- A historic, creative founder, nurturing and personifying this Utopia, who, having been supplanted, returns to save the now-declining company.
- A temporal dimension that now solidifies over time: Apple is a saga, that of a messianic creator, ousted from his own company and replaced by traditional marketing, then recalled to give the same company a new creative lease of life.
- A status component: when you use an Apple, you show it off proudly. Moreover, the famous Apple logo has been inverted on laptops so that everyone around can identify it in a meeting, when it is open. We all know users who stick an 'apple' on their computer cover in order to cover the brand of the (non-Apple) product they are using.
- A collective cultural dimension (as anyone who has attended Steve Jobs's annual jamboree can testify), and a personal one (any Apple fan can spend hours explaining to you to what extent their computer is different from, and nicer than, that of any other brand), the exceedance of pure functionality through an aesthetic dimension and sensual materials (glass and aluminium for the iMac).
- A relationship to art, since the brand is worshipped by design professionals, its most faithful clients and believers.
- Personalization taken to the extreme (the thousands of different possible covers for the iPod, even crocodile or python skin), and the 'iPod-ization' of your car.
- The systematic creation of virtual rarity, hence the queues of clients waiting an entire night for the opportunity to buy an iPhone as soon as it comes out.
- Increasingly controlled distribution: exclusive boutiques (the Cube) and dedicated Apple stands are multiplying, which enables them to remain

in direct contact with their clients, and never in direct comparison with other PC brands. Apple distribution took a further step with the launch of the iPhone, which is granted to a single telephone operator per country, at a high price (30 per cent of turnover) or a considerable royalty rate, which speaks volumes about the gross margin. We can understand the rush of sharp minds and hackers around the world to unlock this device and render it compatible with all operators. For Apple this is the equivalent of the counterfeiting or grey market typical of the luxury market.

- The prices clearly higher than all competitors and never reduced.
- Clients set at a distance: Apple was revolutionary in its day through its open invitation to 'techies' on all sides, to the 'nerds' to freely create with and for Apple. With iPhone and iTunes, we are moving into another logic, closed and aiming to manage demand.

The fact that Apple's strategy is clearly a strategy copied from what we call 'luxury' is likewise confirmed by the failure of John Sculley to return the 'Apple collective' to the straight and narrow of classic marketing, a failure that demonstrated the specificity of the brand, or better yet, the fact that Apple is not only a brand, but above all a universe, that of the original dream of 'human, user-friendly computing' of 1970s California.

In contrast, the most recent incident, due to the price positioning of the first offer, illustrates how difficult it is to manage a luxury strategy in 'non-luxury' trades: the iPhone was introduced at $599 (and not $600, as would have been the rule in luxury) on 29 June 2007 in New York, with great success. Despite this, and against our anti-law no. 13, 'Raise your prices as time goes on in order to increase demand', Apple abruptly lowered its price to $399 (and not $400) shortly afterwards, placing it at the level of other 'smartphones' and taking a major risk for its image.

Luxury according to Mini

When we think of luxury cars, the famous brands Bentley, Maserati and BMW immediately come to mind. However, the latter fought hard to buy the moribund Rover: because Mini was being sold along with it. Although BMW quickly lost money with Rover, which it had to sell on to the Chinese, the reverse was true with the little Mini, thanks to a strategy directly inspired by luxury.

Paying €23,000 for a car whose direct competitors are sold at €15,000 and which has more in common with a go-kart, with difficulty in getting in and out and limited luggage space (even in the estate version) appears something of a gamble. In reality BMW is applying a luxury strategy to the Mini, even if this car is not a luxury car. The essential facets of this strategy are visible:

- A strong temporal anchor point that grounds its authenticity: the 1960s. It was created in 1959.
- A strong geographic anchor point, maintained even though Mini is managed by BMW: England. Moreover, the Mini is produced close to Oxford.
- A strong cultural anchor point: that of creativity and moral liberation associated with the 1960s (the miniskirt, the Mini, pop music).
- A status dimension: the Mini has become a bijou car, and less of an everyman's car, the status it held in its first lifetime.
- Exceeding functionality through aestheticization, with the Mini becoming a style accessory, an element of one's own personalization, through its multiple options. The design of the Mini is the first purchasing criterion among its owners.
- The maintenance of a handmade element: the leather on the front seats.
- A relationship to art: the Mini quickly became an iconic shape of its century, adopted by contemporary artistic milieus. This led to partnerships with FIAC (Foire Internationale de l'Art Contemporain), Apple Expo, etc.
- A progressive beginning based on a single product ('the Mini'), which created a cult thanks to an unparalleled design and the enthusiasm of opinion leaders.
- Nowadays it has been brought up to date technically but the heritage is respected. The Mini is 60mm bigger than the historic Mini, but has respected the proportions of the latter down to the last micron. The increased length has enabled it to accommodate a larger engine, and to achieve more sporting performances, even without the Cooper S version.
- Ultra-personalization (300 exterior and 320 interior options): there is also a profusion of accessories. This creates high profitability owing to the fact that it prevents distributors from having stock: Minis are built to order, which leads clients to await 'their Mini' (once more the temporal dimension) and does not encourage them to haggle over the price – Mini offers zero reductions in any case. Profitability is all the higher as a result.
- The staging of desire through celebrities with Minis, photographed in their daily lives, all acting as 'buzz' factors.
- A feeling of exclusivity conferred by the two factors above, not to mention the exclusive distribution, close to the mythical BMW brand.
- The maintenance of a community of believers: people who collect Minis in the same way that others collect watches

A little-known fact that confirms through its absurdity the association of the Mini with luxury: before its acquisition by BMW, this car had never made money throughout its 41 years of existence. Today it is very profitable.

The strategies we discussed before were strategies in 'B to C' (business to customer), and in which the whole brand was concerned. But it is also possible to go further, and to apply those luxury strategies to part of a brand (we call them 'mixed strategies'), and even to B to B business.

Mixed strategies

We took a firm line on the indispensable coherence of all the elements of the marketing mix in luxury, meaning that you cannot successfully pursue a strategy mixing elements of the luxury '4 Ps' with elements of the classic '4 Ps', for example a luxury price policy and a traditional product policy. It is imperative to choose one or the other at a given moment.

Having said this, a purely luxury strategy is difficult, and often costly, to pursue; in particular, as we have already seen, it is highly demanding in terms of distribution. We might therefore wonder if it is not possible to pursue both strategies in parallel, within the same brand; this is what we will call 'mixed strategies', characterized by the fact that they are practised under the same brand name, one part using the classical '4Ps', the other the '4Ps of luxury'.

The 'two-tier' system: Caudalie

In a so-called 'two-tier system' strategy, one of the tiers is luxury, the other premium. The tiers are clearly separated, but within the same house.

For example, in cosmetics, new brands are continually being born, close to luxury, but in reality only part of their business is inspired by luxury. Two are symptomatic of this: Nuxe and Caudalie. Caudalie is a brand born in the Bordelais region, the high place of French wine. It is based on 'vinotherapy', the exploitation of the benefits of molecules and essences drawn from the vine itself. We find both the luxury, in the brand's exclusive hotels and spas based on the universe of the vine, and the premium dimension, in the self-care products, deriving from viticulture and sold in the classic perfumery networks. In this case, there is no possible confusion: the products of the two tiers bear the same brand name (Caudalie), share the same concept (vinotherapy), but are completely different. Despite having the same name, the joint use of which makes it possible to exploit genuine synergies, nobody confuses a spa and a packaged cosmetic cream.

True mixed strategies (linked products)

In this case, the product offer itself comprises a 'luxury' part and a 'premium' part, the two being closely intertwined: unlike the previous case, you do not buy one product or the other, you must buy both.

A particularly enlightening example is that of Nespresso, in which two strategies are pursued simultaneously.

A luxury strategy on the capsule

Here we find all the elements of the luxury marketing mix:

- the complete control over distribution, Louis Vuitton-style, maintaining the direct contact with the client and subtly using the internet for 'repurchase' and personalized dispatch;
- the product strategy (limited series, specific patented technology, the quality of the coffee obtained, the look of the capsules);
- the price strategy (very high, since the choice of competitive universe is coffee consumed at a restaurant, rather than the 'home coffeemaker' competitors, etc).

A premium strategy on the machine

Co-branding with upper-range brands such as Krups and open distribution made it possible to conquer Nespresso's target (the home) more quickly and less expensively than if a luxury strategy had also been chosen for the machine. It would then have been necessary to 'reinvent' internally at Nestlé the competences that already existed among manufacturers such as Krups. Once the machine has been bought, the brand is installed at home, and since the machine and the capsule are interdependent, a loyal client base, which is the first stage of success in luxury, is quickly created, for a reasonable investment cost. After this, the base does the demonstrating at home: it becomes the proselyte.

Since there is one common brand, it is in terms of communication that it was necessary to choose between the two strategies: luxury or premium. By using George Clooney as the 'star' in its advertising, Nespresso chose the 'premium' strategy. Nespresso could equally have used a 'luxury' strategy, without using a 'star', but rather by communicating on the dream of coffee, a cultural and sophisticated product dating back to recent antiquity, and all of whose characteristics lend themselves to luxury communication. By way of complement, George Clooney could have been used as a 'brand ambassador': his image, more 'man' than 'star', allows for this.

This choice of a premium and not a luxury communication strategy is a strong strategic choice, since it implies the choice of direct confrontation with competitors. It is coherent with belonging to a mass consumption goods group, Nestlé, which can bring all its firepower to bear in the service of the Nespresso brand, which fits well into its global strategy... but it leaves the luxury field open to the competition. Today, a house such as Jura (founded in 1931) is attacking the luxury niche, and now leads Nespresso in Germany and is hard on its heels in Switzerland in terms of provision of domestic machines.

Having said this, even in its choice of 'premium' advertising strategy, Nespresso retains a spice of luxury, in the way it is treated. In the advertisement, it is the Nespresso that attracts the client and not George Clooney: anti-law number 16, 'Keep stars out of your advertising', that is, 'The brand is above the stars', is therefore applied, as in luxury.

The future will tell whether the choice of a mixed, and therefore ambiguous in communication terms, strategy will last, whether Nespresso will align itself with a 'premium' strategy in order to continue to grow in the environment of a major group, or on the contrary choose luxury, in order to maintain its originality and its exceptional profitability.

The considerable success of Nespresso shows the relevance of this mixed approach; to successfully apply it, two conditions must be met:

- the offer must comprise at least two complementary elements and both must be indispensable: they must be overlapping;
- it must be possible to place the brand name on both, even if it is co-branding on the part of the offer that is managed as 'premium'.

Managing a luxury strategy in 'B to B'? Think 'B to B to C'

Given that a luxury house is in close contact with its client, a luxury strategy derives specifically from 'B to C' (business to customer); all that has been said in this book therefore does not appear to concern 'B to B'.

Nevertheless, 'B to B' represents a major part of the industry, and is facing considerable challenges in the context of globalization. If, for the 'B to C', there is always a possible choice between a 'low-cost' strategy on the one hand and upper-range or luxury strategies on the other, in order to escape the 'squeeze' in the middle of the range, it would appear that 'B to B' has no other alternative but to constitute an oligopoly (steel, paper, glass) or outsource.

In fact, the example shows that the classic strategies of 'creating shared value with the client' do not last: the client is quick to grab all of the value creation, and then to seek to shave down prices and margins. If you try to shelter behind patents, they will be quickly overturned, or even disregarded; how many small companies have died before the end of a counterfeiting lawsuit that they would have won?

It would therefore seem that for a developed country producer active on the 'B to B' market, the search for a monopoly, via the classic acquisition/restructuring strategies, is the only way to maintain a position of strength vis-à-vis its clients.

In fact, there is another path to be explored. In certain cases, an industrial 'B to B' may successfully pursue a luxury marketing strategy, or rather than a 'luxury product' marketing strategy: it is clear that, in this case, not all elements of the marketing mix are present (no distribution or public price policy), which means that a luxury strategy, as we have previously defined it, insisting on the total coherence of the '4 Ps', is clearly not applicable. However, it can be applied on the part of the '4Ps' which are relevant in 'B to B'.

For this strategy to work, it is imperative that:

- the product is a major component of the finished product;
- it arrives in the client's hands as such;
- it is an important part of the image perceived by the client;
- the supplier is not easily replaceable.

In order to shed further light on this subject, let us take a revealing example, experienced by one of the authors: glass bottles for perfumery.

At first glance this is hardly exciting: glass is a heavy industry, and therefore in contradiction with artisanship and creation, and the luxury part of the trade is that in which finished objects, destined for the end consumer, are made by hand (Baccarat, Daum, Cristal de Bohème), essentially for the decoration and tableware markets.

How can the business of glass packaging, essentially focused on the production of an enormous quantity of disposable objects (beer or wine bottles, yoghurt pots), become a business of producing luxury objects?

In fact, as we saw in Chapter 13 (perfume business model), the bottle is a key element of the perfume: it is what you pick up, it is what appears in advertising; it is therefore in some senses the 'transactional object' of the perfume product; it is, together with the name, the carrier of the product's luxury. Moreover, since time immemorial, perfumes have been placed in precious vessels. The key, for the glassmaker, is not to be caught in the trap of the simple packaging supplier who is subjected to competition, but to cross the barrier of the perfumer to understand what the end clients want, what their motivations are, to carry out its own market research on the ground, and to work upstream with the bottle designers to create original forms and colours. If this is well managed, the perfumer is obliged to work through this specific glassmaker if they wish to access rapidly an original, high-quality bottle, corresponding to the dreams of their potential clients, and therefore making a strong contribution to the perfume's success. In the launching of a perfume, it is the bottle that is on the 'critical path', since the other elements of the product (the scent, the advertising) are easy to carry out quickly. In our time-poor society, the glassmaker and the designer who arrive together to present a handsome, rapidly manufacturable product will win the contract. There is no longer any question of being subjected to savage competition... especially on price. Owing to this 'luxury product strategy in B to B', or rather 'luxury strategy in B to B to C', the French glassmakers of the Picard valley of la Bresle, and in particular Pochet du Courval and Desjonquères, have become world-leading and highly profitable companies, in a trade – glass packaging – where profitability is difficult to achieve.

This case is interesting for its marketing subtlety: a crystal Lalique bottle for the perfume L'Air du Temps by Nina Ricci, or a Baccarat bottle for the Louis XIII cognac by Rémy Martin, are luxury objects in themselves, which the glass bottles of Pochet or Desjonquères are not. The fact that they are key elements in a product relating to a luxury strategy (perfume, fine spirits) does not mean that these simple glass bottles can automatically become major actors in this luxury universe; It is the application of this original 'B to B to C strategy of luxury', and the progressive diminution of the perfume brands' capacity to properly manage a proper luxury strategy that strengthened the relative position of the manufacturers.

This example shows that it is possible to concentrate on only one of the elements of the marketing mix (the '4 Ps') of our luxury strategy as we have proposed it (in this case the product), always provided that it is not in contradiction with the others. It is in fact only possible if you are not in 'B to C' and therefore not in direct competition at the end client level.

This example relates to a supplier to a luxury trade and there are similar suppliers to many trades: among these, packaging, high-tech (founders such as Intel), technical car supply (Bosch, Valeo) or service (health) lend themselves particularly well to this exercise. Having said this, it is still necessary for the product to be perceived by the end consumer as a luxury, and therefore unique, and not as a premium product, and therefore substitutable, in which case the protection is illusory, as Valeo has found out.

The basic approach for a 'B to B luxury strategy' consists of:

- Finding out how and for whom your product can be luxury, and therefore have an existence of its own in the eyes of the end consumer, not only as a component, even of high quality.
- Beginning with the principle that your client is not the company to which you are selling your product, but the end consumer. This is what we call moving from 'B to B' to 'B to B to C'. It is necessary to break through the fence that your industrial client erects between you and the consumer, to understand directly how the final demand (quantitative and qualitative)

relates to your product. It is then necessary to develop products in response to this demand, and only then to go and sell these products to your industrial client, relative to whom you are in a position of strength to seize an important part of the value added by the 'dream part'. It is a question of leading an offer policy towards your client, but an offer already tested among the end consumers, and not simply being content to respond to your client's demands.

It is sometimes even possible to also lead a mass audience brand policy, which is a considerable strategic support; of course, it is necessary to communicate in luxury codes and not premium codes (dreams and not desire). Here we are entering fully into the true 'B to B to C', where the producer can master all elements of the marketing mix, right up to the end client. This is how Du Pont de Nemours built a reputation for Lycra, its luxury name for the fibre known as elastane: by working first and foremost with the luxury houses, which are always seeking to enrich their products with added value, it bypassed the first level of its clients (textile manufacturers) and directly addressed their clients, right up to the end client, through advertising.

Luxury marketing as the future of classic marketing?

In analysing how a luxury marketing strategy was possible, we have in fact used the research and discoveries of classic marketing, even if we have often arrived at conclusions and recommended practices opposed to those of classic marketing; in this way, classic marketing has brought a great deal to luxury.

In the opposite sense, luxury has already enriched classic marketing, by bringing new concepts and new techniques to it, which have been adapted to mass consumption products, with the personal relationship with the client becoming CRM, the lending of an object becoming 'product placement', 'word of mouth' becoming 'buzz marketing'.

This mutual enrichment therefore began some decades ago; now, to pick up on our Darwinian analogy from Chapter 1, the first hybrid species is appearing: the almost standard use by luxury perfumers of mass consumption marketing tactics today, to the detriment of luxury marketing tactics, makes perfume a hybrid, neither pure luxury nor pure premium, for which the neologism 'masstige' is suitable.

What marketing issues of today could luxury marketing help to resolve?

- In companies where there is overabundance, marketing is increasingly accused of playing a perverse role: instead of capturing and analysing the consumer's needs, it would seek to create them.
- Investment in the advertising (including the packaging) and not in the product: the client does not get more for their money, hence the rise of hard discount.
- The brand is no longer a guarantee of quality, but a 'mug's game', serving only to sell an often inferior product at a higher price, hence the success of unbranded products, Meiji and basic cars, such as the Logan; a study, carried out at the end of 2004, concluded that 80 per cent of French respondents felt that all brands were alike.
- Today's cars are differentiated only through the badge on the radiator grille.
- The systematic 'benchmarking' induces a mimetic crisis, hence the success of comparative advertising where, often, since there is nothing good to be said of your product as it has no originality, you are reduced to speaking ill of the competition.
- the marginal profitability of investment in advertising is shrinking, even negative (see the case of launching new perfumes above).

In the luxury concepts of searching the dream of the customer, keeping a personal contact with them, being ethical both with the producer and the customer, looking for quality of product and service before price, refusing to relocate, insisting on the qualified human input in production, communicating to create the dream and not to sell, and so forth, lots of ideas can be found to rejuvenate the brand and gain high-profitability.

The Lacoste example

Admittedly Lacoste is not a luxury brand. Since it was created by René Lacoste in 1933, the brand has been marketed as a luxury product within everyone's reach, an oxymoron in itself.

As a matter of fact, under the leadership of the world tennis champion René Lacoste, then of his sons – Bernard, and now Michel – the brand has continued with the same medium-price strategy.

Even if they are considered as the best-quality polo shirts in the world thanks to their first-rate long-threaded cotton, high-quality workmanship and a sense of detail, Lacoste polo shirts cost less than €80.

Not only can they be found in 1,000 Lacoste boutiques around the world, but also in sales points in department stores. Nowadays the production has been relocated and the number of licences has increased.

And yet, the Lacoste management follows the model of most luxury brands. On analysis, one can find the ingredients of the management of luxury brands and many of its guiding principles:

- A real story, that of tennis champion René Lacoste, who was one of the French Tennis Musketeers. At that time tennis was an upper-class game, similar to golf, and a sport his wife and then their daughter, Catherine, excelled at, since they were world champions. Rene Lacoste, nicknamed 'the crocodile' (Kapferer and Gaston-Breton, 2008) became the symbol of sports achievement, as well as of elegance.
- A historic, iconic product, the 12×12, still the top seller, a concept typical of luxury brands, which make a very high profit, is regularly given a more modern look, and is the centre of many advertising campaigns.
- Constant concern for quality, with hand-finishing, genuine mother-of-pearl buttons, and the embroidered crocodile, the brand's symbol.
- An advertising campaign that does not aim to sell a product but rather to make people dream: 'a touch of air'.
- The opening of exclusive Lacoste stores on the most fashionable avenues around the world (Rodeo Drive in Los Angeles, 5th Avenue in New York, the Champs-Elysées in Paris). Since Devanlay, the historic partner in charge of production and distribution, was taken over by Mauss, priority has been given to upgrading the quality of the boutiques, making them look more soberly classy, and increasing their average surface area.
- The constant reference to the brand's founder René Lacoste, who even appears in adverts, and has inspired many publications (Kapferer and Gaston-Breton, 2002, 2008).
- The brand's presence in sporting events, mainly through sponsoring, which revitalizes its historic tennis and golf roots and puts it in the news.
- The growing importance given to creativity, thanks to a fashion designer, Lemaire, whose collections are now shown during New York fashion week.
- The launching of limited series, created by fashionable designers: for example the metal or plastic-stitched polo shirt.
- A booming worldwide expansion, especially in the USA, and now in China, India, Russia and Brazil.
- A wider range of products associated with fashion: shoes, accessories (glasses, watches) and of course perfume. Some licensees have been partners since the beginning of the brand, which proves that time and tradition are major components of the Lacoste management.

Consequently it can be easily understood why, despite the reasonable prices of its products Lacoste is seen as a prestige brand. Indeed, this is the result of its being faithful to the management strategy found in the luxury business, as defined and explained in this book.

This strategy makes the company's medium-price strategy all the more remarkable and accounts for its excellent financial results.

16 Conclusion: Luxury and sustainable development

We have arrived at the end of our long voyage through luxury.

We hope that we have convinced you that the image of luxury that is so often bandied about, that of 'luxury and sequins', does not correspond in any way to what luxury is, at least as we see it. Moreover, far from being useless, luxury has a profound role in our societies: what might at first glance pass for superfluous is in fact profoundly useful.

We also hope that we have convinced you that, from our psycho-sociological standpoint on luxury and our long professional experience, it is possible to put in place concrete, effective and clearly explicable industrial strategies: luxury is not only the subject of vague and mysterious discourses, but can also be the subject of effective marketing practices, always provided that you have understood what marketing is, fundamentally, in luxury, which is to say not the classic brand marketing. To conclude, let us touch again on two always current topics.

Luxury and ethics

Luxury is ethical or not depending on how societies read it (Sparta or Athens), but it is neutral in itself. Our statement is clear: if something is addictive (as fashion was for Emma Bovary in *Madame Bovary*), it is no longer luxury, and if it is pure flaunting (the fancy yacht moored at St Tropez or Portofino), it is no longer luxury.

For us, therefore, luxury is refinement and not ostentation, communication and not proclamation. It therefore moves away from the domain of 'having' (possession, accumulation, slavery to the object) towards the domain of 'being', both for yourself (dreams) and for others (recognition, esteem).

Under these conditions, it fulfils a fundamental ethical role: that of pacifying society. In what is luxury, man does not escape the 'triangular desire' so dear to René Girard, since this is an integral part of the human being; however, he escapes the dramatic social consequences of triangular desire: the mimetic crisis.

A society where luxury is democratized is a society that is pacified.

Luxury and sustainable development

Are luxury and sustainable development compatible? Yes and no. Can you be both 'green' and 'gold'? At first glance, few subjects seem to present such a challenge to luxury as sustainable development, often associated with a Rousseau-like return to nature and a rejection of the Western way of life and of the usual concept of luxury. But the situation is more complex.

In fact, in certain senses luxury is shocking: we can rail against the fuel consumption of private helicopters or of huge saloon cars, and their CO_2 emissions, which turn their possessors into polluters. But luxury is also ahead in terms of sustainable development: luxury cars will be the first to offer hydrogen fuel cells, or hybrid engines, to rich clients who are indifferent to the additional cost. Today building a passive house, energy-independent, is a luxury. Today, it is the wealthy who can afford technologies that are not profitable in terms of energy savings, but so pleasant in terms of peace of mind, ecological satisfaction, and social restratification. Luxury can therefore be on the side of the planet. However, sustainable development will only be effective if it is democratized and even generalized. Initially, a hybrid engine is a luxury of the rich; but over time, thanks to these early buyers, a larger production is made economically viable, and as a result it will be present in most cars, without losing its aura. In this book we have examined the strategies that make democratisation of luxury possible, while avoiding vulgarization; they are strictly applicable in this case.

In terms of food, it is one of luxury's privileges to flout the time of year: buying fruit and vegetables out of season. Sustainable development, however, supposes a return to the local, as required by a reduction in the consumption of fuel per kilo transported. This would spell the end of cherries from Chile at Fauchon in January, a luxury of the greatest restaurants. On the other hand, as we have emphasized, luxury is never relocated. It therefore satisfies the need to return to buying locally that will accompany the wakening ecological conscious- ness. Here again, the strategies proposed in this book are perfectly suitable.

The notion of sustainability does not only cover optimal management of the planet's limited resources, or controlling climate change and CO_2: already many luxury brands are adding foundations for restricting global warming to their charitable programmes. We will also worry much more about the well- being of those in the shadows, who work in the workshops, factories or mines. The conditions of miners in South Africa will weigh heavily on the image of the diamond, in the same way as that of the factory workers of Calabria or Asia, who work in wretched conditions for the great names of fashion (but never of luxury), or mass audience brands. Conditions of the miners will remain a big issue, but luxury's respect for its artisans makes it safe from blameful behav- iour in manufacturing.

Since our concept of luxury adapts to the dreams of any human society, it is perfectly compatible with sustainable development; more, even, it is an inte- gral part of it: a luxury brand strategy is based on the client's dream, and not on the consumer's artificially created desire. Communication in luxury is personal, interactive; it is not an advertisement where the consumer is passive.

A sustainable luxury product has a long lifespan, and is produced by a qual- ified human worker, and not by soulless machines or exploited workers on the other side of the world.

One particularly significant example: organic products fit perfectly into a luxury marketing strategy. They carry a dream (mankind integrating harmo- niously with Nature), and are the result of qualified work; they are distributed in a selective manner, and the producer–consumer link is maintained; they are more expensive than ordinary products, but the client pays the difference in full awareness of the reasons why.

The Western world has experienced several decades of abundance; tradi- tional marketing corresponded to this world of abundance. We are now entering permanently into a finite world, a world of rarity. The Western model of consumption cannot be generalized to the whole planet, and its preferred tool, traditional marketing, even less so. Luxury strategies are also rarity strategies where humans again find their true place, both in time as a producer and as free and responsible consumer. They are the tool of the future for managing this new universe.

Bibliography

Abeles, M (2008) *Anthropologie de la Globalisation*, Payot, Paris

Abric, J-C (2003) *Pratiques Sociales et Representations*, PUF, Paris

Alleres, D (1995) *Luxe: un management spécifique*, Economica, Paris

Alleres, D (2003) *Luxe...: Stratégies marketing*, Economica, Paris

Arnault, B (2001) *La passion créative*, Pocket, Paris

Barthes, R (1967) *Le Système de la Mode*, Le Seuil, Paris

Bataille, G (1967) *La part maudite*, Les éditions de Minuit, Paris

Baudrillard, J (1970) *La société de consommation*, Gallimard, Paris

Baudrillard, J (1972) *Pour une critique de l'économie politique du signe*, Gallimard, Paris

Baudrillard, J (1976) *L'échange symbolique et la mort*, Gallimard, Paris

Becker, C (2002), *Du Ricard dans mon Coca*, Editions d'Organisation, Paris

Benjamin, W (2008 [1935]) *The Work of Art: in the age of its technological reproducibility*, Belknap Press, Harvard

Berry, C (1994) *The Idea of Luxury*, Cambridge University Press, Cambridge

Berry, C (2005) La construction libérale du luxe, in *Le Luxe: essais sur la fabrique de l'ostentation*, O Assouly ed, Editions du Regard, Paris

Besson, M and Gurviez, P (2000), La vente dans un contexte relationnel: l'exemple du luxe, *Décisions Marketing*, **20**, pp 47–55

Beverland, M (2004) Uncovering 'the theories-in-use': building luxury wine brands, *European Journal of Marketing*, **38** (3/4), pp 446–66

Blanckaert, C (2007) *Le Luxe*, Cherche-Midi, Paris

Bourdieu, P (1970) *La distinction: critique sociale du jugement*, Minuit, Paris

Castarède, J (2003) *Le Luxe*, PUF, Paris

Catry, B (2006) Manager la rareté du luxe, *Revue Française de Gestion*, **30**, Décembre

Chadha, R and Husband, P (2006) *The Cult of the Luxury Brand*, N Brealey International, Boston MA

Chevallier, M and Mazzalovo, G (2008) *Management et Marketing du Luxe*, Dunod, Paris

Danziger, P (2005) *Let them eat the cake*, Kaplan Books, Dearborn

DeJean, J (2005) *The Essence of Style*, Free Press, New York.

Dior (2007) *60 Années Hautes en Couleur*, Edn Artlys, Versailles

Doyle, P and Stern P (2006 [1994]) *Marketing Management and Strategy*, Prentice Hall, London

Dubois, B and Czellar, S (2001) Prestige brands or luxury brands? An exploratory inquiry on consumer perceptions, *Marketing in a Changing World: Scope, Opportunities and Challenges*, Proceedings of the 31st EMAC Conference, University of Minho, Portugal, 28–31 May

Dubois, B and Duquesne, P (1990) *Existet il un consommateur de luxe européen*, HEC Working Papers, Paris

Dubois, B and Laurent, G (1994) Attitudes towards the concept of luxury: an exploratory analysis, *Asia Pacific Advances in Consumer Research*, **1**, pp 273–78

Dubois, B and Paternault, C (1995) Understanding the world of international luxury brands, *Journal of Advertising Research*, **35** (4)

Durkheim, E (1930) *De la division du travail social*, PUF, Paris

Elias, N (1974) *La société de cour*, Flammarion, Paris

Floch, J M (2004) *L'indémodable total look de Chanel*, IFM-Regard, Paris

Forden, S G (2000) *The House of Gucci*, Perennial, London

Frank, R H (1999) *Luxury Fever*, PUP, Paris

Frank, R H (2007) *Richistan*, Piatkus Books, London

Girard, R (1961) *Mensonge Romantique et Verité Romanesque*, Grasset, Paris

Girard, R (1972) *La Violence et le Sacré*, Grasset, Paris

Girard, R (1978) *Des choses cachées depuis la fondation du monde*, Grasset, Paris

Haie, V (2002) *Donnez nous notre luxe quotidien*, Gualino Editeur

Hanna, J (2004) Luxury isn't what it used to be, *Harvard Business School Bulletin*, **80** (2)

Heilbrunn, B (2005) Le marché du Luxe à l'Aune de la démocratisation, in *Le Luxe: essais sur la fabrique de l'ostentation*, O Assouly ed, Editions du Regard, Paris

Hobbes, T (1997 [1651]) *Leviathan*, Touchstone

Holt, DB (2004) *How Brands Become Icons*, Harvard University Press, Boston MA

Hume, D (1752) *Of Luxury* in *Essays, Moral, Political and Literary*

Jensen, R (1999) *The Dream Society*, McGraw Hill

Kapferer, J-N (1987) *Rumeurs: le plus vieux media du monde*, Le Seuil

Kapferer, J-N (1990) *Rumors: processes, uses and image*, Transaction Books, New Brunswick

Kapferer, J-N (1997) Managing luxury brands, *Journal of Brand Management*, **4** (4), pp 251–60

Kapferer, J-N (1998) Why are we seduced by luxury brands, *Journal of Brand Management*, **6** (1), pp 44–49

Kapferer, J-N (2000) *Reinventing the Brand*, Kogan Page, London

Kapferer, J-N (2007) *Les Marques : capital de l'entreprise*, Eyrolles, Paris

Kapferer, J-N (2008) *The New Strategic Brand Management*, 4th edition, Kogan Page, London

Kapferer, P and Gaston-Breton, T (2002) *Lacoste: the legend*, Cherche Midi, Paris

Kapferer, P and Gaston-Breton, T (2008) *The Style René Lacoste*, Editions l'Equipe

Knafo, J (2008) *Pub de Luxe*, Alban Editions, Paris

Letzelter, P, Weil, G and Valesio, C (1996) Le luxe: acte créatif ou satisfaction client, *Décisions Marketing*, **9**, pp 7–14

Lipovetsky, G and Roux, E (2003) *Le Luxe éternel*, Gallimard, Paris

Marion, G (2005) Objets et marques de Luxe, in *Le Luxe: essais sur la fabrique de l'ostentation* , O Assouly ed, Editions du Regard, Paris

Marseille, J (2000) *France, Terre de Luxe*, La Martinière, Paris

Maus, M (1950) *Sociologie et anthropologie*, PUF, Paris

Mergen, R and Terblanche, N (2005) How not to extend your luxury brand, *Harvard Business Review*, December

Michel, G (2004) *Les Stratégies d'Extension de Marque*, Vuibert, Paris

Moore, CM and Birtwistle, G (2005) The Burberry business model: creating an international luxury fashion brand, *International Journal of Retail and Distribution Management*, **32** (8), pp 412–22

Morand, P (1996) *L'allure de Chanel*, Hermann Editeurs, Paris

Nueno, JL and Quelch, JA (1998) The Mass Marketing of Luxury, *Business Horizons*, **41** (6), pp 61–69

Okonkwo, U (2007) *Luxury Fashion Branding*, Palgrave Macmillan, Basingstoke

Okonkwo, U (2008) *Luxury and Internet*, Palgrave Macmillan, Basingstoke

Pande, A (2005) Traditions de Luxe en Inde, in *Le Luxe: essais sur la fabrique de l'ostentation*, O Assouly ed, Editions du Regard, Paris

Pannekoucke, S (2005) Un condensé du paraître aristocratique, in *Le Luxe: essais sur la fabrique de l'ostentation*, O Assuly ed, Editions du Regard, Paris

Paquot, T (2005) *Eloge du Luxe*, Bourin Editeur, Paris

Pedraza, M and Bonabeau, E (2006) What is luxury without variety? *Harvard Business Review*, **1** (April)

Phan, M (2007) Service innovations: the case of the Plaza Athénée Paris Hotel, *Décisions Marketing*, **48**, pp 9–20

Phau, I and Prendergast, G (2000) Consuming luxury brands: the relevance of the rarity principle, *Journal of Brand Management*, **8** (2), pp 122–38

Quemin, A (2005) Une lecture contemporaine de T. Veblen, in *Le Luxe: essais sur la fabrique de l'ostentation* , O Assouly ed, Editions du Regard, Paris

Radon, A (2002), The paradoxical relationship between the exclusiveness of luxury goods and profit maximization, Working Paper School of Business, Stockholm University, 25 March

Reicheld, F (2006) *The Ultimate Question*, Harvard Business School Press, Cambridge MA

Remaury, B (2005a) Luxe et identité culturelle américaine, in *Le Luxe: essais sur la fabrique de l'ostentation* , O Assouly ed, Editions du Regard, Paris

Remaury, B (2005b) L'objet de luxe à l'ère de la reproducibilité technique, in *Le Luxe: essais sur la fabrique de l'ostentation* , O Assouly ed, Editions du Regard, Paris

Richou, S and Lombard, M (1999) *Le luxe dans tous ses états*, Economica, Paris

Roux, E and Floch, J-M (1996) Gérer l'ingérable: la contradiction interne à toute maison de luxe, *Décisions Marketing*, **9**, pp 15–23

Salmon, C (2007) *Storytelling*, La Découverte, Paris

Sapori, M (2005) Les marchands de mode parisiens, in *Le Luxe: essais sur la fabrique de l'ostentation* , O Assouly ed, Editions du Regard, Paris

Saussure, Ferdinand de (1972) *Cours de linguistique générale*, Paris, Payot

Schutz, P and Cook, J (1986) Porsche on nichemanship, *Harvard Business Review*, **2** (March–April)

Sicard, M-C (2005a) *Les ressorts cachés du désir*, Village Mondial, Paris

Sicard, M-C (2005b) Les perceptions internationales des produits de luxe, in *Le Luxe: essais sur la fabrique de l'ostentation* , O Assouly ed, Editions du Regard, Paris

Sicard, M-C (2006) *Luxe, mensonges et marketing*, 2nd edition, Village Mondial, Paris

Silverstein, M and Fiske, N (2003) Luxury for the masses, *Harvard Business Review*, **1** (April)

Silverstein, M and Fiske, N (2005) *Trading Up*, Portfolio, London

Simmel, G (2004) *The Philosophy of Money*, Routledge, London

Sukhdial, A S, Chakraborty, G and Steger, E K (1995) Segmentation in the US Luxury Auto Market, *Journal of Advertising Research*, **35** (1)

Süskind, P (2001) *The Perfume*, Vintage, London

Tarde, G (1890) *Les Lois de l'Imitation*, Slatkine, Geneva

Teil, G (2005) Les procédures de qualification des produits de luxe, in *Le Luxe: essais sur la fabrique de l'ostentation* , O Assouly ed, Editions du Regard, Paris

Thomas, D (2007) *De Luxe: How Luxury Lost its Lustre*, Penguin Books, London

Tungate, M (2005) *Fashion Brands*, Kogan Page, London

Twitchel, JB (2001) *Living It Up*, Columbia University Press, Cambridge

Usunier, J-C (1997) Consommation ostentatoire et valeurs asiatiques, *Décisions Marketing*, **10**, pp 45–53

Veblen, T (1970 [1899]) *The Theory of the Leisure Class*, Gallimard, Paris

Vettrano-Soulard, M-C (1990) *Luxe et Publicité*, Retz, Paris

Vigneron, F and Johnson, LW (1999) 'Review and a conceptual framework of prestige-seeking consumer behavior, *Academy of Marketing Science Review*, **3** (1)

Vincent, C and Monnin, P (1990), *Guerre du Luxe*, Bourin Edn, Paris

Weber, M (1964 [1893]) *L'éthique protestante et l'esprit du capitalisme*, Plon, Paris

Weber, M (1993) *The Sociology of Religion*, Beacon Press

Weber, M (2003) *The Protestant Ethic and the Spirit of Capitalism*, Dover Publications

Weber, M (2006 [1913]) *Sociologie de la religion*, Flammarion, Paris

Wilcox, C and Mendes, V (2007) *Modern Fashion in Detail*, V&A Publications, London

Index